WE STILL HOLD THESE TRUTHS

WE STILL HOLD THESE TRUTHS

Rediscovering Our Principles,
Reclaiming Our Future

Matthew Spalding

Wilmington, Delaware

Spalding, Matthew.

    We still hold these truths : rediscovering our principles, reclaiming our future / Matthew Spalding.
    p. cm.
    Includes index.

    ISBN 978-1-935191-67-4 (cloth bound : alk. paper)

        1. National characteristics, American. 2. United States—Civilization. 3. United States—Politics and government. 4. United States—Moral conditions. 5. Social values—United States. I. Title.

E169.1.S714 2009
973—dc22   2009028260

Published in the United States by:

ISI Books
Intercollegiate Studies Institute
3901 Centerville Road
Wilmington, Delaware 19807-1938
www.isibooks.org

To Elizabeth:
as Lysander wrote to his Diana,
you soften and warm my heart,
and form my happiness.

Contents

Contents

Freedom is never more than one generation away from extinction. We didn't pass it on to our children in the bloodstream. It must be fought for, protected, and handed on for them to do the same, or one day we will spend our sunset years telling our children and our children's children what it was once like in the United States when men were free.

—Ronald Reagan

Foreword

William J. Bennett

Our country seems to be in the midst of an identity crisis, divided, confused, and adrift. Change is the watchword of the moment, yet there is little consideration about where it is that we may be going. Everything is rapidly moving forward, despite a general sense among us that we are entering uncharted territory. Nevertheless, there are increasing calls for America to get back to its first principles—to reset its compass, so to speak—as a way to give direction to our rudderless politics.

It has long been fashionable to believe that American culture has become too fragmented and pluralistic to justify our faith in a common creed, and few of our academic elites have shown an inclination to think seriously about what our age-old political principles mean for modern society—despite broad popular agreement about the importance of these principles and of making just such an effort.

When I was chairman of the National Endowment for the Humanities many years ago, I invited several hundred educational and cultural leaders to list ten books that every educated high school graduate should have read. Hundreds of texts received a few mentions, but the principal documents of American history—the Declaration of Independence, the Constitution, and *The Federalist*—were cited again and again by most respondents. This reflected a widespread belief that in reading these core documents, and other early American writings, students would learn something important not only about America, but also about politics simply, which would shed light on the great issues both then and now.

Is it possible that the guidance we are looking for—the framework for the change we seek—and the most compelling vision for true American progress is to be found in the principles declared by a fledgling nation more than two hundred years ago?

At a time when there is no shortage of books that argue for specific policies or political agendas, *We Still Hold These Truths* is refreshingly *radical*, according to the original meaning of that word: It looks to the *root* of what we believe and seek to conserve—the liberating principles, practical wisdom, and constitutional insights of the American Founding. It makes a clear and compelling case for America's principles as an enduring source of real, practical guidance for today, explaining how we got so far off track, and laying out how to get our nation back on course.

Matthew Spalding argues that America's principles form a consistent, meaningful, and universally true understanding of human liberty, and that an understanding of the permanent truths about man—"the Laws of Nature and Nature's God"—supplies us with standards and ends of political life. He reminds us that constitutional government derives its legitimacy from the consent of the governed and exists to secure the natural rights with which we are endowed by our Creator. He explains how the great principle of human equality is expressed in the constitutional rule of law and in the forms and institutions of limited constitutional government. The principles of liberty, he demonstrates, culminate in our understanding of self-government—of the character and moral institutions that make for *self*-government, as well as the political institutions and free markets of a self-governing people. It is this model of national independence and human freedom that we uphold, and defend, at home and in the world.

Some argue that our founding principles mean nothing more than that each generation can decide for itself the meaning of equality and liberty, of the Declaration of Independence and the Constitution. And so they claim the mantle of the American Founders when they advocate new rights and more centralized government power. But the fact of the matter is that we got where we are today by rejecting the principles of our founding, not by following them. *We Still Hold These Truths* shows that modern liberalism proceeds upon a thoroughgoing critique of our founding, and that it attempts to define America in a different way, based on ideas found outside of America. The progressive thinkers of the early twentieth century, having rejected the very idea of self-evident truths and enduring principles, created a theory of a "living," evolving Constitution, allowing government to expand and implement "progress" through more and more governmental control over everyday life. This philosophy of government defined and continues to shape contemporary American liberalism.

We now face a choice. One path is change for the sake of change, of continued travel along the road of decline—for this future, just witness the political and cultural implosion of modern Europe. The other is the path of renewal, based on what I have long called a great relearning, which seeks to rediscover America's principles and restore them to their proper place in our political life, as the cornerstone of America's public philosophy.

We Still Hold These Truths shows that the way forward is to transcend the partisan ideologies and the special interests that divide us, and instead re-create the deep and abiding national consensus that defines us by appealing to the principles that unite all Americans in our common purpose.

In his last Annual Message to Congress, one month before he issued the Emancipation Proclamation, Abraham Lincoln spoke of how "we shall nobly save, or meanly lose, the last best hope of earth." I firmly believe that we are still that hope, and that it is still in our power and still our responsibility to uphold and advance the truths of human freedom. The source of that belief, and that hope, is America's eternal capacity for rededicating itself to these truths that we hold, applicable to all men and all times.

Former Secretary of Education William J. Bennett is the Washington Fellow of the Claremont Institute and the author of America: The Last Best Hope, *a multivolume history of America.*

Introduction

～⁓

Curiosities in Glass Cases

Not far from the United States Capitol, just down Pennsylvania Avenue in Washington, D.C., is the magnificent building of the National Archives of the United States. Designed by the great American architect John Russell Pope, its façade, columns, massive bronze doors, and central rotunda are intended to evoke classical Greek themes as well as the neoclassical style of the Roman Pantheon.

The temples of the ancient world were grand monuments constructed to provide sacrifices to the pagan gods, and the Pantheon was to be the grandest—the temple of all the gods, where the victorious Romans kept their conquered deities and worshipped their Caesars. The difference between these two structures—the Pantheon and the National Archives—could not be more striking, or more significant.

At the entrance of the Pantheon were huge statues of Caesar Augustus, the first emperor, and Marcus Vipsanius Agrippa, the Roman general responsible for most of Caesar's military triumphs. The reigning emperor was to be enthroned in its rotunda, wielding power at the center of the Roman Empire, around which the world and the heavens revolved.

In the rotunda of the National Archives building there are no statues of dead rulers, symbols of political power, or emblems of military glory. Instead, in the center of this temple, upon a simple marble altar, are two faded documents enshrined in glass cases. Mere words, handwritten on a few sheets of parchment.

"We hold these truths to be self-evident . . ."

In 1776, when it announced itself to the world, America was little more than a potential nation of thirteen small colonies on a barren continent, thousands of miles from their ancestral homeland, surrounded by hostile powers.

Well over two centuries later—having won its independence from the British Empire, established its sovereign nationhood, completed its continental expansion and brought unprecedented prosperity to its citizens, survived a devastating Civil War that threatened its very life, abolished slavery and raised up the emancipated to be citizens equal to their one-time masters, and triumphed in two world wars fought on foreign soil and a decades-long struggle against worldwide communism—the United States has become the freest, wealthiest, and most powerful nation in the world.

What is to account for this monumental success?

Every nation derives meaning and purpose from some unifying quality—an ethnic character, a common religion, a shared history. America is different. Unique among the nations of the world, America was founded, at a particular time, by a particular people, on the basis of a particular idea. At its birth, this nation justified its independence by asserting truths said to be self-evident, according to "the Laws of Nature and Nature's God." Working from the great principle of human equality, the men who launched this experiment in popular government claimed a new basis of political legitimacy: the consent of those governed. Through a carefully written constitution, they created an enduring framework of limited government based on the rule of law. With this structure, they sought to establish true religious liberty, provide for economic opportunity, secure national independence, and maintain a flourishing society of republican self-government—all in the name of a simple but radical idea of human liberty.

The founding of the United States was indeed *revolutionary*, but not in the sense of replacing one set of rulers with another, or overthrowing the institutions of society. "What do we mean by the American Revolution?" queried John Adams. "The revolution was in the minds and hearts of the people. . . . This radical change in the principles, opinions, sentiments, and affections of the people, was the *real* American Revolution."*

Our revolution was about the ideas upon which a new nation was to be established. Permanent truths "applicable to all men and all times," as Abraham Lincoln later said, proclaimed that *principle* rather than *will* would be the ultimate ground of government. What is truly revolutionary about America is that, for the first time in human history, these universal ideas became the foundation of a particular system of government and its political culture. It was *because* of these principles, not despite them, that, rather than ending in tyranny, the American Revolution culminated in a constitutional government that has long endured.

To this day, so many years after the American Revolution, these principles—proclaimed in the Declaration of Independence and promulgated by the United States Constitution—still define us as a nation and inspire us as a people. They are responsible for a prosperous and just nation unlike any in the world. They are the highest achievements of our tradition, serving not only as a powerful beacon to those throughout the world who strive for freedom and seek to vindicate self-government but also a warning to tyrants and despots everywhere. It is *because* of these principles, not despite them, that America has achieved its greatness.

Can a nation so conceived and dedicated endure? From the beginning this has been the key question.

When Benjamin Franklin departed the Constitutional Convention, he was asked by an acquaintance if the framers meeting in Philadelphia had created a monarchy or a republic. "A republic," he famously replied, but then added, "*if you can keep it.*" Our nation's Founders knew that the perpetuation of liberty would always depend on spirited citizens and patriotic statesmen actively engaged in the democratic task of governing themselves, holding to the truths of 1776.

Today, according to numerous studies, most of our high-school and college students do not know the basic facts of American history. They consistently score poorly in virtually every measure of civic knowledge.

---

* All the quotes in this book can be found in a searchable database at: WeStillHoldTheseTruths.org.

But while there is much that we have forgotten, this is not simply a case of national amnesia. This distressing state signals a larger systemic problem.

In many circles, especially among the learned elites of our universities and law schools—those who teach the next generation, shape our popular culture, and set the terms of our political discourse—the self-evident truths upon which America depends have been supplanted by the passionately held belief that no such truths exist, certainly no truths applicable to all time. Over the past century the federal government has lost much of its mooring, and today acts with little regard for the limits placed upon it by the Constitution, which many now regard as obsolete. On both the Left and the Right, our political leaders are increasingly unsure of their way, speaking in inspiring generalities, all the while mired in small-minded politics and petty debates. As a nation, we are left divided about our own meaning, unable—perhaps unwilling—to defend our ideas, our institutions, and maybe even ourselves.

From the decline of civic education to the rise of a politics of government dependency, these societal problems are rooted in a deep confusion about the meaning and status of America's core principles. In the midst of the many challenges we face—unsustainable spending and increasing debt, the future burden of social welfare entitlements, national security in a dangerous world—the real crisis that tears at the American soul is not a lack of courage or solutions as much as a loss of conviction. Do we still hold these truths? Do the principles that inspired the American Founding retain their relevance in the twenty-first century? We will find it difficult to know what to do and how to do it as long as we are not sure who we are and what we believe.

We must restore America's principles—the truths to which we are dedicated—as the central idea of our nation's public philosophy. But before we can rededicate ourselves as a nation to these principles, we must rediscover them as a people. That is the purpose of this book: to recall America's first principles as they were understood by our Founders, in the context of our nation's history and its constitutional development from roots deep in Western civilization.

The following chapters seek to explain and bring to life ten core principles that define our national creed and common purpose: *liberty* is the grand, overarching theme of our nation's history; *equality, natural rights*, and the *consent of the governed* are the foundational principles that set the compass of our politics; *religious liberty* and *private property* follow from these, shaping the parameters of our nation's day-to-day life; the *rule of law* and a *constitutionalism* of limited government define the architecture that undergirds our liberty; all of these principles culminate in *self-government*, in the political sense of republican governance and the moral sense of governing ourselves; and lastly, *independence* encompasses the meaning of America's principles in the world.

Only when we *know* these principles once again can we renew America. Only when we understand the significance of these principles can we grasp the nobility of our accomplishments as a people and see how far we have strayed off course as a nation. Only then can we realize the societal choices before us and begin to develop a strategy to reclaim our future.

The National Archives building was designed to publicly house and display together for the first time the Declaration of Independence and the United States Constitution. There was a solemn ceremony when it was dedicated in 1952. The chief justice of the United States presided and the chaplain of the Senate gave an invocation, but the main speaker was the president of the United States, Harry S. Truman.

Recall that these were the dark days of the Cold War. An iron curtain had descended across Europe, the Soviet Union had exploded an atomic bomb, and China had fallen to communism. The United States was bogged down in a military stalemate in Korea. The West seemed to be fighting rear-guard battles against a steadily advancing enemy. Truman wondered whether liberty could ever be lost in this country. His answer to his own question had nothing to do with world events.

Liberty "can be lost, and it will be," Truman observed, "if the time ever comes when these documents are regarded not as the supreme expression of our profound belief, but merely as curiosities in glass cases."

This cannot—this must not—be allowed to happen. We may take some comfort in recognizing that every generation finds it necessary to relearn our history and the heritage of freedom. As it was with our forefathers, so it is now our task to ensure that the principles of liberty are securely enshrined in the hearts and minds of the American people.

LIBERTY

EQUALITY

NATURAL RIGHTS

CONSENT OF THE GOVERNED

RELIGIOUS FREEDOM

PRIVATE PROPERTY

THE RULE OF LAW

CONSTITUTIONALISM

SELF-GOVERNMENT

INDEPENDENCE

1

A New Nation, Conceived in Liberty:
The Roots of American Freedom

In the early spring of 1775, the members of the Virginia legislature were meeting to consider the results of a Continental Congress that had convened recently in Philadelphia, and to ponder the next steps in the brewing controversy between England and the American colonies. Many expected—most fervently hoped—that London would back down.

Three days in, having gathered at St. John's Church in Richmond, a strong and eloquent advocate of the patriot cause named Patrick Henry argued that it was time to prepare the colony for the war that may be coming—and that unbeknownst to them would break out in less than a month's time.

Before George Washington, Thomas Jefferson, Richard Henry Lee, and other prominent state leaders, the young backcountry lawyer rose to defend the momentous proposition. "We have done everything that could be done to avert the storm which is now coming on," he argued in building to the close of his powerful address. "The next gale that sweeps from the north will bring to our ears the clash of resounding arms! Our brethren are already in the field! Why stand we here idle? What is it that gentlemen wish? What would they have?"

"Is life so dear, or peace so sweet," he cried, "as to be purchased at the price of chains and slavery?" Henry raised his hands, crossed at the wrists, as though he were bound. "Forbid it, Almighty God!"

"I know not what course others may take," he calmly professed, and then he paused. Slowly, deliberately, and in a firm voice, Henry concluded to the hushed audience, "But as for me, *give me liberty . . .*"

Then with clenched fist, he struck his chest as if he were thrusting a dagger: " . . . or give me death."

The Cause of Liberty

Liberty is the essential idea that is America. It is at once our greatest inheritance, our greatest achievement, and our greatest bequest to posterity. The Declaration of Independence asserts unalienable rights to "life, liberty, and the pursuit of happiness," and the Constitution is meant to "secure the blessings of liberty." In his Farewell Address, Washington reminded Americans of "the love of liberty" that is "interwoven with every ligament of your heart." At Gettysburg, Abraham Lincoln noted that before this nation was dedicated to the proposition of human equality, it was "conceived in *liberty.*"

To this day, the United States is a magnet for those seeking opportunity and prosperity, attracting the talented and enterprising, rich and poor alike. The Founders knew that this would be the case. James Madison predicted that this country "will be the workshop of liberty to the civilized world." After all, it had been in the name of liberty—political liberty, religious liberty, economic liberty—that many had come to America in the first place.

So important is the concept that English—unlike any other language—has two words to describe it: *liberty* as well as *freedom.* We tend to use the term *freedom* more nowadays, for it has a powerful and evocative ring to it. But the words are often used interchangeably, as when the patriotic hymn sings of "My country, 'tis of thee, sweet land of liberty," and at the same time proclaims, "From every mountainside, let freedom ring." The Founders preferred and widely used the word *liberty.*

There is a difference between these two terms that helps us understand the Founders' concept of the principle. Freedom is understood as more expansive, and suggests a general lack of restraint, especially a lack of political restraint, as when we speak of the United States as a "free society." It is often used to suggest a more open-ended sense of autonomy, meaning that we are free to do whatever we want. But from the

Founders' view, freedom must be understood within the context of constitutional and moral order, which meant reasonable limits and cultural bounds. Liberty means the rightful exercise of freedom, the balancing of rights and responsibilities.

Consider how we use the two words. All animals can be said to have freedom. Men can be free, but so can fish in the ocean or birds in the sky. But liberty is an inherently *human* word. While we say man has liberty or is at liberty to do something, we do not say the same of animals, because animals lack a rational capacity to choose their own actions. This distinction reflects a much larger and more significant point. In the American tradition, liberty was never understood to mean anything and everything, but came with duties and obligations appropriate for human self-government.

The view of liberty appropriate for self-government did not appear spontaneously. The moment in which this nation was conceived was not a chance occasion in time; rather, it was the culmination of a larger tradition, stretching back well before this nation began, that forms the foundation upon which America is built—and without which it would not have come into being. This foundation was the tradition and history of art, custom, philosophy, and political thought, originating thousands of years ago with Greco-Roman culture and its descendants, fundamentally shaped by Judeo-Christian theology and spiritualism, that came to be called Western civilization and that formed western Europe and then North America. The United States is a product of this great development.*

The American Founders understood themselves in the context of the ideas and institutions that came out of this tradition, out of that profound learning and wide experience that had been transmitted over time from Athens, to Jerusalem, to Rome, to London—and now to Philadelphia. A deep realization of this civilization and their gratitude for its inheritance gave the American Founders a profound sense of their responsibility to the past and to the future. It is reflected in the art, architecture, rhetoric, and symbols of the early republic: The Founders saw America continuing, and potentially surpassing, the greatest civilizations of the West.

---

* This argument is made at greater length in Russell Kirk's *The Roots of American Order* (1974).

So we begin our understanding of this first principle of liberty by reference to the deep roots of human freedom as they took hold in America. The four core roots that provided the most definition and nourishment to America's liberty are the "Britishness" of America, the importance of religious faith and the development of religious liberty, the intellectual influences that shaped the American mind, and America's unique experience in democratic governance.

The Roots of American Liberty

Though the peopling of America began much earlier, the American Founding can be said to begin with the end of the French and Indian War in 1763, after which the British began to more actively govern their American colonies. The founding period encompasses two pivotal events in the history of liberty. The American Revolution opens at the Battle of Lexington in 1775 and concludes with the Treaty of Paris in 1783. The creation and establishment of the Constitution begins in earnest in 1785 (the Constitutional Convention was held in the summer of 1787) and can be said to conclude with the passage of the Bill of Rights in 1791, or perhaps at the end of Washington's formative presidency in 1797. The centerpieces of those events are two monumental documents, the Declaration of Independence and the United States Constitution.

Most colonists were from northern and western European stock. The first and most plentiful European immigrants were English. Together with the Welsh, the Scots, and the Scots-Irish, they made up the vast majority of the population. Nearly all the New Englanders were of English stock, while the Scots-Irish were strung from Pennsylvania to Georgia. Then came the Dutch, the Swedes, and the French Huguenots. As much as a third of the population of Pennsylvania was German. There was some immigration of free blacks from the West Indies in the eighteenth century, though nearly all blacks were brought to the colonies unwillingly as slaves, whose very presence—as shall be discussed at length in the chapters ahead—would mark the struggle for liberty with poignancy, tragedy, and nobility.

More than anything else, the Americans were *British*. In 1790, 60 percent of the free population was English derivative, mostly second- or third-generation immigrants, and 18 percent came from Ireland and

Scotland, which meant that almost 80 percent were from Great Britain. The eminent historian David Hackett Fischer argues that the foundation of American culture was formed from four mass emigrations from four different regions of Britain: the Puritans from East Anglia to New England, southern English cavaliers to the Chesapeake Bay region, North Midland Quakers settling in the Delaware Valley, and Scots-Irish settlers from the borderlands of Britain and Northern Ireland migrating to Appalachia.*

In only a bit of an overstatement, John Jay was not too far off the mark when he wrote in *Federalist* 2 of "one united people . . . descended from the same ancestors, speaking the same language, professing the same religion, attached to the same principles of government, very similar in their manners and customs."

Nor can we forget that the Americans lived in *colonies*, established, supported, defended, and ruled by England. Early settlements were often formed by compact, a temporary agreement between a group consenting to form a community, as in the Mayflower Compact made by the Puritans at Plymouth or the compacts that established Providence, Connecticut, and New Haven (all eventually incorporated into the Massachusetts Bay colony). The colonies themselves, however, were all formed by charters from the king of England, who formally granted governing rights in accordance with his sovereign authority. Pennsylvania, Delaware, and Maryland had "proprietary" charters giving such authority to individuals; Connecticut and Rhode Island possessed "commercial" charters; and the other colonies had "royal" charters and were ruled by governors, judges, and legislatures appointed or authorized by the king.

In 1776 there were some two and a half million people in America, 20 percent of the population of England, a little more than 10 percent of the population of France. There were no great metropolises, like London or Paris, and only five cities of any magnitude—Philadelphia, Boston, New York, Charleston, and Newport. The largest was Philadelphia, with a minuscule population of 20,000 compared to London's 800,000 inhabitants. The vast majority of the population lived in small villages or frontier settlements up and down the eastern seaboard. But America was growing, and would double its population in twenty-five years. The population was just under four million at the time of the first census in 1790.

* See David Hackett Fischer's *Albion's Seed: Four British Folkways in America* (1989).

In the early 1770s, the colonies were a loyal and important component of the British Empire. There were three regional groupings: New
England (Massachusetts, New Hampshire, Connecticut, and Rhode
Island); the Middle Colonies (New York, New Jersey, Pennsylvania, and
Delaware); and the Southern Colonies (Virginia, Maryland, North and
South Carolina, and Georgia). The economy of New England was based
on fishing and shipbuilding, Pennsylvania was highly agricultural, Virginia's major industry was tobacco farming, and the Carolinas primarily grew rice and later indigo. Consistent with English laws and policy,
most of America's economic trade dealt with Britain directly or indirectly through the British West Indies, and most exports were handled
by British merchants. Almost 50 percent of all English shipping dealt
with American commerce, while the colonies bought 25 percent of all
English exports. For the colonies, this meant that in exchange for their
raw materials, almost all of their imported manufactured goods—tex-
tiles, clothing, china, metalware—were British. As a result, the American colonies were quickly turning into an economic dynamo: Over the
course of the 1770s, the colonial economy expanded tenfold.

God and Liberty

Of the many influences that shaped the American concept of liberty, the
first and most formative was faith. From the earliest settlements, Americans were a strongly religious people. More than anything else, religion
formed the backbone of colonial culture and defined its moral horizon.

This religious character was largely a product of the fact that many
came to the New World for religious liberty—to freely practice and
spread their faith. A small group of pilgrims granted land by King James
arrived in New England in 1620. They had landed outside the charter
territory they had been granted, and so wrote out the Mayflower Compact creating their own political community "for the Glory of God and
advancement of the Christian Faith and Honour of our King and Country." This was, in essence, a social contract to form a body politic for the
sake of survival. A greater number of Puritans arrived there in the following decade. Governor John Winthrop's "Model of Christian Charity"
address in 1630 set forth a stern moral code and spoke of the colony as a
covenant with God established to do service to the Lord: "For wee must

consider that wee shall be as a citty upon an hill," he famously declared. "The eies of all people are uppon us."

The Puritans came to America believing that "their errand was not a mere scouting expedition: it was an essential maneuver in the drama of Christendom," according to Perry Miller, the preeminent historian of the subject. "These Puritans did not flee to America; they went in order to work out that complete reformation which was not yet accomplished in England and Europe."*

In 1624, the Dutch established a small settlement in the Middle Colonies called New Amsterdam that developed a Dutch Reformed church, which continued to thrive as a religious minority even after being taken by the British and renamed New York. Further south, the Englishman George Calvert founded Maryland in 1632 to provide Roman Catholics a colony free from religious persecution. The Baptist theologian Roger Williams, a staunch proponent of broad religious liberty (including freedom of worship for Roman Catholics and non-Christians), established Providence (eventually Rhode Island) in 1636. William Penn founded Pennsylvania with a 1681 proprietary charter proclaiming that all who believe in God "shall, in no ways, be molested or prejudiced for their religious persuasion, or practice, in matters of faith and worship." The first Jewish immigrants settled in New York (still New Amsterdam) sometime around 1654 and in Rhode Island in 1658. There were scattered Jewish communities throughout colonial cities like New Haven, Savannah, Richmond, and Philadelphia; the largest Jewish population was in Charleston, South Carolina.

The British colonists were overwhelmingly Christian, and overwhelmingly Protestant. Congregationalists dominated New England, where their church was established. New York had more Presbyterian and Dutch Reformed churches, along with the Church of England in some of the lower counties. The South was largely Anglican, with some Presbyterian, Quaker, and Baptist populations. The Baptists began to take a much more visible role in the South, particularly in the Carolinas, in the mid-1700s. During the early decades of the eighteenth century, as the population was expanding, the main churches in American grew at a rapid and astonishing rate, according to research done by Dr. James Hutson of the Library of Congress. This growth was fueled in large part

---

* See Perry Miller, *Errand into the Wilderness* (1956).

by the religious revival movement in the 1730s and 1740s known as the Great Awakening, but it continued beyond that. Hutson estimates that throughout the 1770s, some 70–80 percent of the population attended church on a regular basis.*

As a whole, the Founders were strongly religious. The religious culture surrounding them profoundly shaped their ideas and lives. While some were more traditional (such as John Jay and John Witherspoon) and some more skeptical of religious institutions and doctrines (such as Thomas Paine and Thomas Jefferson), the vast majority were firmly in the mainstream of religious belief, viewing God as having created man with an immortal soul, actively involved in human affairs, and as "the Supreme Judge of the world," as it says in the Declaration of Independence. Even the deists among them—and it is by no means the case that they were mostly deists, as some have claimed—held that God created the world and determined the rules of human action. "It is a fool only, and not the philosopher, nor even the prudent man, that will live as if there were no God," wrote Paine. "Were a man impressed as fully and strongly as he ought to be with the belief of a God, his moral life would be regulated by the force of belief; he would stand in awe of God and of himself, and would not do the thing that could not be concealed from either." While one can always speculate about the details of each individual's religious faith, it doesn't require such a determination to know that the Founders as a whole took religious beliefs seriously and understood that religion was a necessary component of republican government.

It is crucial to understand the great influence of religion in general, and of Christianity in particular, on the thought and culture of Europe and America. That there are laws of God that exist prior to, outside of, and above the laws of the state necessarily means that the laws of the state are limited and controlled by a higher or transpolitical authority. The injunction in the Bible (Matthew 22:21) to "render unto Caesar the things which are Caesar's, and unto God the things that are God's" means that while there are responsibilities to legitimate government authority, the state must not negate or replace man's responsibilities to God. The distinction also demanded a space for other institutions—church and religious communities, families and tribes—to exist and flourish.

---

* See James H. Hutson, *Religion and the Founding of the American Republic* (1998).

The idea of human dignity, that we are created in the image of God, forms the theological underpinning of the ideas of human nature and human equality—core principles of liberty. The notion that all men are sinners is the theological equivalent of the commonsense observation that human beings are drawn to their passions and prone to be selfish, and it informs the political idea that no one is to be trusted with absolute power or tempted to misuse it for personal gain. At the same time, the idea that all are redeemable—that there is a divine spark in each person, as a young George Washington wrote in his childhood copybook— grounds the notion that all can govern themselves and are capable of justice and benevolence toward one another.

All of these concepts—informed and encouraged by the moral individualism and independence of the reform Protestantism that overwhelmingly shaped the early American religious consciousness—were crucial to the beginnings of liberty and the creation of the conditions for democratic constitutionalism.

The American Mind

Colonial America was a highly literate society, despite its overwhelmingly rural population. The two books likely to be found in every home were a well-worn copy of the Bible and a volume of Shakespeare, Milton, or other great literature. Benjamin Franklin created the first public library (in Philadelphia) in 1731; by 1776, two dozen newspapers were being published throughout the thirteen colonies. "A native American who cannot read or write is as rare as a comet or an earthquake," John Adams once commented. Thomas Paine's *Common Sense*—America's first best-seller—sold 125,000 copies in the first three months of 1776, and the total quickly reached 500,000. Not bad for a population of only some four million.

By all accounts, the American Founders were an especially well-read and well-educated lot. They were avid and conscientious readers of the many articles, journals, and pamphlets regularly circulating in the colonies. Much of their education in political ideas came from reading and debating the major political works of the day, such as Paine's *Common Sense*, Jefferson's *A Summary View of the Rights of British America*, and John Adams's *Defence of the Constitutions of Government of the United States of America*.

More than anything, Americans were steeped in history. "The minds of youth are perpetually led to the history of Greece and Rome or to Great Britain," observed Noah Webster of early American education. "Boys are constantly repeating the declamations of Demosthenes and Cicero, or debates upon some political question in the British Parliament."

Nine colleges existed in the colonies before the revolution, and all but one (the nonsectarian school founded by Benjamin Franklin that would become the University of Pennsylvania) were established by religious denominations. The earliest were founded by the Congregational Church in 1636 (Harvard College in Cambridge, Massachusetts) and the Anglicans in 1693 (the College of William & Mary in Williamsburg, Virginia). John Adams attended Harvard; Thomas Jefferson and John Marshall studied at the College of William & Mary; James Madison attended the College of New Jersey (now Princeton); Alexander Hamilton went to King's College (now Columbia). Thirty-seven of the fifty-five delegates to the Constitutional Convention attended college.

The curriculum at the time was classically based, so many of the Founders received instruction in Latin and Greek language in order to read classical literature and history. Two-thirds of the signers of the Declaration of Independence had studied the classics, half of them formally. Others got the classics informally, in private, or by studying in Europe. Richard Henry Lee, for instance, was tutored at home and then sent to England, where he studied Latin and Greek, while Samuel Chase and George Wythe (who taught Jefferson and Marshall law at William & Mary) were homeschooled in the classics.

Others got it indirectly through the culture. Washington read some of the works of Cicero, the great Roman statesman, and especially liked Roger L'Estrange's *Seneca's Morals*, a popularization of stoicism. His favorite theater production—he had it performed for his men several times during the Revolutionary War, and it was the source of many of his favorite phrases and quotations—was Joseph Addison's play *Cato: A Tragedy*, about Cato's refusal to submit to the tyrannical rule of Julius Caesar. It was also the source of Patrick Henry's line, "Give me liberty, or give me death."

You see the influence of the classics in the pen names they took for their writings. The Anti-Federalists (who opposed the Constitution) often took the names Brutus and Cassius, assassins of Caesar, to suggest that the Constitution and its supporters were monarchical and oligarchic. The Federalists (who advocated the Constitution) countered with their own pseudonyms, the most noted being Publius—after Publius Valerius Publicola, the consul who played a key role in establishing the Roman republic—the pen name of James Madison, Alexander Hamilton, and John Jay in writing the *Federalist* essays. Classically derived pseudonyms appear in the private writings of the Founders, too, as in the lengthy (and delightful) correspondence between John Adams and his wife, Abigail, who wrote under the names Lysander, the great Spartan general, and Diana, the Roman goddess of love.

From ancient Greece, the Founders learned mostly what to avoid. In preparation for the Constitutional Convention, James Madison wrote "Notes on Ancient and Modern Confederacies," in which he describes the failures of the confederacies of ancient Greece. Alexander Hamilton voiced their collective assessment in *Federalist* 9: "It is impossible to read the history of the petty republics of Greece and Italy without feeling sensations of horror and disgust at the distractions with which they were continually agitated, and at the rapid succession of revolutions by which they were kept in a state of perpetual vibration between the extremes of tyranny and anarchy." Fortunately, the science of politics had seen "great improvement": Various new ideas that were well understood and developed by the Founders—such as the distribution of powers, checks and balances, an independent judiciary, representation—"were either not known at all, or imperfectly known to the ancients."

There were some instructive lessons as well. The idea of separating the powers of government had beginnings in Aristotle's *Politics*, and the concept of balancing power among different public offices developed under the Romans, something the Founders knew from reading Polybius's *Histories*. Especially from the stoic thinkers like the Roman statesman Cicero, they knew of the classical concepts of nature and natural law. They also learned from the Greeks and Romans to fear conspiracies against liberty, and of the enduring importance of virtue and honor, which the ancients had taught is the end of political life. To the extent that American constitutionalism is designed to produce a certain kind of citizen, that constitutionalism cannot be understood apart from the ancient account of politics.*

---

* See *The Founders and the Classics: Greece, Rome, and the American Enlightenment*

Perhaps the most significant manifestation of classical ideas was the fact that these individuals generally understood themselves to be "founding" a new nation, hence the use of the term "founders" as we refer to them today. The concept recalls the great lawgivers of ancient history, who founded Athens, Sparta, and Rome. It implies that nations can be established or "founded," and that the act of founding permanently imprints the identity of the regime. In *The Federalist Papers*, the Constitutional Convention (the gathering of lawgivers who formed the governing Constitution) replaces the ancient model, although in many ways George Washington—often portrayed as the Roman Cincinnatus laying down his plow to save the republic—is the better analogy as our "founding father."

The more immediate influence on the American mind, though, was British. The Founders knew well their own history—which is to say British history—especially their "recent" history going back to Elizabethan times. They understood that they were in a position to inherit the achievements and learn from the mistakes of that history. "The history of Great Britain is the one with which we are in general the best acquainted, and it gives us many useful lessons," John Jay wrote in *Federalist* 5. "We may profit from their experience, without paying the price which it cost them." At the Constitutional Convention, delegates regularly spoke—several gave lectures, sometimes lasting hours—of the lessons to be drawn from ancient and modern history. History was the essence of their national identity. It was the touchstone of their common political, social, and cultural lives as loyal colonists of the British Empire.

By far their greatest inheritance from their mother country was the concept of liberty itself, which had come to be associated with and protected by English rule. Beginning with Magna Carta in 1215—when the barons of England forced King John to guarantee certain liberties in exchange for their loyalty to him—up through "modern" documents such as the Petition of Right (1628), the Habeas Corpus Act (1679), and the Bill of Rights (1689), it had come to be understood that there were certain rights that all subjects of the English monarch everywhere possessed and could expect to be protected.* Indeed, it was these rights of

---

(1994) by Carl J. Richard.

* For more on this, see *The Road from Runnymede: Magna Carta and Constitutionalism in America* (1968) by A. E. Dick Howard.

Englishmen—legal due process, trial by jury, security in one's home from unlawful entry, no taxation without consent—that the American colonists would argue were violated by the British themselves in the years before the American Revolution, leading them to assert their own ideas of constitutional government. Despite this break, the Americans always saw themselves as continuing and extending the great achievements of British constitutionalism.

The British "constitution" did not exist in one written document in the way we think of the term today. Instead, it was a combination of the numerous decrees, conventions, laws, royal charters, and accumulated legal opinions that had evolved over centuries. This difference will be important in the development of the United States Constitution. The British common law, likewise, was a body of judicial decisions developed over time that defined the limits on government and the privileges given to the people in these documents. Early American legal ideas were deeply shaped by the British common-law tradition. John Adams wrote that "the liberty, the unalienable, indefeasible rights of men, the honor and dignity of human nature, the grandeur and glory of the public, and the universal happiness of individuals, were never so skillfully and successfully consulted as in that most excellent monument of human art, the common law of England." Early American legal thought was influenced by the great jurists and writers of British legal history, especially Sir Edward Coke (pronounced "Cook") and Sir William Blackstone, the author of the landmark *Commentaries on the Laws of England.*[*] Lastly, it is important to keep in mind the great extent to which colonial government and laws in America were modeled on British institutions—the primary one being parliament, the great English legislative body—and designed to uphold the rights and liberties guaranteed under the British rule of law.

The French Revolution

In the broadest sense, the American Founders were men of the Enlightenment. Based on the scientific revolution that began in the seventeenth century, the Enlightenment was a worldwide philosophical movement—led by thinkers in France, England, Scotland, and Germany

---

[*] See James Stoner's *Common Law and Liberal Theory: Coke, Hobbes, and the Origins of American Constitutionalism* (1992).

over the course of the eighteenth century—that was characterized by a strong belief in the advance of scientific knowledge and a confidence that this reasoning would come to reshape much of human life. Writers and thinkers of the day, "enlightened" by reason, called for great innovations in the ideas, politics, and culture of Western society. A healthy skepticism abounded, as well as a broad humanitarianism.

The American Founders firmly believed in individual freedom, in the pursuit of economic well-being, and in benefiting from the material fruits of modern science. They welcomed the technological innovations developing in the modern world. Nevertheless, the Enlightenment that flourished in America—powerfully expressed in the American Founding—was not the same Enlightenment as that which came to dominate and then disfigure the European continent. The differences are critical, not only to understanding the American Founding but also to realizing the divergences between American and European history even in our day.

France was the intellectual and practical focus of the more extreme version of the Enlightenment. Driven by the view that pure scientific reason would radically change every institution of human society, French *philosophes* (thinkers such as Diderot, Voltaire, and Rousseau) were not only highly skeptical of classical reasoning and traditional philosophy but also deeply and even violently antireligious and anticlerical. They aspired to free humanity from the "prejudice," "custom," and "authority" associated with the "irrational" ideas of the past. In order to reform society and politics to reflect their new ideas, they criticized accepted ideas and advocated the overthrow of every vestige of the existing social and political order. They were truly revolutionary in all things. "Man will never be free," to use the vivid line attributed to Diderot, "until the last king is strangled with the entrails of the last priest." Jean-Jacques Rousseau (who did not entirely agree with the early Enlightenment) dramatically opened *The Social Contract* of 1762 with the announcement, "Man is born free, and everywhere he is in chains." Yet once the Enlightenment's political reforms are put in place, Rousseau declared, "Whoever refuses to obey will be forced to be free."

The French Revolution (1789–99) claimed the American Revolution as its predecessor but in fact was inspired by radical Enlightenment ideology. Considered the first of the modern revolutions, it sought to liberate mankind from the shackles of the old order—and crush anyone and anything that stood in its way. Beginning with the abolition of the aristocratic and religious privileges that dominated French politics, as well as a social program to formally redistribute land and wealth, the political and social upheaval that continued in the name of *liberté, égalité,* and *fraternité* was quickly accompanied by riots, chaos, and violent turmoil. What seemingly began as a constitutional monarchy soon suspended the monarchy, and then condemned and beheaded the French king. Once in control, the revolutionaries repressed their perceived enemies, held tens of thousands of public executions, and eventually devoured their own during an official Reign of Terror.* It all culminated in the dictatorship of Napoleon and his wars of imperial expansion, which did not end until his defeat in the Battle of Waterloo in 1815.

One of the earliest and fiercest critics of the French Revolution was the great British statesman Edmund Burke, who saw it as a total rebellion against society—"a revolution in sentiments, manners and moral opinions"—that would inevitably become violent and uncontrolled. "Justifying perfidy and murder for public benefit, public benefit would soon become the pretext, and perfidy and murder the end, until rapacity, malice, revenge, and fear more dreadful than revenge could satiate their insatiable appetites," Burke wrote in his *Reflections on the Revolution in France.* "Such must be the consequences of losing, in the splendor of these triumphs of the rights of men, all natural sense of wrong and right." The denial of right and wrong at the heart of the French Revolution left it unable to check the violent passions it had unleashed.

The American Enlightenment

The American Enlightenment—and so the American Revolution—was very different. While the French *philosophes* were abstract and speculative, and wanted to create a new kind of man for a new kind of social order, the American Founders were practical and constructed a new constitutional order that was based on the traditional concept of a fixed human nature. The reasonableness and moderation of the American Revolution contrasts sharply with the radical ideas and violent character of the French Revolution.

---

* A compelling and comprehensive account is *The Oxford History of the French Revolution* (1990) by William Doyle.

This had much to do with the fact that the Americans were influenced by the moderate Enlightenment that had flourished especially in Great Britain. In her work comparing the various forms of the Enlightenment, the social historian Gertrude Himmelfarb writes that "the skeptical Enlightenment *à la France* had had virtually no influence on America in its formative years." In 1984, two professors studied the sources cited by the founding generation in their major writings between 1760 and 1805. Their findings are revealing, to say the least. The most-referenced work by far was the Bible, accounting for 34 percent of all citations. The next grouping, making up 22 percent of the citations, was dominated by three writers associated with the moderate Enlightenment: John Locke, the author of *Two Treatises of Government* (1689); Baron de Montesquieu, or the "celebrated Montesquieu," as Madison called him, who praised the forms of England's government and advocated small republics and the separation of government powers; and William Blackstone, the great English jurist. Citations of Locke were highest in the 1760s and 1770s, when the colonists were considering the ground of their constitutional rights and the justification of their impending independence; in the 1780s the Founders turned more to Montesquieu as they focused on constitutional design; in the 1790s they looked to Blackstone during the early years of the new government.*

Locke was especially influential in America, so it is important to understand how the Founders viewed him and his work. In 1688, King James II had been overthrown in what came to be called the Glorious Revolution, replaced on the English throne by William of Orange. The greatest consequence was to make the king subject to the legislature, a monumental step in the development of constitutional government. The resulting English Bill of Rights (1689) is a milestone in British constitutionalism. Nevertheless, England still had a hereditary monarch and a landed aristocracy that controlled parliament's House of Lords. While there was some religious toleration—again, a notable improvement—there was still an established church, headed by the monarch, who appointed the church leadership. As a result, England was divided

---

* See Gertrude Himmelfarb's *The Roads to Modernity: The British, French, and American Enlightenments* (2004). "The Relative Influence of European Writers on Late Eighteenth-Century American Political Thought" by Donald Lutz and Charles Hyneman, can be found in the *American Political Science Review* (1984).

between the dominant guardians of traditional monarchy and those reformers who saw the Glorious Revolution as a legitimate, popular resistance to government tyranny based on what was then a new idea of the consent of the governed.

In this split, the Americans took the side of the republican Whig reformers rather than the Tory defenders of the throne. The great martyr of the republican cause was Algernon Sidney, who had been executed for attacking absolute monarchy and defending republican principles in his *Discourses Concerning Government* (1698). By the mid-1760s, the Whig interpretation had become part of the British constitutional position as espoused by William Blackstone in his authoritative *Commentaries*. But the expositor par excellence of the argument was John Locke.

In his *Two Treatises of Government*, Locke taught that all men were by nature free and equal, that legitimate government came into existence through a social contract, that political power required consent, and that government should be constitutionally limited to protecting fundamental rights of life, liberty, and property. The Americans learned these political ideas both directly from reading Locke and through intermediaries like John Trenchard and Thomas Gordon (the British authors of *Cato's Letters*) and other Whig writers such as Algernon Sidney. Most Americans learned the argument in popular form through the writings of their own political thinkers—Jefferson, Adams, Hamilton, Madison, and others. These arguments even showed up in American church sermons, right alongside and understood to be perfectly consistent with the arguments of biblical theology.

Throughout these American writings, Lockean arguments for natural rights are presented not in the context of the Enlightenment per se but rather as part of the larger intellectual horizon that encompassed the American mind. There is little if any evidence, for instance, that the Americans went beyond Locke's political principles to the more problematic epistemological ideas expressed in his *Essay on Human Understanding*. That is, the American Founders understood Locke in light of classical political reason and biblical revelation, as part of the English Whig republican thinking and the natural law tradition in which they understood themselves.

Colonial Experience

Perhaps the most overlooked influence on the Founders was their own practical experience, accumulated through grappling with and adapting their conditions and applying the ideas and the principles they knew to the world around them.

In the half century leading up to 1763, parliament rarely intervened in the governance of the colonies, and loosely enforced its trade regulations with them. It was only after their victory in the French and Indian War that the British, needing money and resources to maintain their empire, abandoned the hands-off policy Edmund Burke once described as a "wise and salutary neglect." For decades, the American colonies had essentially been governing themselves under the guise and protection of imperial rule. During this period, as Burke noted in his 1775 speech in the House of Commons defending the colonies, "A generous nature has been suffered to take her own way to perfection." That is, the British policy of generally neglecting the American colonies created a situation in which the Americans learned to take care of themselves.

The rule of law, fundamental rights and liberties, constitutional limits on government—all of these ideas had been slowly developing over the centuries. But the particular circumstances of the colonies, in which they had to make their own way on a vast continent of untamed wilderness and eventually assert their own freedom in defiance of a distant and unreasonable ruler, encouraged and allowed these ideas to advance more rapidly and take unique shape in British North America.

Most of the great practical questions the Americans would later face were implicit from the beginning. Their charters entitled the colonists to the rights and privileges of Englishmen—"as if they had been abiding and born in this our realm of England," as the 1609 royal charter of Virginia put it. As we shall see, a significant controversy arose regarding the nature of those rights and the authority and responsibility of the king and parliament in the colonies, and that debate played a central role in the revolution. Charters also gave them the significant experience of written agreements—contracts, if you will—about fundamental political questions, preparing the ground for formal, written constitutions of government.

The charters of the colonies formed governments strongly resembling the structure of the English government. For most of the colonies, the governor was appointed by the king. All but one of the colonies had bicameral legislatures that were considered to be small-scale models of the English Parliament, with an upper chamber usually appointed in England and a colonially elected lower chamber. As might be expected, the appointed governor often came in conflict with the local legislators, but the legislature generally prevailed because it controlled government funding and appropriations—including the governor's wages. The concept of representation that developed in the colonies differed from that of the British: A representative in America acted to promote the common good of his colony as a whole but also represented the people of his particular district. Not so in England, where there was no actual relationship between the member of parliament and his constituents. This distinction is crucial to understanding the argument over consent and representation leading up to the revolution. The Americans would also conclude, based on their experience, that there needed to be significant new checks on legislative power, well beyond those imposed on the British Parliament.

Most importantly, the colonial experience of generally managing their own affairs taught Americans the difficulties and importance of participatory government and the institutions of democratic politics. Such institutions, which existed and thrived throughout the colonies down to the local level of government, were considered the practical manifestation of liberty. It was through these institutions, by which the American colonials "acquired from their infancy the habit of discussing, of deliberating, and of judging of public affairs," John Adams wrote, "that the sentiments of the people were formed in the first place." This well-established habit, built on town hall meetings and local governance, gave rise to the many conferences, congresses, and conventions that were the deliberative structures wherein were forged the argument and action of the American Founding.

Novus Ordo Seclorum

In one sense, the American Revolution was about old ideas and inherited liberties that had been denied the Americans by their British rulers. It was not a revolution to overthrow society, not the upheaval that is associated with the French model—or the Spanish, Russian, and Chinese

revolutions of the twentieth century. The American Founders understood themselves as part of a larger culture of Western civilization, and
sought to preserve that great bequest.

But the past could tell them only so much. They had to make their
own decisions as best they could, in light of the times in which they
found themselves, in keeping with the specific character of the American people. "The establishment of our new Government seemed to be
the last great experiment for promoting human happiness by reasonable
compact in civil Society," George Washington later wrote in reflecting
upon the accomplishment. "It was to be, in the first instance, in a considerable degree a government of accommodation as well as a government of Laws. Much was to be done by *prudence*, much by *conciliation*,
much by *firmness*." We must always keep in mind that the accomplishment of the American Founding was the work of statesmanship.

"Is it not the glory of the people of America, that, whilst they have
paid a decent regard to the opinions of former times and other nations,
they have not suffered a blind veneration for antiquity, for custom, or for
names, to overrule the suggestions of their own good sense, the knowledge of their own situation, and the lessons of their own experience?"
James Madison asked in *Federalist* 14. Had they listened exclusively to
the advice from history and previous political theorists and not trusted
their own educated instincts and practical reason, the American Founders might well have given up on the prospect of launching their experiment in liberty. After all, the history of republican governments was one
of unrelieved failure, and virtually every serious political thinker since
ancient times held that self-government was unstable and could not
endure. "Happily for America, happily, we trust, for the whole human
race, they pursued a new and more noble course," wrote Madison.

Those who achieved the American Founding understood themselves
to be engaged in a momentous project to secure liberty for themselves and
their posterity, and by proving it possible, to determine the future of republican government. "They accomplished a revolution which has no parallel
in the annals of human society," Madison continued. "They reared the fab-
rics of governments which have no model on the face of the globe." It was
to be, if it succeeded, a *novus ordo seclorum*—a new order of the ages.

In the end, the American Founding was a test to see whether free
men could govern themselves.

But it is not a test that, once taken and passed, is over and done with. America remains a proposition, as Abraham Lincoln said in his greatest speech, meaning that the validity of its claims is to be tested again and again and again.

It is in that spirit that we now join these great statesmen—who dedicated their lives, liberties, and sacred honor to the cause of American liberty—in their collective effort, thinking through the first principles of liberty and constitutional government, to answer the all-important question, posed by Alexander Hamilton in the opening of *Federalist* 1, "whether societies of men are really capable or not of establishing good government from reflection and choice, or whether they are forever destined to depend for their political constitutions on accident and force."

2

~~~

We Hold These Truths:
Equality, Natural Rights, and
the Consent of the Governed

O n the night of April 18, 1775, a force of British light infantry and grenadiers slipped out of their Boston encampment with the objective of seizing rebel military supplies thought to be hidden at Concord, Massachusetts. A well-organized team of riders, signaled by lanterns hung in the steeple of Boston's Old North Church and visible across the harbor, alerted the awaiting countryside. One determined rider, a silversmith named Paul Revere, warned John Hancock, head of the Massachusetts Provincial Congress, and everyone else along the way of the troop movements. The British were coming.

On the way to Concord, in the predawn hours of April 19, the British force passed through the small village of Lexington. There, a number of citizens—less than 150 men, ranging in age from sixteen to sixty-six, including eight pairs of fathers and sons—had mustered on the town green. "Stand your ground," Captain John Parker told his volunteer militia. "Don't fire unless fired upon, but if they mean to have a war, let it begin here." One can only imagine their fear—nervously anticipating, hearing, and then catching sight of the long columns of well-armed soldiers approaching them.

Upon entering Lexington that morning and seeing the armed colonials, the British forces quickened their march to a slow run. As they had been trained, the advance units deployed to a line of battle across the field. Major John Pitcairn of the Royal Marines charged up from behind and ordered the rebels to disburse. Moments later, shots were fired, then a series of volleys. The War for Independence had begun.*

The Battle of Concord followed later that morning, with the Americans holding their ground and then engaging the British all the way back to Boston. News of the fighting—and what the poet Ralph Waldo Emerson would call "the shot heard 'round the world"—spread quickly throughout the colonies.

It was an amazing turnaround. Just a decade earlier, the British colonies in North America were a loyal part of the freest, richest, and most powerful empire that the world had ever known. Now they were in open revolt, and the king of England had declared them to be in rebellion.

How had it come to this? The answer is to be found in the tumultuous decade leading up to these events. It was between 1763 and 1776, during the "long train of abuses" which led the colonies to declare themselves an independent nation, that the Americans were forced as never before to think through fundamental questions about the basis of liberty and constitutional government. Key debates—about the legitimate process of representation and, beyond that, about the ultimate source of their rights—led to the definition of three closely connected foundational principles: that the just powers of government are derived from the consent of the governed; that the source of constitutional legitimacy is found in equal natural rights; and that these rights are grounded in the self-evident truth that all men are created equal.

The Road to Revolution

In 1763, with the British victory over France in the Seven Years' War (which began in North America as the French and Indian War), Great Britain controlled—in addition to the thirteen American colonies— New France (Canada), Spanish Florida, and all the lands east of the Mississippi River. It also had massive debts, incurred in large part in the defense of that empire, and so the English Parliament looked for the first time to the American colonies as a source of revenue.

The American Revenue Act (sometimes called the Sugar Act) expanded various import and export duties and created additional

---

* The story is wonderfully told in *Paul Revere's Ride* (1994) by David Hackett Fischer.

courts and collection mechanisms to strictly enforce trade laws. Then parliament went a step further and passed the first direct tax levied on America, requiring all newspapers, almanacs, pamphlets, and official documents—even decks of playing cards!—to have stamps (hence it was called the Stamp Act) to show payment of taxes.

The colonists—who by this point were very used to their independence and Britain's benign oversight of their affairs—were none too pleased with the new imperial policies. Colonial merchants instinctively began a movement to boycott British goods, and a new group called the Sons of Liberty was formed to foment and organize opposition. Several legislatures called for united action, and nine colonies sent delegates to a Stamp Act Congress in New York in October 1765.

The American Revolution began as a tax revolt. But it is important to understand from the start that the debate was never really over the *amount* of taxation (the taxes were actually quite low) but the *process* by which the British government imposed and enforced these taxes. As loyal colonists, the Americans had long recognized parliament's authority to legislate for the empire generally, as with colonial trade, but they had always maintained that the power to tax was a legislative power reserved to their own assemblies rather than a distant legislature in London. You'll remember their slogan: no taxation without representation.

In making this argument, the colonials were objecting to being deprived of an important historic right: The English Bill of Rights of 1689 had forbidden the imposition of taxes without legislative consent, and since the colonists had no representation in parliament they complained that the taxes violated the traditional rights of Englishmen.

The British ended up repealing the tax, but in the Declaratory Act of 1766 they flatly rejected the Americans' general argument by asserting that parliament was absolutely sovereign and retained full power to make laws for the colonies "in all cases whatsoever." To the British, "no taxation without representation" was indeed a well-established right, but it was understood to mean no taxation without the approval of the British Parliament. And, they argued, it never literally meant—not for the Americans and not even for the overwhelming majority of British citizens—representation in that body. The colonists, like all British subjects, enjoyed "virtual representation" of their interests by the aristocrats that voted in and controlled parliament.

To the Americans, this was as absurd as it was unacceptable. Their commonsense notion of consent required actual representation—elected representatives of the governed making laws. So the declaration of the Stamp Act Congress—the first statement of the united colonies—argues that because the colonists were "entitled to all the inherent rights and privileges of his natural born subjects within the kingdom of Great Britain," no taxes could be imposed without colonial consent. And since as a practical matter they couldn't participate in a parliament thousands of miles away, the Americans concluded that this authority could only be vested in their local legislatures.

In 1767, the British government passed a new series of revenue measures (called the Townshend Acts) which placed import duties (external taxes) on a number of essential goods including paper, glass, lead, and tea—and once again affirmed the power of British courts to issue undefined and open-ended search warrants (called "writs of assistance") to enforce the law. Asserting that the sole right of taxation was with the colonial legislature, Virginia proposed a formal agreement among the colonies banning the importation of British goods—a practice that quickly spread to the other local legislatures and cut the colonial import of British goods in half. So parliament eventually repealed those duties, too, except—in order to maintain the principle that it could impose any taxes it wished—for the tax on tea.

It was at Boston in the spring of 1770 that, tensions running high, British soldiers fired on a large crowd of protesters, wounding eleven colonials and killing five. The Boston Massacre, as it was quickly called, marked the final downturn in the relationship between Britain and the American colonies. By late 1772, Samuel Adams and others were creating new Committees of Correspondence that would link together patriot groups in all thirteen colonies and eventually provide the framework for a new government. They would soon form Committees of Safety as well to oversee the local militias and the volunteers who had begun calling themselves Minutemen.

In December 1773, a group of colonists disguised as Indians boarded ships of several British merchants and in protest of British colonial policies dumped overboard an estimated £10,000 worth of tea in Boston Harbor. "The die is cast," reported John Adams. "The people have passed the river and cut away the bridge. Last night three cargoes of tea were emptied into the harbor. This is the grandest event which has ever yet happened since the controversy with Britain opened."

The British government responded harshly by punishing Massachusetts—closing Boston Harbor, virtually dissolving the Massachusetts Charter, taking control of colonial courts and restricting town meetings, and allowing British troops to be quartered in any home or private building. In response to these "Intolerable Acts" the various Committees of Correspondence banded together and planned an even larger congress of all the colonies to meet in Philadelphia in September 1774.*

Rights of Englishmen and of Nature

Ever since Magna Carta, British subjects had petitioned for justice according to their long-held rights as Englishmen. This was the case with the colonies as well, as when the assembly of colonial Maryland in 1639 claimed the rights of "any naturall born subject of England" or William Penn in 1675 spoke of "the ancient and undoubted rights of Englishmen." When the British imposed the Stamp Act in 1765, the British-appointed governor reported that "[the] prevailing reason at this time is, that the Act of Parliament is against the Magna Charta, and the natural rights of Englishmen, and therefore, according to Lord Coke, null and void."

But as the conflict developed the American colonists faced a real, practical dilemma: In fighting England to secure their rights as *Englishmen*, what better authority to define the extent and application of those rights than the king of England and the British Parliament? Without access to the ultimate grounding of those rights—what John Adams called the "foundation of right"—they were left fighting on England's terms without a higher authority to which they might appeal. And that made them more susceptible to British tyranny.

So from almost the beginning, and then with increasing emphasis, the Americans deepened and extended the British argument to focus on the inherent rights of human nature that were the original root of their historic privileges as Englishmen. Consider this early example from the

---

* The classic work on these British measures and colonial opposition to them is *The Founding of a Nation: A History of the American Revolution 1763–1776* (1968) by Merrill Jensen.

colonial leader James Otis in 1764: "Every British Subject born on the continent of America, or in any other of the British dominions, is by the law of God and nature, by the common law, and by act of parliament, (exclusive of all charters from the crown) entitled to all the natural, essential, inherent and inseparable rights of our fellow subjects in Great-Britain."

The revolutionary import of this argument becomes clear in a 1766 essay by John Dickinson of Pennsylvania:

> Kings or parliaments could not *give* the *rights essential to happiness*, as you confess those invaded by the Stamp Act to be.... They are not annexed to us by parchments and seals. They are created in us by the decrees of Providence, which establish the laws of our nature. They are born with us; exist with us; and cannot be taken from us by any human power, without taking our lives. In short, they are founded on the immutable maxims of reason and justice.

Meeting at Carpenter's Hall in Philadelphia in the fall of 1774, the First Continental Congress set a clear tone from the start. The congress set aside a loyalist-proposed reconciliation plan that would have created an American legislative body subject to parliament and instead unanimously adopted what were called the Suffolk Resolves (proposed by a convention in Suffolk County, Massachusetts), declaring the Intolerable Acts to be "unconstitutional," resolving to boycott British imports, instructing Massachusetts to form a government free of British authority, and calling on the colonies to prepare for the possibility of war.

Delegates also discussed the basis upon which to defend their rights. It was increasingly clear that appeals to common law and charters, to parliament and to the king, and to the rights of Englishmen were crucially important but ultimately insufficient in defending their liberties. Richard Henry Lee, for instance, observed that the rights of the colonists "are built on a fourfold foundation; on nature, on the British constitution, on charters, and on immemorial usage," but then advocated "lay[ing] our rights upon the broadest bottom, the ground of nature." In the end, delegates agreed that their strongest case was based on this ground, and that meant making human nature—"a resource to which we might be driven by parliament much sooner than we are aware," noted John Adams—the true foundation for their claims. The classic statement of this argument would be the Declaration of Independence.

This was not some abstract theory that the colonists had invented out of thin air. Nor were they repudiating their own past. In making this argument, they were recalling that the momentous rights protected by the British constitution and tradition, and held in common by all British subjects, were not exclusively *English* but were in fact derived from something more fundamental that applied to all human beings everywhere. Their rights were not a coincidence of history, and did not merely stem from the fact that they just happened to be British.

In turning to this argument, the Americans could look to several sources of support. John Locke and his influential *Two Treatises of Government*, written in the 1680s, argued that liberty was grounded in nature, and that the British constitution should be understood as the embodiment of that concept. But they could also point to William Blackstone in his *Commentaries on the Laws of England*, an authoritative English source on the laws and statutes that made up the British constitution:

> This law of nature, being co-eval with mankind and dictated by God himself, is of course superior in obligation to any other. It is binding over all the globe, in all countries, and at all times: no human laws are of any validity, if contrary to this; and such of them as are valid derive all their force, and all their authority, mediately or immediately, from this original.

And this from Edward Coke, the great English jurist: "The law of nature is that which God at the time of creation of the nature of man infused into his heart, for his preservation and direction; and this is *lex aeterna*, the moral law, called also the law of nature."

When loyalists criticized the actions of the First Continental Congress, a New Yorker named Alexander Hamilton—not yet twenty years old—defended the colonial cause in a series of spirited writings. In a pamphlet called *The Farmer Refuted*, Hamilton gave a powerful explanation of this understanding of the natural law and natural rights informing the actions of the congress. Quoting Blackstone as his authority, he spoke of "an eternal and immutable law, which is indispensably obligatory upon all mankind, prior to any human institution whatever."

Upon this law, depend the natural rights of mankind: the Supreme Being gave existence to man, together with the means of preserving and beatifying that existence. He endowed him with rational faculties, by the help of which, to discern and pursue such things, as were consistent with his duty and interest, and invested him with an inviolable right to personal liberty, and personal safety. . . .

The Sacred Rights of Mankind are not to be rummaged for, among old parchments, or musty records. They are written, as with a sun beam, in the whole volume of human nature, by the Hand of the Divinity itself; and can never be erased or obscured by mortal power.

A Declaration of Independence

A second continental congress convened just one month after fighting had broken out at Lexington and Concord, and only days before the Battle of Bunker Hill. War was now upon the land. One of the delegates' first acts was to recognize the various local militias that had instinctively surrounded the British at Boston as a Continental Army and appoint George Washington of Virginia—the only one among them with any real military experience—as its commander. The appointment "fills me with inexpressible concern," Washington wrote his wife, Martha. "But as it has been a kind of destiny that has thrown me upon this service, I shall hope that my undertaking is designed to answer some good purpose."

The Continental Congress sent to the king one last attempt at reconciliation, called the Olive Branch Petition. To make sure there was no confusion about its absolute seriousness, though, the congress also issued a "Declaration of the Causes and Necessities for Taking Up Arms," avowing that, if necessary, the colonists were "resolved to die Free men rather than live slaves." King George III refused to receive the colonial petition, issuing instead a Royal Proclamation of Rebellion regarding his disloyal subjects and promising "to bring the Traitors to Justice." The break was now complete and irreparable.

Thomas Paine's *Common Sense* in January 1776 issued the first clarion call: "Everything that is right and natural pleads for separation.

The blood of the slain, the weeping voice of nature cries, 'TIS TIME TO PART.'" The sentiment for independence was building, and hostilities made the decision all the more imperative.

And so on June 7, 1776, Richard Henry Lee, a delegate from Virginia, proposed a resolution to declare that "these United Colonies are, and of right ought to be, free and independent states," to establish a formal confederation of the colonies and to seek alliances between the united colonies and other nations. Each of these matters was referred to a select committee; the last two would lead to the Articles of Confederation and the Franco-American Treaty of 1778, which was crucial to fighting and winning America's War of Independence.* "We must be unanimous, we must hang together," the body's president, John Hancock, is reported to have said, to which Benjamin Franklin quipped: "Yes, we must indeed hang together, or most assuredly we shall all hang separately."

Congress extensively debated and eventually passed Lee's resolution in favor of independence on July 2, and then took two more days to debate and amend a committee's draft declaration, approving it on July 4. The separate consideration of Lee's resolution of independence and the committee's language to declare that independence suggests that more was required than a simple announcement of withdrawal from the British empire. Had that been the objective, Lee's resolution itself would have been sufficient. A "decent respect for the opinions of mankind," however, demanded a broader statement of the principles that justified their actions.

The Declaration of Independence is structured in the form of a common-law legal document: preamble, statement of principle, indictment, and conclusion. The stated purpose is to "declare the causes" that impelled the Americans to separate from the British. The document's famous second paragraph is a succinct and powerful synthesis of American constitutional and republican ideas. All these years later, its familiar opening words remain striking:

> We hold these truths to be self-evident, that all men are cre-
> ated equal, that they are endowed by their Creator with certain
> unalienable Rights, that among these are Life, Liberty and the

---

* Samuel Flagg Bemis's *The Diplomacy of the American Revolution* (1935) remains the standard work on this aspect of American history.

pursuit of Happiness.—That to secure these rights, Governments are instituted among Men, deriving their just powers from the consent of the governed,—That whenever any Form of Government becomes destructive of these ends, it is the Right of the People to alter or to abolish it, and to institute new Government, laying its foundation on such principles and organizing its powers in such form, as to them shall seem most likely to effect their Safety and Happiness.

The bulk of the document is a bill of indictment accusing King George III of some thirty offenses: some constitutional, some legal, and some matters of policy. In general, these grievances not only track the colonial complaints but also foreshadow many of the protections included twelve years later in the United States Constitution. A perennial favorite: "He has erected a multitude of New Offices, and sent hither swarms of Officers to harass our People, and eat out their substance." But the key charge was that the king had conspired with parliament to subject America to a "jurisdiction foreign to our constitution."

At this point in their constitutional development, the Americans argued that a common king with authority over each of the colonies was their only binding legal connection with Great Britain. Parliament was not a party to the various original compacts with the individual colonies and thus could not tax them or regulate their internal affairs. This explains why the colonists' final appeals—and the Declaration of Independence itself—were addressed to the king and not to parliament. Through his own actions (and inactions) leading up to the American Revolution, intentionally violating those agreements and explicitly placing America outside his protection, George III had himself rebelled, thereby dissolving the colonists' obligations of allegiance.

The combined charges against the king were intended to demonstrate a history of repeated injuries, all having the object of establishing "an absolute tyranny" over the colonies. And while the previously loyal subjects were "disposed to suffer, while Evils are sufferable," the time had come to acknowledge that the relationship had come to an end: "But when a long train of abuses and usurpations, pursuing invariably the same Object, evinces a design to reduce them under absolute Despotism, it is their right, it is their duty, to throw off such Government."

As a practical matter, the Declaration of Independence announced to the world the unanimous decision of the thirteen American colonies to separate themselves from Great Britain. But its greatest significance—then as well as now—was its enduring statement of the limits of political authority and the proper ends of government, and its proclamation of a new basis of political rule in the sovereignty of the people. The Americans' final appeal was not to any positive law or evolving theory but to rights inherently possessed by all men and "the separate and equal station to which the Laws of Nature and Nature's God" entitled them as a people.

The Declaration of Independence is revolutionary not because a particular group of Americans declared their independence under particular circumstances but because they did so by appealing to—and promising to base their particular government on—a universal and permanent standard of justice. As such, the Declaration's meaning transcends history and the particulars of the time. Self-evident truths are not restricted to any one era or nation; they are as true today as they were in 1776. It is in this sense that Abraham Lincoln in 1859 praised the author of the Declaration as "the man who, in the concrete pressure of a struggle for national independence by a single people, had the coolness, forecast, and capacity to introduce into a merely revolutionary document, an abstract truth, applicable to all men and all times, and so to embalm it there, that to-day, and in all coming days, it shall be a rebuke and a stumbling-block to the very harbingers of re-appearing tyranny and oppression."

The Laws of Nature and of Nature's God

Although Congress had appointed a distinguished committee to draft the Declaration of Independence—including John Adams, Benjamin Franklin, Roger Sherman, and Robert Livingston—the document is chiefly the work of Thomas Jefferson. Jefferson originally proposed that John Adams draft the Declaration, but Adams made the case to Jefferson that he must be the writer: "Reason first—You are a Virginian, and a Virginian ought to appear at the head of this business. Reason second—I am obnoxious, suspected, and unpopular. You are very much otherwise. Reason third—You can write ten times better than I can."

By his own account, Jefferson was neither aiming at originality nor taking from any particular writings but was expressing what he called

the "harmonizing sentiments of the day." The basic theory of the document reflected English Whig thought as it had been developed in the pre-
ceding century and a half. By 1776, the ideas of the Declaration—about
nature, rights, and government—were well established in the colonies.
George Mason had anticipated much of its substance in his draft of the
Virginia Declaration of Rights one month earlier. Jefferson stressed that
he had written the Declaration to be "an expression of the American
mind," and used language so as to "place before mankind the common
sense of the subject, in terms so plain and firm as to command their
assent." He did his job well.

So what did the Continental Congress mean in asserting—going so
far as to say it is "self-evident"—that all men are *equal*? This seems to
make no sense. Ordinary experience tells us the exact opposite: There
are innumerable differences—in size, shape, color, intelligence, you
name it—and no two individuals are exactly alike. But these kinds of
differences are not what Jefferson (or the Continental Congress that
approved the Declaration) had in mind. Let us try to understand the
matter as they understood it.

The Declaration of Independence makes its claim for American
independence based on "the Laws of Nature and of Nature's God." In
looking to nature, the Founders did not mean the outdoors—the trees,
lakes, and animals that make up the natural environment. They meant
nature as in the design or purpose of things, as birds by nature fly just
as fish by nature swim. Different things have different natures. Man has
a distinguishing nature as well; it has to do with distinctive capacities
and characteristics. Other species follow instinct and, as a result, are not
responsible for their actions. Wolves, for instance, cannot be said to be
responsible for killing sheep—that's what wolves do. But human beings
are different: They are capable of imagination, deliberation, judgment,
and choice in their actions and so can be held morally accountable. It is
this ability to contemplate right and wrong and to act accordingly that
distinguishes men from other animals. In this sense, man is by nature
unique among animals, and alone has the capacity for liberty.

That "all men" are created equal is not a reference to males as
opposed to females but means the whole human species. Indeed, the
observed inequalities of individual men and women (such as size, shape,
and color) are insignificant and dramatically underscore the ways in

which all human beings, as a species, are equal in their nature.* It says in the Declaration of Independence that this equality is "self-evident." In what sense? To say that something is self-evident does not mean that it is *obvious*, but means that something is evident in itself once one understands the terms involved. Once we understand that "man" has a certain nature, for instance, it becomes self-evident that all men, by sharing the same nature, are equal. We can understand this to be "self-evident" regardless of whether we believe nature to have been created (as in "all men are *created* equal") or observed by reason, as in the language of the Virginia Declaration of Rights ("all men are by nature equally free and independent").

This understanding of human nature reaches back to both classical philosophy and biblical theology—as in "the Laws of Nature" as well as "nature's God"—and represents a profound agreement between reason and revelation about man and the proper ground of politics. The Founders understood the argument for natural rights to be a continuation of both the English republican tradition—in writers such as John Locke and Algernon Sidney, whose *Discourses Concerning Government* was widely read and admired in America—and a natural law tradition dating back to medieval thinkers such as Thomas Aquinas and further to classical thinkers such as Aristotle and Cicero. The "harmonizing sentiments" expressed in the Declaration of Independence, Jefferson wrote, could be found in conversation, letters, essays, and "the elementary books of public right, as Aristotle, Cicero, Locke, Sidney, etc." One can also see these arguments woven together in religious sermons of the day, associating human nature and natural rights with theological views of creation and moral obligation, pointing out that God created man and is the author of the laws of nature.

Because of this nature, each man is his own natural ruler, with the capacity to govern himself. Unlike an animal, man can make decisions about how to live his own life and conduct his affairs. Because man is rational and seeks relationships with others to fulfill that nature, men can live in communities based on agreed purposes and common understandings of justice. At the same time, man is a bundle of desires and emotions, and is prone to allow his passions to overrule his reason. It is with this inclination in mind that Madison famously wrote in *Federalist* 10 that

---

* Hadley Arkes's *First Things* (1986) investigates this concept in greater depth.

"the latent causes of faction are sown in the nature of man." And recall his memorable observation from *Federalist* 51: "It may be a reflection on human nature, that such devices should be necessary to control the abuses of government. But what is government itself, but the greatest of all reflections on human nature? If men were angels, no government would be necessary."

The Founders' view of nature was by no means wholly negative. "As there is a degree of depravity in mankind which requires a certain degree of circumspection and distrust," Madison observed in *Federalist* 55, "so there are other qualities in human nature which justify a certain portion of esteem and confidence." The choosing of moral actions shapes habits and gives rise to virtue. But it was a sober view consistent with classical philosophy as well as the Christian concept of man fallen from divine grace. The givens of human nature—the highs, the lows, and the in-betweens—had to be accounted for in forming government, and its weaknesses moderated and corrected by moral education and character formation.

The emphasis on nature is profoundly significant, as it provided the philosophical mooring for everything else.* It was the concept that defined the grounds and legitimate ends of politics and political community. As such, it is the necessary premise of the foundational and operational first principles of American liberty.

Equal Rights

The idea of grounding the first principles of liberty on the equal human nature of all persons has great implications. The natural relationship between man and horse, for instance, is that of master and servant, because in the order of nature man is rationally superior to beast. But no such relationship exists, by nature, between man and man. Jefferson once described this relationship using a powerful analogy from Algernon Sidney: "[T]he mass of mankind has not been born with saddles on their backs, nor a favored few booted and spurred, ready to ride them legitimately, by the grace of God."

---

* On the importance of foundational concepts in American political thought, see James Ceaser's *Nature and History in American Political Development: A Debate* (2006).

That man is unique in the scheme of creation also means that man is entitled to certain rights that result from that common humanity.* A right is something that justly belongs to someone and creates a claim against those who deprive one of that right. One person's right implies an equivalent duty in others not to interfere unjustly with that right. In terms of these fundamental rights (called "natural rights"), we are all equal—no one has more and no one less—and equally free.

While there are, of course, dramatic differences in abilities and talents, all persons are equal before the law and are to be given equal protection of the same fundamental rights. John Adams articulated this case in his *Discourses on Davila* when he wrote that "among men, all are subject by nature to equal laws of morality, and in society have a right to equal laws for their government, yet no two men are perfectly equal in person, property, understanding, activity, and virtue—or ever can be made so by any power less than that which created them."

Two things should be noted in this context. First, it is important to understand that the philosophical grounding in natural rights does not create a radical and unlimited sense of freedom, as some claim today. The argument of the American Founders is of rights derived from a human nature understood in accord with the classical or traditional view of man. The Declaration of Independence says that "all men are created equal and endowed by their creator with *certain* unalienable rights." These are the truly fundamental things, not just anything or everything we want or claim. You may *want* a better job, but that does not mean you have a natural right to it. Rights are those things that are self-evident from an understanding of man and his place in the nature of things. Foremost among these are the right to one's own life and the right to pursue the purposes or ends of man's nature—that is, the pursuit of happiness. As we will learn, two other very important core rights that stem from our nature are the right of conscience or religious liberty, and the right to property. We also have a natural right to govern ourselves as a sovereign people.

Second, these rights are not the creation or indulgence of government. While additional positive or civil rights (more correctly termed

---

* On the unique American understanding of rights, see Charles Kesler, *The Nature of Rights in American Politics: A Comparison of Three Revolutions* (Heritage First Principles Essay #18).

civil liberties) are enshrined in the Constitution—like the rights of free speech and freedom of the press recognized in the Bill of Rights—and Congress can legislatively create "civil" rights, natural rights preexist the institution of government, precisely because they arise out of the natural equality that is the essence of human liberty. Congress (or more likely today, the courts) can't just make up rights as it sees fit. Nor can these rights be taken away—they are "unalienable" and can't be given over (alienated) to someone else. In the end, it is this sense of rights that ultimately limits government. The law of nature, as Hamilton explained, is "an eternal and immutable law, which is indispensably obligatory upon all mankind, prior to any human institution whatever." Jefferson was more to the point when he wrote that the colonists claimed "their rights as derived from the laws of nature, and not as the gift of their Chief Magistrate."

The Contradiction of Slavery

It is impossible to go any further without discussing the existence of slavery in America, which clearly and blatantly contradicts this nation's dedication to liberty and equal rights. Does the continuation of human slavery after the American Founding make the United States or its principles less defensible as a guide for just government? Does it make the nation ill-founded and so not worth our support?

A brief review of some history is in order.* At the time of the American Founding, there were about half a million African slaves in the United States, mostly in the five southernmost states, where they made up 40 percent of the population. Many of the leading American Founders—most notably Thomas Jefferson, George Washington, and James Madison—owned slaves, but many did not. Benjamin Franklin thought that slavery was "an atrocious debasement of human nature" and "a source of serious evils." He and Benjamin Rush founded the Pennsylvania Society for Promoting the Abolition of Slavery in 1774. John Jay, who was the president of a similar society in New York, believed that "the honour of the states, as well as justice and humanity, in my opinion, loudly call upon them to emancipate these unhappy people. To contend for our own liberty, and to deny that blessing to others, involves an

---

* Thomas G. West addresses this issue (and others) in *Vindicating the Founding: Race, Sex, Class, and Justice in the Origins of America* (1997).

inconsistency not to be excused." John Adams opposed slavery his entire life as a "foul contagion in the human character" and "an evil of colossal magnitude." And they were right.

It is clear from his letters that George Washington struggled with the reality and inhumanity of slavery in the midst of the free nation he was helping to construct. In 1774, he wrote that Americans must assert their rights against the British or else submit to being ruled "till custom and use shall make us as tame and abject slaves, as the blacks we rule over with such arbitrary sway." When he took command of the Continental Army in 1775, there were both slaves and free blacks in its ranks. (About five thousand blacks served in the Continental Army.) At one point, Alexander Hamilton proposed a general plan to enlist slaves in the army and "give them their freedom with their muskets," and Washington supported the policy (with the approval of Congress) in South Carolina and Georgia, two of the largest slaveholding states.

In 1786, Washington wrote of slavery, "There is not a man living who wishes more sincerely than I do, to see a plan adopted for the abolition of it." He devised a plan to rent his lands and turn his slaves into paid laborers, and at the end of his presidency he quietly left several of his slaves to their freedom. In the end, he could take it no more, and decreed in his will that family slaves (most came to his estate by marriage) would become free upon the death of his wife. The old and infirm were to be cared for while they lived, and any children among them were to be taught to read and write and trained in a useful skill until they reached age twenty-five. Washington's estate paid for this care until 1833.

The case of Thomas Jefferson is more troubling. During his first term in the House of Burgesses, Jefferson proposed legislation to emancipate slaves in Virginia, but the motion was soundly defeated. His 1774 draft instructions to the Virginia delegates of the First Continental Congress, A Summary View of the Rights of British America, called for an end to the slave trade: "The abolition of domestic slavery is the great object of desire in those colonies where it was unhappily introduced in their infant state." That same year the First Continental Congress agreed to discontinue the slave trade and boycott other nations that engaged in it. The Second Continental Congress affirmed the policy in 1776.

Jefferson's original draft of the Declaration of Independence—written at a time when he owned about two hundred slaves—included a paragraph condemning the British king for introducing African slavery into the colonies and continuing the slave trade:

> He has waged cruel war against human nature itself, violating its most sacred rights of life and liberty in the persons of a distant people who never offended him, captivating & carrying them into slavery in another hemisphere, or to incur miserable death in their transportation thither. This piratical warfare, the opprobrium of INFIDEL powers, is the warfare of a CHRISTIAN king of Great Britain. Determined to keep open a market where MEN should be bought & sold, he has prostituted his negative for suppressing every legislative attempt to prohibit or to restrain this execrable commerce.

Despite his noble words attacking the institution, Jefferson never freed his slaves. His own hypocrisy, however, does not remove the powerful meaning of the language. The words of the draft Declaration were especially offensive to delegates from Georgia and South Carolina, who were unwilling to acknowledge that slavery went so far as to violate the "most sacred rights of life and liberty," and so, like some of Jefferson's more expressive phrases attacking the king, they were dropped in the editing process for the sake of maintaining unanimous support of the document. Nevertheless, the central principle—that all men are created equal and endowed with unalienable rights—remained as an obvious rebuke and condemnation of the institution.

From very early in the movement for independence it was understood that calls for colonial freedom from British tyranny, especially the arguments grounded in equal rights and human nature, had clear implications for ending domestic slavery. "The colonists are by the law of nature free born, as indeed all men are, white and black," James Otis wrote back in 1761. "Does it follow that it is the right to enslave a man because he is black?" The Founders knew that human slavery violated the self-evident truths of human liberty. Indeed, it is difficult, if not impossible, to find a statement to the contrary.

In the wake of independence, state after state passed legislation restricting or banning the institution. In 1774, Rhode Island had already passed legislation providing that all slaves imported thereafter should be freed. In 1776, Delaware prohibited the slave trade and removed restraints on the liberation of slaves, as did Virginia in 1778. In 1779, Pennsylvania passed legislation providing for gradual emancipation, as did New Hampshire, Rhode Island, and Connecticut in the early 1780s, and New York and New Jersey in 1799 and 1804. In 1780, the Massachusetts Supreme Judicial Court ruled that the state's bill of rights made slavery unconstitutional. By the time of the U.S. Constitution, every state (except Georgia) had at least proscribed or suspended the importation of slaves. These steps, as incomplete as they were, suggest that the cultural and political rejection of slavery had already begun.*

By any and all accounts and measures, slavery was the great flaw in the American Founding. But consider the achievement. Having inherited the institution of slavery, those who founded this nation established in principle a country dedicated to the proposition that all men are created equal. The principle necessary to destroy slavery was the cornerstone of the new nation. The alternative, given the facts of the day, was no such nation. "The inconsistency of the institution of slavery with the principles of the Declaration of Independence was seen and lamented," John Quincy Adams readily admitted in 1837. Nevertheless, he argued, "no charge of insincerity or hypocrisy can be fairly laid to their charge. Never from their lips was heard one syllable of attempt to justify the institution of slavery. They universally considered it as a reproach fastened upon them by the unnatural step-mother country and they saw that before the principles of the Declaration of Independence slavery, in common with every mode of oppression, was destined sooner or later to be banished from the earth."

The Consent of the Governed

Having considered the philosophical principle of equality, and of natural rights that follow from that concept, let us return to the other first principle that develops practically in parallel over the course of the American Revolution: the consent of the governed. This follows from man's natural equality and equal rights. If we are all equal, and no one (king, a ruling class, intellectual elites) possesses a right to rule by nature, then

* This case is made in great detail by Don E. Fehrenbacher in *The Slaveholding Republic: An Account of the United States Government's Relations to Slavery* (2001).

we must proceed in a way that gives everyone as much as possible an equal say in how political rule is formed and operates. Because of our status as equals, it is also the case that legitimate government—that is, government that respects that fundamental equality—must be based on common agreement or consent.

Americans understood government not as a relationship between the ruler and the ruled but a voluntary agreement among the sovereign people about how they shall govern themselves to secure the rights they possessed by nature. This was referred to as the "social compact." The idea was espoused by (and came to Americans through the writings of) John Locke and others. Americans saw much of their own history in terms of contract and compact—from the religious view of covenant theology applied in the context of political governance, to the fact that individual colonies began with charters between the king and the colonies. For well over a century, Americans developed and became accustomed to the idea of government as having been created through fundamental agreement authorized by popular consent.

The concept can be seen in the Massachusetts Constitution of 1780, which declares: "The body politic is formed by a voluntary association of individuals; it is a social compact by which the whole people covenants with each citizen and each citizen with the whole people." But it is summarized very simply in the words of the Declaration of Independence, which posits as a self-evident truth "that to secure these rights, Governments are instituted among Men, deriving their just powers from the consent of the governed."

In addition to the formation of government in the first place, consent also gives guidance concerning the processes by which legitimate government operates. Among the charges lodged against the king in the Declaration of Independence is that he assented to parliament's "imposing Taxes on us without our Consent" and "has kept among us, in times of peace, Standing Armies without the Consent of our legislatures." Indeed, the first six charges against the king address interference with local legislation and legislatures, violating "the right of Representation in the Legislature, a right inestimable to them and formidable to tyrants only."

Consent does not necessarily mean pure democratic rule, but it does require some sort of process of popular agreement to lawmaking and governance. In America, this was understood to mean a popular form of representative government. Only a government that derived its power from "the great body of the people," according to *Federalist* 39, was compatible with the "genius of the American people," "the fundamental principles of the revolution," and a determination to "rest all our political experiments on the capacity of mankind for self-government."

On the other hand, consent does not mean mere majoritarianism—that anything and everything the majority demands is right. Lawmaking by consent is not the simple translating of majority will into public policy but is the product of settled public reasoning consistent with a proper understanding of the first principles of liberty. Consent is the legitimate or just means for securing equal rights, but in the end it remains the *means* rather than the *end* of democratic government.

Just because a government is based on consent does not mean that it is incapable of violating equal rights. In 1934, for instance, 90 percent of German citizens officially approved Adolf Hitler as Führer of Germany. To itself be legitimate, popular consent must understand and respect the rights and the responsibilities of constitutional government, often despite the passions of the temporary majority. "All, too, will bear in mind this sacred principle," Jefferson wrote in his First Inaugural, "that though the will of the majority is in all cases to prevail, that will to be rightful must be reasonable; that the minority possess their equal rights, which equal law must protect, and to violate would be oppression." We are bound to accept the rule of the majority, but consent is always limited by the higher principle that the rights of all must be equally respected and enforced.

While the Declaration of Independence supports a wide range of choice in the form of government, those choices must ultimately be judged in terms of the ends of government. Prudence may dictate otherwise for a time, but that does not weaken a profound preference for popular government as the form most consistent with the principles of equal rights and consent of the governed. We can see the principles of consent reflected in the creation of government and in the institutions of representative democracy, as well as in the ability of the people to amend their constitutions to better reflect their sovereignty.

One last consideration here, underscoring the connection between rights and consent. The Declaration of Independence says that whenever government becomes destructive of its ends (that is, does not secure our rights), the people have a collective right "to alter or abolish it, and to institute new Government, laying its foundation on such principles and organizing its powers in such forms, as to them shall seem most likely to effect their Safety and Happiness."

This ultimate form of consent is called the "right of revolution" and was the final justification of the colonists in their case for breaking away from Great Britain. The right is immediately qualified, mind you: Governments should not be changed for "light and transient reasons" and problems must be insufferable before "abolishing the forms to which they are accustomed." It is not the right of any individual to use force or unjust means outside the legitimate political process to change or destroy the government; as much as one might dislike Congress, the Supreme Court, or the president, no one has a natural right to use violence to alter or abolish the rule of law. And the right to abolish government is connected to the obligation to institute new government; it is not a right to create anarchy. Nevertheless, it is a clear and powerful reminder that, in the end, it is the people who are sovereign, that each person possesses equal natural rights, and that the enlightened consent of the people—and not the opinions of presidents, congresses, or courts—determines the legitimacy of government.

3

～～

Of Faith and Reason:
The Establishment of Religious Freedom

In the fall of 1774, as the First Continental Congress was convening in Philadelphia, British military forces occupied the city of Boston and British naval ships filled Boston Harbor. By that time, parliament had all but disbanded the Massachusetts colonial government, and outlawed meetings without prior approval of the royal governor. Six months before the battles of Concord and Lexington, hostilities looked increasingly imminent, and a general sense of impending war weighed heavy on the delegates.

At such a trying moment, to no one's surprise, one of the delegates, Thomas Cushing from Massachusetts, suggested that the members of the Continental Congress pray for divine guidance and protection. There were discussions, and then some debate. John Jay of New York opposed the motion, as did Edward Rutledge of South Carolina. How were they to proceed? The members were divided in their religious denominations, what with Episcopalians and Quakers, Anabaptists, Congregationalists, and Presbyterians. Everyone seemed to disagree about matters spiritual. How could they possibly come together?

Then Sam Adams, one of the early firebrands of the revolution, rose and said he would hear a prayer from anyone of piety and good character, as long as he was a patriot. Instead of focusing on their many differences, the delegates should focus on what they held in common, Adams suggested. And so the next morning an Episcopal clergyman led the members of the Continental Congress, ending with "an extraordinary prayer, which filled the bosom of every man present."

For the next ten years two continental congresses and the Confederation Congress that followed appointed chaplains, attended religious services, endorsed the first English-language Bible published in North America, and exhorted the American people in general religious language about the rightness of their cause.

Among the American Founders, there was a profound sense that faith and freedom were deeply intertwined. "The God who gave us life, gave us liberty at the same time," Thomas Jefferson once wrote. "The hand of force may destroy, but cannot disjoin them." They also believed that God favored liberty and their cause: Anyone of "pious reflection," wrote Madison in *Federalist* 37, could not fail to perceive "a finger of that Almighty hand which has been so frequently and signally extended to our relief in the critical stages of the revolution."

Nowadays, we are often told that religion is divisive and ought to kept away from politics for the sake of liberty. Religion somehow is opposed to liberty, and so liberty requires a diminution of religion in the public square. The traditional view long consistent with our historical practice, though, is that of America's Founders, who advanced religious liberty so as to strengthen religious faith and its influence on American self-government. All had a natural right to worship God as they chose, according to the dictates of their consciences. At the same time, the Founders upheld religion and morality—to paraphrase Washington's Farewell Address—as indispensable supports of good habits, the firmest props of the duties of citizens, and the great pillars of human happiness. Religious liberty, and the proper understanding of the relationship of religion and politics, is a key principle of liberty.

Failed Efforts to Reconcile Politics and Religion

Throughout human history, there have been many attempts to reconcile the realms of religion and politics. Such a reconciliation was an important objective of the American Founding. In order to understand the great significance of this principle of religious liberty, a brief historical background is in order.

In the civic life of the ancient world, among the many different Greek city-states, each city claimed its own local gods and deities. The laws were understood to be of divine origin, and thus there was no conflict between the citizens' obligations to obey the city's laws and to follow divine commands. Religious beliefs were not a matter of a citizen's choosing but were determined by the city. An Athenian, for instance, worshiped the gods of Athens, and not those of neighboring Sparta. And when one city was defeated by another, its gods too were defeated by the gods of the conquerors. In short, there was no concept of religious liberty as we understand it.*

Most ancient peoples believed in a multitude of deities; think of the many gods, half-gods, and demigods of Greek and Roman mythology. The Jewish people, however, believed there is only one God who created and who governs everything that exists. Repeatedly conquered by pagan kings, the Jewish people stubbornly refused to accept the victory of the conquerors' divinities over their one God, whom they insisted on worshiping even in defeat. The ancient world was transformed most significantly by the birth of Christianity and its spread throughout Europe, Asia, and northern Africa. According to this new teaching, one God rules over every polity alike, calling on every person in every community to believe in Him and follow His commands; Christianity did not identify with any particular polity or ethnic community. Faith in the biblical God gave every person a dazzling new freedom from the local political divinities. Yet the new faith also created a profound conflict in the heart and soul of every human being: where does the citizen's first duty rest—with the city of man or the city of God?

It was inevitable that the claims of this spiritual community would create tension between universal monotheistic religion and the official polytheism of most nation-states. Rulers could not depend upon Christians to obey laws derived from their pagan divinities. Christian faithful repeated the command of the one God of Judaism: in any conflict between the demands of the polity and those of religion, the higher law of God rather than the law of man was to be obeyed. This conviction threatened to subvert and abolish the traditional sanctions on which law and order depended, and so Christians were seen as divisive.

---

* Written in 1864, Fustel de Coulanges's *The Ancient City: A Study on the Religion, Laws, and Institutions of Greece and Rome* is the classic work on pagan religion and the rise of Christianity.

The rise and expansion of Rome complicated matters further. At first, it persecuted believers of biblical monotheism: In Rome and its far-flung provinces, Christians were forced to decide between offering public worship to the Roman divinities or being brutally executed (or thrown to the lions as games of sport). Eventually, Rome came to adopt Christianity as the official imperial religion, and for the next thousand years the Roman empire and other polities with large Christian populations lived in intertwined but uneasy relationships with the universal or Catholic Church.

During the medieval period, a religious doctrine of the "two swords" argued that political leaders had the right to direct the police and military power for the community's earthly benefit while the church had the right to determine the spiritual, otherworldly direction of the community, including its rulers. In practice, political rulers influenced church policy by bribing the clergy with money, lands, and titles, by sending armies into church-ruled territories, and by capturing religious leaders and jailing priests. The Church could invoke the fearful instrument of "excommunication" against disobedient princes (as with King John of England in 1209 and Holy Roman Emperor Frederick II in 1239), which absolved Catholic subjects of their loyalty to that government.

In the fourteenth and fifteenth centuries, some religious thinkers and clergymen, particularly Martin Luther in Germany and John Calvin in Geneva, disturbed by religious corruption and growing political-religious tension, promoted the "reformation" of Christianity, including the creation of independent Christian institutions separate from the Catholic Church. This eventually divided nations and communities across Europe into rival Protestant and Catholic camps, with states committed to one or the other engaging in bloody warfare and mutual persecution for over a century. The "divine right of kings" argument—claiming that the monarch was ordained to rule as God's absolute surrogate on earth—was developed in order to counter the traditional Catholic doctrine on papal supremacy over political rulers.

Before the American Revolution, the generally accepted argument was that every territory's ruler determined the religion of its people. If the king of England was Anglican, then so were his subjects. While this policy did help to end the international warfare over religion, it caused displacement of populations as dissenting groups moved from land to land in search of communities that would accept their form of faith. It also intensified domestic religious persecution by justifying each religion in its efforts to forcefully convert or eliminate other believers in the same nation.

Sixteenth-century England had seen some of history's worst religious persecution. After King Henry VIII broke away from the Church of Rome and ransacked Catholic churches and monasteries, his daughter Mary tried to restore the Catholic faith by punishing and executing reformers, only to be followed by Queen Elizabeth, who punished and executed Catholics (and many others, such as the Puritans) in order to suppress all religions except the reformed Church of England. Catholic France and Spain launched plots against Elizabeth and sent naval forces to overthrow her, but all they accomplished was to reinforce her determination. There was some easing of the harshest persecutions after the death of Elizabeth in 1603, but long-suffering communities began to look across the Atlantic for empty lands where they could worship God as they wished without fear of religious oppression.

The Establishment of Religious Freedom

In light of this past, what happened in America was of fundamental importance for the spiritual and political history of the world. As we have discussed, the British colonists and the early immigrants to America were strongly religious. Many religious groups—Puritans, Quakers, Roman Catholics, Jews—came to the New World to escape persecution and otherwise freely practice their faith. This made for a religious people, to be sure, but also a diversity of religious sects within the Judeo-Christian tradition and a general desire to prevent the religious battles that had bloodied the European continent from spreading to the New World.

Now recall the American argument for political sovereignty and government legitimacy discussed in the previous chapter. It was not a claim of divine authorization to rule, or a particular sectarian assertion of religious authority in this world. The new ground of political sovereignty was that all men are created equal, endowed with equal rights by nature, and that legitimate government is based on the consent of those governed. One of the most fundamental of the rights guaranteed by nature to all—inherent in man's equal humanity—is the freedom of religion. What liberty is more fundamental to human nature than to freely pursue one's deepest convictions of faith? This is why the United States is deeply committed to *religious* liberty as well as civil liberty.

What did the American Founders—especially those who established the new nation under the Constitution—mean by religious liberty, and how did they reconcile religion and politics? In general, the line they drew was between religious doctrine—particular dogmas, forms of worship, church governance—and lawmaking. The great questions of religious truth were not to be determined in the political realm—settled by princes, clergy, or majority opinion, and imposed by government. The law would not define the doctrines of religious faith, or take sides in sectarian disagreements. Individuals would be free to believe and worship as they chose. At the same time, religious doctrine would not determine the laws. While several states still had "established" churches at the time of the Constitution (Massachusetts's establishment continued until 1833), no one church or denomination would be established as the official or preferred religious faith of the nation and no particular doctrine of faith would be imposed by the federal government. What this reconciliation of religion and politics did *not* mean is equally important, and crucial to understanding the meaning and significance of religious liberty: This official separation of church doctrine and the new federal government never meant—was never intended to imply—the separation of religion and politics, or the expunging of religion from public life.

Soon after he became president, George Washington wrote an important series of letters to different religious congregations in the United States. To the United Baptists, for instance, he wrote that he would be a zealous guardian against "spiritual tyranny, and every species of religious persecution," and that under the federal Constitution every American would be protected in "worshiping the Deity according to the dictates of his own conscience." He told the Presbyterians that America would provide an example of "an enlarged and liberal policy" concerning "liberty of conscience and the immunities of citizenship." But the most moving statement of this principle is the letter Washington sent to one of the most persecuted religious minorities in all history. Up to that time, the best a dissenting religious believer could hope for was to be "tolerated" (put up with but not approved of) and not actively persecuted for his faith. Not so in America, said Washington. In the letter to the Hebrew Congregation at Newport, Rhode Island, he beautifully explained a distinctive understanding of religious liberty:

> The citizens of the United States of America have a right to applaud themselves for having given to mankind examples of an enlarged and liberal policy—a policy worthy of imitation. All possess alike liberty of conscience and immunities of citizenship.
>
> It is now no more that toleration is spoken of as if it were the indulgence of one class of people that another enjoyed the exercise of their inherent natural rights, for, happily, the Government of the United States, which gives to bigotry no sanction, to persecution no assistance, requires only that they who live under its protection should demean themselves as good citizens in giving it on all occasions their effectual support.

The argument here is twofold. On the one hand, political legitimacy and citizenship are disconnected from religious doctrine and church membership—the possession of rights does not depend on a particular profession of religious faith. On the other hand, a vast sphere of liberty for different religious beliefs and practices is protected—all possess alike liberty of conscience. All that was required and expected from believers of every religion in return was to support free government by obeying the law to which all have consented. Washington concluded his letter using his favorite biblical image from the Book of Micah:

> May the children of the stock of Abraham who dwell in this land continue to merit and enjoy the good will of the other inhabitants—while every one shall sit in safety under his own vine and fig tree and there shall be none to make him afraid. May the father of all mercies scatter light, and not darkness, upon our paths, and make us all in our several vocations useful here, and in His own due time and way everlastingly happy.

A Common Morality

This argument for religious liberty neither settles nor dismisses the claims of reason and revelation to teach the most important things for human beings to know. Such theological and philosophical matters remain questions of the highest order. But it does create a practical solution—after thousands of years of failed attempts—at the level of politics and political morality.* It established a form of government that is sanctioned by human nature and open to moral reasoning, but the legitimacy of which does not depend on the truth of any particular religious denomination. One does not have to be a Christian, a Jew, or a Muslim to believe that all have equal rights and are equal before the law.

This solution is possible because the American Founders recognized general moral precepts that are understandable by human reason and no less agreeable to faith in the form of a general revelation of creation. This morality common to both natural reason and divine revelation, usually termed "natural law" or natural theology, is the philosophical ground of the American Founding.

We can see this agreement of reason and revelation in the Declaration of Independence. The liberties recognized therein are deduced from a higher law to which all human laws are answerable and by which they are limited. This higher law can be understood by man's practical reason—the truths of the Declaration are held to be "self-evident"—but also by the revealed word of God. There are four references to God in the document: to "the Laws of Nature and Nature's God"; to all men being "created equal" and "endowed by their Creator with certain unalienable rights"; to "the Supreme Judge of the world for the rectitude of our intentions"; and to "the protection of divine Providence." The first term suggests a deity that is knowable by human reason, but the others—God as creator, as judge, and as providence—are more biblical, and add (and were assuredly intended to add) a theological context to the document.

In his work, Blackstone equated the two terms "Law of Nature" and "Nature's God" with natural law and revealed law: "Upon these

---

* The American Founding as the Best Regime: The Bonding of Civil and Religious Liberty (1990) by Harry V. Jaffa is a brief but powerful argument for the significance of America as the first regime in Western civilization to provide for the coexistence of the claims of reason and revelation.

two foundations, the law of nature and the law of revelation, depend all human laws." Locke, in his writings, spoke of the "law of nature" as general revelation in nature observable by reason and the "positive law of God" or revelation proper. The Anglican divine Richard Hooker (whom Locke often cited) made similar arguments. Other writings at the time of the Declaration attest that this was the general understanding of the phrase.

"The law of nature is immutable; not by the effect of an arbitrary disposition, but because it has its foundation in the nature, constitution, and mutual relations of men and things," James Wilson wrote in his *Lectures on Law*. "The law of nature is universal. For it is true, not only that all men are equally subject to the command of their Maker; but it is true also, that the law of nature, having its foundation in the constitution and state of man, has an essential fitness for all mankind, and binds them without distinction."

In his First Inaugural Address, George Washington made an extraordinary claim. He said that the public policy of the country would depend on the sanction of every individual's moral beliefs and behavior: "The foundation of our national policy will be laid in the pure and immutable principles of private morality." Why? Because "there exists in the economy and course of nature, an indissoluble union between virtue and happiness." No nation can prosper that "disregards the external rules of order and right, which Heaven itself has ordained." Human nature provides common moral precepts about virtue and happiness which can be understood, and upon which everyone could agree.

The connection between private morality and public policy is not made for merely utilitarian purposes—far from it. There is "no truth" more thoroughly established in the economy and course of nature than the "indissoluble union" between virtue and happiness. The "external rules of order and right"—in the draft of the address, Washington's words were "the eternal line that separates right from wrong"—suggest that morality and policy are informed by principles that are fixed and permanent, available by both reason and revelation, and applying to both private and public life. While the separation of church and state disentangled the doctrines of theology from political authority, it nevertheless does not free men (or politics) from "the external rules of order and right, which Heaven itself has ordained." The Founders saw the ground of civil and religious liberty in the doctrine of equal natural rights, but always maintained that the legitimate exercise of those rights must nevertheless remain in accord with the larger moral order that gave rise to those rights in the first place, regardless of whether that moral order is derived from the ground of natural reason or biblical revelation.

And from the perspective of religious faith, the basic principles of the Founding, at the level of political principles, were understood to be in essential agreement with the core precepts of the Bible. That this is the case can be seen throughout the many church sermons published from the founding era.* Consider this from a sermon by the Congregationalist minister Reverend Samuel Cooper in 1780:

> We want not, indeed, a special revelation from heaven to teach us that men are born equal and free; that no man has a natural claim of dominion over his neighbours. . . . These are the plain dictates of that reason and common sense with which the common parent of men has informed the human bosom. It is, however, a satisfaction to observe such everlasting maxims of equity confirmed, and impressed upon the consciences of men, by the instructions, precepts, and examples given us in the sacred oracles [i.e., the Bible].

There was a general understanding of natural laws—derivative from and consistent with Western philosophical and religious traditions—that could be understood by all and by which all must abide. Jefferson put it succinctly: The people, who are the source of all lawful authority, "are inherently independent of all *but the moral law.*" America does not require a common theology, but it does depend on a common morality shared by all people that is rooted in both faith and reason.

Religion and Republican Government

While it is often thought that religion and politics must be discussed as if they are radically different spheres, the Founders' conception of religious liberty was almost exactly the opposite. The separation of church

---

* A good edition of such works is *Political Sermons of the American Founding Era, 1730–1805* (1991), edited by Ellis Sandoz.

and state *authority* actually allowed—even required—the continual influence of religion upon public life. In a nation of limited government, religion is the greatest source of the virtue and moral character required for self-rule.

The health and strength of liberty depend on the principles, standards, and morals shared by nearly all religions. In his First Inaugural, Thomas Jefferson praised America's "benign religion, professed, indeed, and practiced in various forms, yet all of them inculcating honesty, truth, temperance, gratitude, and the love of man; acknowledging and adoring an overruling Providence, which by all its dispensations proves that it delights in the happiness of man here and his greater happiness hereafter." In recognizing the need for public morality and the prominent role that religion plays in nurturing morality, the Founders invited the various religious communities to cooperate at the political level in sustaining the moral consensus they share despite their theological differences. While this does not exclude any religious denomination that agreed with this consensus, in America as a practical matter it overwhelmingly meant the Protestant denominations of the Christian faith and a religious tradition formed by Christian theology.

What the "separation of church and state" does, then, is liberate America's religions—in respect to their moral forms and teachings—to exercise unprecedented influence over private and public opinion by shaping citizens' mores, cultivating their virtues, and in general, providing a pure and independent source of moral reasoning and authority. This is what Alexis de Tocqueville meant when he observed that even though religion "never mixes directly in the government of society," it nevertheless determines the "habits of the heart" and is "the first of their political institutions."

This sense of religious liberty—by which faith is accorded maximum freedom while government gives no preference to any one particular religion—is clearly reflected in the United States Constitution. Usually taken for granted, the simplest articulation of the principle, and the starkest difference with earlier failed attempts to combine church and state, is found in Article VI: " . . . [N]o religious Test shall ever be required as a Qualification to any Office or public Trust under the United States."

The full dynamic of religious liberty in America is expressed in the first words of the First Amendment: "Congress shall make no law respecting an establishment of religion, or prohibiting the free exercise thereof." The constitutional language here reflects two interconnected ideas, distinguished as the Establishment Clause and the Free Exercise Clause. Often thought to be in tension, these clauses are actually two sides of the same coin of religious liberty.

The Establishment Clause prohibits Congress from passing a law to establish a national church or to disestablish a state religion. Six of the thirteen original colonies had established churches, and the First Amendment was designed not to disallow those churches, or displace them with a national church. Many opposed an established church because it was seen as a threat to free exercise of religion, which the Constitution's framers were most concerned to protect.

The Free Exercise Clause safeguards one's freedom to believe and to practice one's religious faith as a matter of right, without coercion or obstruction, regardless of whether one's religion is traditional or at odds with tradition. Of course, this does not provide a free pass to violate the law in the name of religion. While the clause prohibits laws that restrict or discriminate against religion, persons of religious faith—like anyone else—are still obligated to abide by general laws. Human sacrifice, for instance, is not excused as an aspect of the free exercise of religion. This arrangement prevents the federal government from taking sides between religions even as it makes as much room as possible for a diversity of religions to flourish within reasonable and general parameters of civil society.

Religious liberty is sometimes thought to mean not only the prohibition of a religious establishment, but the prevention of any "intrusion" of religion in political life—national, state, or local. At the center of this assumption is a letter Thomas Jefferson wrote to the Danbury Baptist Association of Connecticut in 1802. Jefferson wrote: "I contemplate with sovereign reverence that act of the whole American people which declared that their legislature should 'make no law respecting an establishment of religion, or prohibiting the free exercise thereof,' thus building a wall of separation between Church & State." The letter, written after the First Congress, which Jefferson did not attend, has caused much confusion. Jefferson's purpose was to explain why he was opposed as president to proclaiming national days of public fasts and thanksgiving—a practice that Congress during the revolution, and then presidents

Washington and Adams, had followed, as had Jefferson himself as governor of Virginia. Scholars have generally argued that the letter should be read from the perspective of federalism, illuminating the meaning of the First Amendment, which Jefferson understood to apply only to—and thus limit—the national government and not the state governments.* The Supreme Court nearly a century and a half later seized upon the "wall of separation" phrase, arguing that Jefferson's letter is an authoritative statement of the meaning of the First Amendment, and creating a new theory of religious-liberty jurisprudence around it. This new wall of separation "must be high and impregnable," the Supreme Court decided in 1947. "We could not approve the slightest breach." Thomas Jefferson did not intend such a radical separation, and neither did the other Founders.

While the Constitution officially "separates" church and state at the level of doctrine and lawmaking, it also allows the general (nonsectarian) encouragement and support of religion in public laws, in official speeches and ceremonies, on public property and in public buildings, and even in public schools. Such activities were understood to be part of the free exercise of religion. On the day after Congress approved the Bill of Rights (including the First Amendment's religious-liberty language), it called upon the president to "recommend to the people of the United States a day of public thanksgiving and prayer, to be observed by acknowledging, with grateful hearts, the many signal favors of Almighty God." Washington's proclamation declared that it was "the duty of all Nations to acknowledge the providence of Almighty God, to obey his will, to be grateful for his benefits, and humbly to implore his protection and favor."

Two days after he wrote the "wall of separation" letter, President Jefferson attended a religious service in the U.S. House of Representatives. Indeed, as president, Jefferson regularly attended official church services held in the congressional chambers and allowed executive branch buildings to be used for the same purpose. In general, the Founders saw nothing wrong with the federal government indirectly supporting religion in a nondiscriminatory and noncoercive way. Churches in America, for

---

* See Daniel Dreisbach's *The Mythical "Wall of Separation": How a Misused Metaphor Changed Church-State Law, Policy, and Discourse* (Heritage Foundation First Principles Essay #6).

instance, are tax-exempt, and religious chaplains are paid by Congress to open legislative sessions and minister in the armed services.

Indeed, official recognition of religious faith has always been a central aspect of how we define ourselves as a political community. The Declaration of Independence speaks of men being "created equal" and having been "endowed by their Creator" with certain rights, and the Constitution dates itself "in the Year of our Lord" 1787. The official national motto is "In God We Trust," and the Pledge of Allegiance speaks of "one nation, under God." Every president has made official but nonsectarian religious statements, especially in major speeches and statements. Washington began the practice in his First Inaugural, when he spoke of "that Almighty Being who rules over the universe" and is the "Great Author of every public and private good." In taking the Constitution's oath of office, placing his hand on a Bible, Washington added in closing " . . . so help me God."

The Flourishing of Faith and Liberty

The principle of religious freedom as a natural right is a great achievement, perhaps the greatest, of the American Founding. Here are four reasons why.

First, religious freedom defuses the historic tension between reason and revelation at the political level—freeing political life from sectarian conflict and theology from the temptations of worldly political power. The solution was not to subordinate religion to politics, as some would have, nor to pretend that all religions are equally true (or equally false), but to recognize the transcendent claims of reason *and* revelation without subordinating those claims to political authority.

Second, the fundamental basis of religious freedom in human nature secures our rights and limits government. Without a transcendent foundation in the "Laws of Nature and Nature's God" or by the endowment of the Creator, our rights become the arbitrary gift of government. And what government giveth, government can taketh away. "Can the liberties of a nation be thought secure when we have removed their only firm basis, a conviction in the minds of the people that these liberties are of the gift of God?" Jefferson asked in his *Notes on the State of Virginia*. Without the fundamental right of conscience, our other rights are much less significant.

Third, by acknowledging the space where reason and faith agree and can cooperate about morality and politics, religious freedom unites civic morality and the moral teachings of religion, establishing the common standards of right and wrong required in republican government to guide private and public life. It is by separating sectarian conflict from the political process and then strengthening moral consensus that religious liberty makes free government possible.

And fourth, we mustn't forget that religious freedom itself was understood to serve a transcendent purpose by enhancing, rather than diminishing, the achievement of man's highest ends. James Madison's famous *Memorial and Remonstrance Against Religious Assessments* argues against Patrick Henry's proposal for nondiscriminatory state funding of religion in Virginia on the grounds that it violated the free exercise of religion. Religious freedom is "an unalienable right" because "what is *here a right* towards men, *is a duty* towards the Creator." Protecting the right to religious liberty allows religious believers to keep their sacred obligations of faith. "This duty is precedent, both in order of time and in degree of obligation, to the claims of Civil Society," Madison wrote. "Before any man can be considered as a member of Civil Society, he must be considered as a subject of the Governour of the Universe."

Religious freedom has a larger purpose: it encourages each person to pursue his or her eternal duties and, by extension, invites religion to pursue its divine mission among men on earth. But that larger purpose must be advanced and embraced freely, and not imposed by force or government fiat. Recall the opening clause of the Virginia Statute for Religious Freedom: "Whereas Almighty God hath created the mind free . . ."

The result is that throughout American history, religion has flourished—and so has liberty. When we observe various ethical and social problems in modern American society, it is hard to not to wonder whether these ills are because we have followed the wisdom of the Founders, or largely because we have ignored it.

4

⚝

The Fire of Opportunity:
Private Property and the
Spirit of Enterprise

In many ways, the right to property was the first principle at issue in the American Revolution. When the British began levying the first direct taxes on America, the colonists immediately considered it an unjust seizure of their property: "Can there be any liberty," wrote James Otis in a 1763 essay, "where property is taken without consent?"

Private property—not to mention the free-enterprise system for which it forms the foundation—is sometimes seen as the unfair prize of narrow self-interest, of undemocratic selfishness and greed that is incompatible with equality and the common good. The American Founders saw property (and so free enterprise) very differently. Property was understood not as a mere possession but as an integral component of freedom, deeply intertwined with and derivative of equal rights and human liberty itself.

Not only was it a requirement for securing the just rewards of labor—the key to a true free-market economy—and a necessary ingredient for economic prosperity, it was seen as a precondition for the enjoyment of other liberties and the cornerstone for building a commercial republic. If a man had a bit of property—a home, a piece of land, his own source of food and security—he could be independent, and so he could be free.

As the Founders saw it, the right to property was not simply an economic concept, and was much more than owning a bit of land. It was a first principle of liberty. In order to grasp the full breadth of the concept, think of property less as a static possession and more as the dynamic source of opportunity for all—the engine that allows liberty, prosperity, and civil society to flourish.

The Great Foundation of Property

Throughout history, property distinctions have existed, but they were almost always determined and controlled by the powerful and restricted by inheritance, race, or social status. Property was the possession of kings, barons, and lords, and was generally unavailable to those outside the aristocratic ruling class.

Without property, one person was literally "subject" to the will of another. And since property, which meant wealth, remained fixed by law in the hands of a very few, there was widespread poverty and little, if any, opportunity to advance and make a better life. In short, each person was born to his or her destiny.

Included among the fundamental liberties that came to be the rights of Englishmen was a fundamental right to property. William Blackstone wrote of the "sacred and inviolable rights of private property" as well as of property as an "absolute right, inherent in every Englishman."

But while British property laws generally protected the ownership of property, those laws rested on a political foundation that was both undemocratic and hostile to commerce. Medieval property laws were instituted under European feudalism for the purpose of protecting and securing powerful aristocratic families. By the feudal property laws, the only person who could inherit an estate was the oldest son. The effect of this law of "primogeniture" was to reduce the younger family members to poverty while enriching the eldest. By another law, known as "entail," landed property could not be sold out of the family. This meant that it was very difficult if not impossible for any other person to buy land for personal or commercial purposes such as raising crops for sale, much less to enter the classes of the powerful and wealthy. Primogeniture and entail reinforced the aristocratic nature of society and discouraged private commercial activities.

The American Founders wanted to place the idea of rights on a more secure footing—one not dependent on the will of the sovereign or the coincidences of history, but grounded on the fundamental laws of nature that they considered to be at the root of their chartered rights.

In making this argument, the Americans were especially influenced by political writers like John Locke and Adam Smith. Locke argued in his *Second Treatise of Government* that it is the primary responsibility of government to protect life, liberties, and possessions, all of which he included under the term "property." Each person by nature held a property in himself and naturally controlled his own person, choosing his own actions and exerting his own labor. The "great foundation of property" in the political sense was established when a man mixed his labor—his initiative and work—with materials originally held by mankind in common. Property was not an arbitrary distribution of land made legitimate by the state but instead a matter of natural right that government was instituted to secure. Locke concluded, "The great and *chief end* therefore, of Men uniting into Commonwealths, and putting themselves under Government, *is the Preservation of their Property*."

Adam Smith argued in his great work *An Inquiry into the Nature and Causes of the Wealth of Nations* (1776) that the feudal laws were aristocratic, not republican, and that they discouraged or prevented cultivation and commerce. Smith and Locke sought not only to secure the right to own private property but also to eliminate laws that prevented or discouraged the transfer of property ownership from one owner desiring to sell to any other who offered to buy it. The right of ownership must be opened to all persons. This would have a number of very important effects: first, it would break down the great landed estates into smaller properties; second, it would provide strong incentives through the motive of profit for owners to improve wasted lands, by clearing them and cultivating farms to sell produce; and third, it would advance democracy by ending the aristocrats' stranglehold on land and expanding ownership to the many and the industrious poor.

The First Principle of Association

The American Founders agreed. John Adams defined a "republic" as "a government, in which the property of the public, or people, and of every one of them was secured and protected by law." It is important to understand that the security of property means not just the possession of property, but the freedom to acquire and get rid of property as well. Property "implies liberty," Adams continued, "because property cannot be secure unless the man be at liberty to acquire, use or part with it, at his discretion, and unless he have his personal liberty of life and limb, motion and rest for the purpose."

The British brought with them to the American colonies their feudal property laws. Even before the Revolutionary War ended, Thomas Jefferson led the work of rewriting the law codes for the state of Virginia to abolish the remaining feudal tenure laws of primogeniture and entail, writing that "every fibre would be eradicated of antient or future aristocracy; and a foundation laid for a government truly republican."

The principal reason to protect property and the right of all persons to acquire, use, and part with property is a matter of justice and fairness. Jefferson put it this way: "To take from one, because it is thought that his own industry and that of his father's has acquired too much, in order to spare others, who, or whose fathers have not exercised equal industry and skill, is to violate arbitrarily the first principle of association—the guarantee to every one of his industry and the fruits acquired by it."

Likewise consider this from Justice William Paterson in a 1795 Supreme Court case:

> It is evident that the right of acquiring and possessing property, and having it protected, is one of the natural, inherent, and unalienable rights of man. Men have a sense of property: Property is necessary to their subsistence, and correspondent to their natural wants and desires; its security was one of the objects, that induced them to unite in society. No man would become a member of a community, in which he could not enjoy the fruits of his honest labour and industry.

In an important essay, "On Property," James Madison concludes: "Government is instituted to protect property of every sort; as well that which lies in the various rights of individuals, as that which the term particularly expresses. This being the end of government, that alone is a just government, which impartially secures to every man, whatever is his own."

As the Americans understood it, the scope of property was quite wide and even comprehensive of other rights. We have already seen how the colonists considered taxation without consent—"no taxation without representation"—to be an unjust taking of property. In his essay, Madison goes on to explain that property "embraces every thing to which a man may attach a value and have a right." Individuals have a property in the safety and liberty of their person, as well as their homes and other possessions, but also "a property in opinions and the free exercise of them," including "a property of peculiar value in his religious opinions, and in the profession and practice dictated by them." In short, "as man is said to have a right to his property, he may be equally said to have a property in his rights."

In addition to protecting property in and of itself, the actual securing of private property serves other freedoms as a practical matter: private church property serves religious liberty; private printing presses facilitate freedom of the press; private homes promote freedom of the family and of association; private property in goods encourages freedom of contract; and on and on. In this sense, property is a practical metaphor reminding us of our rights just as it protects them in reality—a tangible reminder of our unalienable rights and the resulting limits on government.

As such, the protection of property creates a line of defense, the violation of which alerts us to threats against our liberties and freedom generally. John Adams put it more directly: "The moment the idea is admitted into society, that property is not as sacred as the laws of God, and that there is not a force of law and public justice to protect it, anarchy and tyranny commence."*

The Commercial Republic

If property was so important, then why was it not specified in the Declaration of Independence? Even though the colonists charged the British king with several offenses against their property—preventing appropriations for new lands, quartering troops in their houses, and burning their towns—the Declaration lists the primary unalienable rights as "life, liberty and *the pursuit of happiness*."

Jefferson certainly considered property to be a fundamental right, and none of the Founders understood property to have been excluded

---

* In general, see *The Decline and Fall of the Right to Property: Government as Universal Landlord* by Edward J. Erler (Heritage First Principles Essay #15).

from the language of the document. The likely reason (in addition to the fact that "the pursuit of happiness" has a better ring to it) is that liberty, happiness, and property were understood to be closely connected: As pursuing happiness is the expression of liberty's purpose, so the ability to acquire and possess property is the primary practical expression of the means of that pursuit. This relationship is clear in the language of the 1780 Massachusetts Bill of Rights: "All men are born free and equal, and have certain natural, essential and unalienable rights; among which may be reckoned the right of enjoying and defending their lives and liberties; that of acquiring, possessing, and protecting property; *in fine*, that of seeking and obtaining their safety and happiness."

Now, it is important to note that we do not have a right to happiness but only to the *pursuit* of happiness. It is the same with property. Our right is not to *possess* property but to *acquire* (and get rid of) property and keep (and sell) what is rightly ours. And as there are differing opinions about property (what one chooses to value, for instance), so there is a great diversity in (and differing ways and degrees of) acquiring and possessing property. This diversity, it turns out, is a requirement of liberty.

Consider the justly famous discussion of the threat to republican government posed by faction (what we might think of as "special interests" today) in *Federalist* 10. The chief source of conflict is differences resulting from economic motives—and especially property:

> The most common and durable source of factions has been the various and unequal distribution of property. Those who hold and those who are without property have ever formed distinct interests in society. Those who are creditors, and those who are debtors, fall under a like discrimination. A landed interest, a manufacturing interest, a mercantile interest, a moneyed interest, with many lesser interests, grow up of necessity in civilized nations, and divide them into different classes, actuated by different sentiments and views.

There are two ways to look at this situation. One is that the unequal distribution of property inevitably leads to division and the age-old conflict between the rich and the poor. Karl Marx, the intellectual father of communism, thought that such divisions were absolutely central to politics. The only way to overcome class struggle and social warfare, he argued, was to overthrow the capitalist system and replace it with social-ism—that is, state ownership of property. (The American progressives of the early twentieth century would advocate a moderated version of this argument.) If government owns everything, there is no conflict.

The Founders' solution was just the opposite. They believed that to outlaw private property, to put all or most property in government hands, or to enforce an equal distribution of property would be to deny liberty itself. The essence of liberty is the freedom to develop one's tal-ents, pursue opportunity, and generally take responsibility for one's own life and well-being. As there are great natural differences in aptitude, talent, and strength, so there are different vocations, occupations, and professions, resulting in different degrees of income and different kinds of property. As Madison notes in *Federalist* 10, it is from "the protection of different and unequal faculties of acquiring property [that] the pos-session of different degrees and kinds of property immediately results."

America's Founders introduced a new model of political economy: Rather than focusing on the distribution of *fixed* wealth (mostly wealth in property that remained in the same family from generation to gen-eration, thus feeding endless class warfare), they developed an eco-nomic system that encouraged a multiplicity of interests and numerous varieties of property. The Federalists, in particular, argued for a large commercial republic—rather than a small and insular republic based on the traditional model—that would encompass many more people and many more interests. This, in turn, would moderate class struggle for two major reasons: first, it would tend to create a large middle class instead of a two-class, rich-versus-poor society; and second, it would favor broad-based free-market competition, and thus spur widespread opportunity.

Distinctions of wealth would still exist, of course, but they would no longer be the basis of legal or political authority. The point was not to maintain a society based on the permanent arbitrary class divisions that characterized the Old World but to form an energetic social order in which every member of society could advance without barrier, based on individual talent and ability. Wealth would correspond as closely as pos-sible to merit and industriousness rather than aristocratic privilege and inheritance. Economic mobility and diversity of the marketplace would promote a greater degree of material equality and growing prosperity throughout society.

Of course, the freedom to succeed also means the freedom to fail. The cost of unlimited opportunity is the risk that some might not succeed, especially if they don't work hard and make good decisions for themselves and their families. But an unequal distribution of property is a necessary component of liberty—inherent in human nature itself. What is crucial is that the *right* to acquire property is guaranteed to everyone, rich and poor alike. Likewise, all must enjoy equal protection of their property.

Poverty might not be eliminated under the liberty of economic freedom, but the Founders understood that it would be vastly diminished. Most importantly, it would no longer be a permanent condition from which there was no hope of escape. The ladder of opportunity would be available for everyone who would work hard, save, invest, prosper, and make a better life. The poor as much as the rich would have an interest in sustaining, rather than opposing, a free society in which they could repose their hopes for a better future for themselves and their posterity.

The Foundation of Prosperity

A regime of property rights is the foundation of prosperity. The guarantee that what you save and acquire will be secure is simply the promise that you can keep what you earn. Is it not the greatest incentive to work hard and pursue opportunity if you have a right to enjoy the rewards of your own labor?

It is an observation going back at least to Aristotle that individuals will better care for things that belong to them. We take personal responsibility for and invest our time, effort, and money in things that are ours, like our home or business, rather than the things that we do not own and for which we get no return on our investment. "By exclusive property," wrote James Wilson in his *Lectures on Law*, "the productions of the earth and the means of subsistence are secured and preserved, as well as multiplied. What belongs to no one is wasted by every one. What belongs to one man in particular is the object of his economy and care."

When property is secure, and cannot be taken away by violence, lawlessness, or arbitrary government decree, there is an incentive to

earn more, save more, and invest in more opportunities for the future—
which encourages enterprise and further economic activity. If you are
guaranteed to reap what you sow, then there will be more people sowing
and reaping, leading to economic growth. This holds true not just for
individual entrepreneurs but for small businesses, companies, and large
corporations as well. As a result of that activity being available to all, and
of the protection of property extending to all, the overall level of wealth
in the whole society will expand. "True liberty, by protecting the exer-
tions of talents and industry, and securing to them their justly acquired
fruits," Alexander Hamilton wrote in his essay *Defence of the Funding
System*, "tends more powerfully than any other cause to augment the
mass of national wealth."

Hamilton aptly described this effect in *Federalist* 12:

> By multiplying the means of gratification, by promoting the
> introduction and circulation of the precious metals, those darling
> objects of human avarice and enterprise, it serves to vivify and
> invigorate the channels of industry, and to make them flow with
> greater activity and copiousness. The assiduous merchant, the
> laborious husbandman, the active mechanic, and the industrious
> manufacturer—all orders of men, look forward with eager expec-
> tation and growing alacrity to this pleasing reward of their toils.

As a result, "The prosperity of commerce is now perceived and
acknowledged by all enlightened statesmen to be the most useful as well
as the most productive source of national wealth, and has accordingly
become a primary object of their political cares."

Hamilton envisioned a strong and growing American economy,
and designed the early components of our market system, based on
this idea of commercial activity. In his 1791 *Report on Manufactures*,
he argued that a commercial economy would allow a "greater scope for
the diversity of talents and dispositions which discriminate men from
each other," leading not only to greater economic rewards but also a new
spirit of enterprise:

> To cherish and stimulate the activity of the human mind, by
> multiplying the objects of enterprise, is not among the least con-
> siderable of the expedients, by which the wealth of a nation may

be promoted. Even things in themselves not positively advanta-
geous, sometimes become so, by their tendency to provoke exer-
tion. Every new scene, which is opened to the busy nature of man
to rouse and exert itself, is the addition of a new energy to the
general stock of effort.

The Founders recognized man's natural self-interest and built an
economic system that harnessed those private interests—by focusing
them on acquiring the goods of the marketplace that served the larger
economy—to work for the benefit of all. By pursuing their own gain in
the context of a free market, in which buyers and sellers freely provide
and trade goods and services based on agreed market prices that meet
common interests, individuals promote the economic gain of others,
and that leads to greater prosperity.

Self-Interest, Properly Understood

Not everyone was as enthusiastic about commerce as Alexander Hamilton. Stemming from classical republican assumptions, the followers
of Jefferson sought a political economy that emphasized equal republican citizenship and lamented the overcommercialization of society,
which they feared would create a laboring class dependent on others for
income and sustenance. They considered self-sufficient farmers rather
than merchants to be the best source of virtuous citizenship. As Jefferson once put it, "Those who labor in the earth are the chosen people
of God, if ever he had a chosen people, whose breasts he has made his
peculiar deposit for substantial and genuine virtue."

Nevertheless, the Jeffersonians realized that these yeoman farmers
would be commercial farmers as well, producing surplus crops to be
marketed for sale, and so they were enthusiastic supporters of free trade
and in general supported the protection of property and the commercial
activity that resulted. In his Second Inaugural, Jefferson reiterated his
wish that "law and order [be] preserved, equality of rights maintained,
and that state of property, equal or unequal, which results to every man
from his own industry or that of his father's."

The Founders were republicans and enemies of hereditary privilege and aristocratic pretensions. The primary way Jefferson and others

sought to moderate the inequalities of property was to break down the artificial economic structures created by government that prevented economic exchange and tied landed property to privileged family dynasties.

Unlike the statist liberalism that was to come later (think of the modern welfare state), the American Revolution was not about the redistribution of wealth. Jefferson opposed the government's taking of wealth and the reallocation of property, favoring measures to encourage a free-market distribution of property: "Legislators cannot invent too many devices for subdividing property, only taking care to let their subdivisions go hand in hand with the natural affections of the human mind." In the long run, free markets would do a better job at spreading wealth.

Nor was central planning of the economy the objective. No government—not the best experts or the most efficient bureaucratic agency—could ever comprehend and coordinate the innumerable preferences, choices, and decisions that routinely arise (and are more efficiently made) in the dynamic context of the free market. "I own myself the friend to a very free system of commerce, and hold it as a truth, that commercial shackles are generally unjust, oppressive and impolitic," Madison argued in a 1789 speech to Congress. "It is also a truth, that if industry and labour are left to take their own course, they will generally be directed to those objects which are the most productive, and this in a more certain and direct manner than the wisdom of the most enlightened legislature could point out." A reasonable argument could be made for temporary government incentives and disincentives in the common good, as when Hamilton favored the protection of infant industries in order to jump-start American manufacturing. In the long run, however, it is essential for economic liberty and prosperity that such choices are made by individuals and private markets. "Were we directed from Washington when to sow, & when to reap," Jefferson once noted, "we should soon want bread."

This is not to suggest, of course, that self-interest was to be left unrestrained by moral responsibility or treated as the central America idea. The Founders generally expected the pursuit of self-interest to be (and depended on its being) kept in check by the rule of law (criminal law, obligations of contract, the protections of property) and moderated and refined by the character-forming institutions of civil society. At the same time, civil society (and in some cases government) has an obligation to provide for those who truly are unable to care for themselves. In this new view of political economy, aided by a culture of civic virtue, the exclusive activity of narrow self-interest is replaced by what Tocqueville called "self-interest, properly understood," by which individuals' interests also serve one's fellow man and contribute to the common good.

In addition to the protection of private property, the primary responsibility of government in the economy is to uphold the rule of law and so protect the inviolability of contracts, those voluntary exchange agreements between individuals that are the key mechanism of a free-market economic system. Upholding contract is a moral obligation, and an aspect of justice: "The obligation of every contract," Joseph Story wrote in his *Commentaries on the Constitution*, "will consist of that right or power over my will or actions which I, by my contract, confer on another. And that right and power will be found to be measured neither by moral law alone, nor by universal law alone, nor by the laws of society alone, but by a combination of the three; an operation in which the moral law is explained and applied by the law of nature, and both modified and adapted to the exigencies of society by positive law." Story argued that contractual agreements are "sacred" not only in themselves, but also because they point back to the establishment of the United States on that most sacred agreement of agreements, the social contract.

Although by no means the first presentation of such arguments—these ideas can be traced back to classical and medieval writers—the first lengthy treatment of this new concept of vast commercial activity and prosperity was published in 1776 (the same year as the Declaration of Independence). In *The Wealth of Nations*, Adam Smith argued that an "invisible hand" of market competition (invisible in the sense that it is not coordinated by any central planning authority) would turn man's natural desire for self-betterment into a socially beneficial "system of natural liberty." Such an economy would not only give rise to an ordered society but also, by creating widespread material prosperity, would liberate mankind from permanent poverty and scarcity. This system later came to be known as capitalism.

The Fire of Opportunity

Instituting a government consistent with these principles, the American Founders established significant protections for private property and extensive powers to foster a commercial republic. The Constitution fundamentally limits government to secure man in his property, broadly understood to include his life, liberty, and possessions, while at the same time it creates an institutional framework that would provide for and encourage a flourishing of human freedom. Jefferson describes this two-fold idea in his First Inaugural:

> Still one thing more, fellow-citizens—a wise and frugal Government, which shall restrain men from injuring one another, shall leave them otherwise free to regulate their own pursuits of industry and improvement, and shall not take from the mouth of labor the bread it has earned. This is the sum of good government, and this is necessary to close the circle of our felicities.

We will discuss the Constitution at length later, but consider for now one specific clause of that document. In Article I, Section 8, Congress is granted the power "to promote the Progress of Science and useful Arts, by securing for limited Times to Authors and Inventors the exclusive Right to their respective Writings and Discoveries." What does this seemingly minor clause have to do with the protection of property?

In early 1859, the year before he was elected president, Abraham Lincoln delivered a lecture about the sources of America's prosperity, focusing on and chronicling the great discoveries and inventions for communicating ideas—speech, writing, the printing press. He concluded that the credit was due to the long advance of the rule of law and more recently to the development of patent laws, culminating in the adoption of the Constitution and this particular clause, which created and secured a patent right to ideas.

Why did Lincoln place such emphasis on this point? Before that time, he observed, "the inventor had no special advantage from his own invention." That is, the inventor had no property right in his invention. Lincoln's conclusion vividly captured the explosive energy contained in the Founders' concept of private property when it is secured under the rule of law: "The patent system changed this; secured to the inventor, for a limited time, the exclusive use of his invention; and thereby added *the fuel of interest to the fire of genius* in the discovery and production of new and useful things."

Markets, profits, and property long existed in various forms prior to the American Founding. The Founders did not discover these things. But by guaranteeing in law the equal liberty to acquire and protect a wide scope of property, they linked the rewards of the marketplace to the creativity of the human mind—unleashing innovation, enterprise, and the vast expansion of prosperity for the well-being of every American, indeed for the benefit of all mankind.

5

≈

Rule of Law:
The Great Foundation of Our Constitution

I n 1783, after the Battle of Yorktown had been won but before the
treaty of peace was concluded, General George Washington sent his
last report as commander of the Continental Army to the state governors.

In his final Circular Address, as it was called, Washington observed
that Americans were now free and in possession of a great continent rich
in "all the necessities and conveniences of life." The potential of the new
nation was virtually unlimited, given the times and circumstances of its
birth. Washington captured the significance of the moment in powerful
language:

> The foundation of our empire was not laid in the gloomy age of
> Ignorance and Superstition, but at an Epocha when the rights
> of mankind were better understood and more clearly defined,
> than at any former period; the researches of the human mind,
> after social happiness, have been carried to a great extent; the
> Treasures of knowledge, acquired through a long succession of
> years, by the labours of Philosophers, Sages and Legislatures, are
> laid open for our use, and their collected wisdom may be hap-
> pily applied in the Establishment of our forms of Government;
> the free cultivation of Letters, the unbounded extension of Com-
> merce, the progressive refinement of Manners, the growing lib-

erality of sentiment, and *above all*, the pure and benign light of Revelation, have had a meliorating influence on mankind and increased the blessings of Society.

One can hardly imagine a better beginning. "At this auspicious period, the United States came into existence as a Nation. . . ." Under such circumstances, it would be hard not to be optimistic about the future. But then, as when a symphony abruptly shifts to the strains of a minor key, Washington struck a jarring note: "and if their Citizens should not be completely free and happy, *the fault will be entirely their own*."

With the war won, the hard work of constructing a nation was upon them. It would be up to the American people, Washington warned, to decide for themselves whether they were to be "respectable and prosperous, or contemptable [sic] and miserable as a Nation." What they did now would determine whether the revolution would be seen as a blessing or a curse—not only for present and future generations of Americans but also for the rest of the world: "This is the time of their political probation; this is the moment when the eyes of the World are turned upon them." One can hear an echo of John Winthrop's famous words, "wee shall be as a citty upon a hill. The eies of all people are uppon us."

It was eleven years after the Declaration of Independence—and four years after American victory in the Revolutionary War—that a small group of delegates would convene in Philadelphia to create a new charter for governing the new nation. In order to comprehend this historic achievement, we must first understand that this moment and the constitutional document that resulted were built on the great foundational principle of the rule of law.

The rule of law may be the most significant and influential accomplishment of Western constitutional thinking. The very meaning and structure of our Constitution embody this principle. Nowhere expressed, yet evident throughout the Constitution, this bedrock concept is the first principle on which the American legal and political system was built.

The Rule of Law

Throughout most of human history, the rules by which life was governed were usually determined by force and fraud: He who had the power—

whether military strength or political dominance—made the rules. The command of the absolute monarch or tyrannical despot *was* the rule, and had the *coercive* force of the law. Rulers made up false stories of inheritance and rationalizations such as "divine right" to convince their subjects to accept their rule without question. This is still the case in many parts of the world, where the arbitrary rulings of the dictator are wrongly associated with the rule of law.

A principle that itself is quite old and long predates the United States, the rule of law is the general concept that government as well as the governed are subject to the law and that all are to be equally protected by the law. Its roots can be found in classical antiquity. The vast difference between the rule of law as opposed to that of individual rulers and tyrants is a central theme in the writings of political philosophers from the beginning. In the works of Plato and as developed in Aristotle's writings, it implies obedience to positive law as well as rudimentary checks on rulers and magistrates.

In Anglo-American history, the idea was expressed in Magna Carta in 1215. In its famous thirty-ninth clause, King John of England promised to his barons that "[n]o free man shall be taken, imprisoned, disseized, outlawed, or banished, or in any way destroyed, nor will he proceed against or prosecute him, except by the lawful judgment of his peers and the Law of the Land." The idea that the law is superior to human rulers is the cornerstone of English constitutional thought as it developed over the centuries. It can be found elaborated in the great seventeenth-century authorities on British law: Henry de Bracton, Edward Coke, and William Blackstone. The ultimate outcome of the Glorious Revolution of 1688 in England was permanently to establish that the king was subject to the law.*

The idea was transferred to the American colonies through numerous writers and jurists, and can be seen expressed throughout colonial pamphlets and political writings. Thomas Paine reflected this dramatically in *Common Sense*:

> But where says some is the king of America? I'll tell you Friend, he reigns above, and doth not make havoc of mankind like the Royal of Britain. Yet that we may not appear to be defective even

---

* This history is found in John Phillip Reid's *Rule of Law: The Jurisprudence of Liberty in the Seventeenth and Eighteenth Centuries* (2004).

in earthly honors, let a day be solemnly set apart for proclaiming the charter; let it be brought forth placed on the divine law, the word of God; let a crown be placed thereon, by which the world may know, that so far as we approve of monarchy, that in America THE LAW IS KING. For as in absolute governments the King is law, so in free countries the law ought to be king; and there ought to be no other. But lest any ill use should afterwards arise, let the crown at the conclusion of the ceremony be demolished, and scattered among the people whose right it is.

The classic American expression of the idea comes from the pen of John Adams when he wrote the Massachusetts Constitution in 1780, in which the powers of the commonwealth are divided in the document "to the end it may be a government of laws, not of men." It is hard to come up with a simpler definition.

Over time, the rule of law had come to be associated with four key components. First, the rule of law means a formal, regular process of law enforcement and adjudication. What we really mean by "a government of laws, not of men" is the rule of men bound by law, not subject to the arbitrary will of others. The rule of law means general rules of law that bind all people and are promulgated and enforced by a system of courts and law enforcement, not by mere discretionary authority. In order to secure equal rights to all citizens, government must apply law fairly and equally through this legal process. Notice, hearings, indictment, trial by jury, legal counsel, the right against self-incrimination—these are all part of a fair and equitable "due process of law" that provides regular procedural protections and safeguards against abuse by government authority. Among the complaints lodged against the king in the Declaration of Independence was that he had "obstructed the administration of justice, by refusing his assent to laws for establishing judiciary powers," and was "depriving us in many cases, of the benefits of trial by jury."

Second, the rule of law means that these rules are binding on rulers and the ruled alike. If the American people, Madison wrote in *Federalist* 57, "shall ever be so far debased as to tolerate a law not obligatory on the legislature, as well as on the people, the people will be prepared to tolerate any thing but liberty." As all are subject to the law, so all—government and citizens, indeed all persons—are equal before the law, and equally subject to the legal system and its decisions. No one is above the law in respect to enforcement; no one is privileged to ignore the law, just as no one is outside the law in terms of its protection. As the phrase goes, all are presumed innocent until *proven* guilty. We see this equal application of equal laws reflected in the Constitution's references to "citizens" and "persons" rather than race, class, or some other group distinction, as in the Fifth Amendment's language that "[n]o person shall . . . be deprived of life, liberty, or property, without due process of law." It appears again in the Fourteenth Amendment's guarantee that "[n]o State shall . . . deny to any person within its jurisdiction the equal protection of the laws." The rights of all are dependent on the rights of each being defended and protected. In this sense, the rule of law is an expression of—indeed, is a requirement of—the idea of each person possessing equal rights by nature.

A striking example of this came in 1770, after British soldiers fired into a crowd of colonists, killing five persons, in what is known as the Boston Massacre. Popular passions were overwhelmingly against the soldiers yet, in a remarkable testament to the significance of the rule of law, these British regulars were acquitted in a colonial court, by a colonial jury, and defended by none other than John Adams, who was to become one of the most committed stalwarts of the patriot cause. Adams wrote that this was one of the most disinterested actions of his life, and considered it one of the best services he ever rendered his country.

Third, the rule of law implies that there are certain unwritten rules or generally understood standards to which specific laws and lawmaking must conform. There are some things that no government legitimately based on the rule of law can do. Many of these particulars were developed over the course of the history of British constitutionalism, but they may be said to stem from a certain logic of the law. Several examples can be seen in the clauses of the U.S. Constitution. There can be no "ex post facto" laws—that is, laws that classify an act as a crime leading to punishment after the act occurs. Nor can there be "bills of attainder," which are laws that punish individuals or groups without a judicial trial. We have already mentioned the requirement of "due process," but consider also the great writ of "habeas corpus" (no person may be imprisoned without legal cause) and the rule against "double jeopardy" (no person can be tried or punished twice for the same crime.) Strictly speaking, none of these rules are formal laws but follow from the nature of the rule of law. "Bills of attainder, ex-post facto laws and laws impairing the obligation of contracts," Madison wrote in *Federalist* 44, "are contrary to the first principles of the social compact, and to every principle of sound legislation."

Lastly, even though much of its operation is the work of courts and judges, the rule of law ultimately is based on, and emphasizes the centrality of, lawmaking. This is why, although we have three coequal branches of government, the legislature is the first among equals. But as those who make law are themselves subject to some law above them, this gives rise to the idea that there are different types of laws, some of which are more significant and thus more authoritative than others. The rule of law—especially in terms of key procedural and constitutional concepts—stands above government. By definition and by enforcement it is a formal restraint on government. It judges government in light of a higher standard associated with those ideas. The more authoritative or fundamental laws have an enduring nature. They do not change day to day or by the whim of the moment, and cannot be altered by ordinary acts of government.

This sense is captured in Magna Carta's reference to "the Law of the Land," a phrase written into all eight of the early American state constitutions, as well as the Northwest Ordinance of 1787. It is reflected in the supremacy clause of the United States Constitution: "This Constitution, and the Laws of the United States which shall be made in Pursuance thereof; and all Treaties made, or which shall be made, under the Authority of the United States, shall be the supreme Law of the Land." The deep importance of this supremacy is seen in the fact that the oaths taken by those holding office in the United States—the president, members of Congress, federal judges—are oaths not to a king or ruler, or even to an executive or to Congress, but to the United States Constitution and the laws.

Constitutional Development

The idea of a constitution was not new at the time of the American Founding, and goes far back in Western political thought. The concept can be found in Greek philosophy, suggested in Aristotle's classification of "regimes" based on the rule of one (monarchy or tyranny), the few (aristocracy or oligarchy), and the many (democracy). It implied certain arrangements of the offices in the city or state. Similar ideas can be found in Cicero and other Roman writers. In Roman law, a special decree of the emperor was called a *constitutio*. But ancient "constitutions" weren't really even laws, but merely records of actions and precedents. It wasn't until later that *constitution* came to mean the structure or framework embodying the rule of law.

During the Middle Ages, the powers of political rulers in relation to some classes of subjects came to be limited by legal agreements, the most prominent example being Magna Carta. But these were merely accidental results of power struggles among various groups and classes. The key turn in constitutional history comes with the development by John Locke and others of a natural law theory including inalienable personal rights. If certain rights belong to each person by nature, then it follows that legitimate governments are to be organized and structured to protect those rights. England moved in this direction in its Glorious Revolution. But the full implications of this constitutional development first appeared in the principles and institutions of the American Founding.

The idea that no man is above the law applies not only to monarchs but also to legislatures, judges, and all who make, interpret, and enforce the law. Sir Edward Coke made this clear in *Dr. Bonham's Case* in 1610: "[W]hen an Act of Parliament is against common right and reason, or repugnant, or impossible to be performed, the common law will control it, and adjudge such an Act to be void." It was the colonists' grievance that the British government had come to reject this ancient argument. "Parliaments are in all cases to *declare* what is good for the whole; but it is not the *declaration* of parliament that makes it so," wrote the American colonial thinker James Otis in his 1764 pamphlet *The Rights of the British Colonies Asserted and Proved*. There must be an authoritative law above parliament as well.

As a practical matter, the Glorious Revolution in England established parliamentary supremacy over the monarch, a crucial step in the development of political liberty. But when that supremacy came to mean complete parliamentary sovereignty and acts of parliament came to be synonymous with the rule of law itself there was no longer any higher, fundamental law to which that legislature was subject and against which its legislation could be judged and held accountable. This became more and more apparent in the decades leading up to the American Revolution. In the Declaratory Act of 1766, parliament declared it "had, hath, and of right ought to have, full power and authority to make laws and statutes of sufficient force and validity to bind the colonies and people of America, subjects of the Crown of Great Britain, *in all cases whatsoever.*"

That marked a break with the older principle that the rule of law and the fundamental rights protected by the rule of law were above government and provided an overall constraint on government, legislatures just as much as monarchs. The British were violating this Anglo-American concept. "There cannot be a more dangerous doctrine in a state, than to admit that the legislative power has a right to alter the constitution," wrote one pamphlet writer in 1776 under the pen name of Demophilus. "For as the constitution limits the authority of the legislature, if the legislature can alter the constitution, they can give themselves what bounds they please." Legislative power that was not based on consent ("no taxation without representation") was just as problematic as an unlimited monarch.

In appealing to their constitutional rights, the Americans were confronted with the practical problem that the British didn't really have a constitution at all—at least not a written constitution as we understand it. The British "constitution" was a combination of the numerous decrees, conventions, laws, royal charters, and accumulated legal opinions that had evolved over centuries to become part of English common law. While many elements of the "unwritten" British constitution were fundamentally important written agreements and laws (such as Magna Carta of 1215, the Bill of Rights of 1689, the Act of Settlement of 1700), and although it formed the historic basis of the American legal system, there was no single authoritative constitution.

Americans demanded a comprehensive written document, within the context of the rule of law, that would create an enduring structure and process for securing their rights and liberties and spell out the divisions of powers within government and its overall limits. What's more, that constitution must be above ordinary legislation and the changing actions of government. That is what they meant by "constitution," and that, by definition, meant a framework of limited government.

If there was one thing upon which there was no disagreement in the colonies it was that there had to be a *written* constitution, for, as Tom Paine put it, "an unwritten constitution is not a constitution at all." *Written* meant written down and conveyed in clear language, publicly available in one supreme constitutional document. We take it for granted today, but the idea of a written constitution of clearly expressed constitutional rules was a major innovation not only for the rule of law but also for government based on the sovereignty of the people.*

Colonial Experience

In 1774, after parliament had shut down the Massachusetts legislature and closed the port of Boston, the First Continental Congress advised Massachusetts to form an independent colonial government. In May 1776, a year after the beginning of hostilities at Lexington and Concord, the Second Continental Congress charged the colonies to develop "such Government as shall, in the opinion of the Representatives of the People, best conduce to the happiness and safety of their Constituents in particular, and America in general." These steps led to the development of state constitutions for many of the colonies. The oldest written constitution in the world is the one John Adams wrote for Massachusetts in 1780.

Roundly skeptical of monarchs and overbearing leaders, the new state constitutions increased the power of the legislature to the diminishment of the executive. Most state legislatures appointed the governor, and largely excluded him from the legislative process. As well, most state constitutions gave the governor minimal veto powers and negligible appointive authority, and limited his term of office to one year.

At the same time, the colonies together began the process of creating the first constitution of the United States. In resolving to declare American independence in July 1776, the Second Continental Congress called for the drafting of a plan to unify the colonies as a confederation. Proposed in 1777 and ratified in 1781, the Articles of Confederation are an important bridge between the government of the Continental Congress and that of the current United States Constitution. The experience of the Articles—during which the nation won the Revolutionary War, formed diplomatic relations with major nations around the world, set-

---

* A brief history of this development is Herman Belz's *Constitutionalism and the Rule of Law in America* (Heritage First Principles Monograph).

tled land claims, and began western expansion through the Northwest Ordinance, while every state remained in the union—was very instructive for the nation.

There had been attempts at national union before, the most serious of which was Benjamin Franklin's Albany Plan in 1754, which proposed a governing body and an independent executive for the purposes of handling defense, trade, and the western lands. But with the coming of independence and the exigencies of war, there was a new urgency to regularize the common identity of the colonies.

Because of the colonies' trepidation of British central authority, and based on their successful experience as united colonies, the Articles created a "Confederation and perpetual union" of sovereign states: "Each state retains its sovereignty, freedom and independence, and every power, jurisdiction, and right, which is not by this Confederation expressly delegated to the United States, in Congress assembled." On paper, Congress had the power to make war and peace, regulate coinage, create a postal service, borrow money, and establish uniform weights and measures. From its inception, however, the inherent weaknesses of the Articles of Confederation made it awkward, and finally unworkable.

Congress under the Articles lacked authority to impose taxes to cover national expenses or enforce requests on the states, and there was no independent executive or judiciary. That is, there was no power to enforce Congress's actions, whether against states or individuals. Because all thirteen states had to ratify amendments, one state's refusal prevented structural reform; nine of thirteen states had to approve important legislation, which meant five states could thwart any major proposal. And although the Confederation Congress could negotiate treaties with foreign powers, all treaties had to be ratified by the states.

By the end of the war in 1783, it was clear that the new system had become, as George Washington observed, "a shadow without the substance." Weakness in international affairs and in the face of continuing European threats in North America, the inability to enforce a peace treaty with Great Britain, and the failure to collect enough taxes to pay foreign creditors all intensified the drive for a stronger national government.*

---

* The classic work on this period is John Fiske's *The Critical Period of American History 1783–1789* (1888), but a more popular and recent work is *The Perils of Peace: America's Struggle for Survival After Yorktown* (2007) by Thomas Fleming.

An immediate impetus to reevaluate the Articles was an armed revolt in 1786–87 called Shays's Rebellion. A group of farmers, objecting to a Massachusetts law requiring that debts be paid in specie, and to increasing farm and home foreclosures resulting from the law, took up arms in protest and attacked a federal armory in Springfield, Massachusetts. The rebellion was put down eventually by local militia, but the federal government had been helpless in defending itself or quelling the uprising.

A Deeper Problem

If that were not enough, the Americans faced a deeper problem. Absolutely committed to the idea of popular, republican government, they were keenly aware that previous attempts to establish such a government had always failed. Indeed, no serious political philosopher defended republican government over a territory much larger than a small city. In *Federalist* 9, Hamilton writes with "horror and disgust" of the constant back-and-forth between tyranny and anarchy that dominated the history of "the petty Republics of Greece and Italy." The problem was that popular governments tended to render government weak, and thus susceptible to majority tyranny, as the domineering many disregarded the rights of the few. Revolution and a complete breakdown of the rule of law followed, which in turn made republics ripe for dictators, military tyrants, and oppression by a small powerful class of nobles.

The problem of tyranny of the majority is famously described in *Federalist* 10 as the tendency of majority faction. Man's self-interest and prejudices—characteristics "sown in the nature of man"—often led him to have narrow views contrary to the common good. "By a faction," James Madison wrote, "I understand a number of citizens, whether amounting to a majority or a minority of the whole, who are united and actuated by some common impulse of passion, or of interest, adverse to the rights of other citizens, or to the permanent and aggregate interests of the community." In a republic, minority factions can be defeated by majority rule. But when decisions are made "by the superior force of an interested and overbearing majority," the rights of the minority as well as the common good are often ignored and trampled, and there may be no legal remedy. When large numbers have the same view contrary to the common good, that can lead to a tyranny, even if it is supported by a majority.

This problem so evident in history had reappeared in the individual states. Agricultural interests were refusing to protect the rights of merchants in the Rhode Island legislature; in Connecticut, one religious faction ran the legislature and another the executive; New York was imposing punitive tariffs on imports from Connecticut and New Jersey. Most states were dominated by popular legislatures that, with weak executives and no independent judiciary, routinely violated rights of property and contract. Madison goes on to note that in the states "the public good is disregarded in the conflicts of rival parties, and that measures are too often decided, not according to the rules of justice and the rights of the minor party, but by the superior force of an interested and overbearing majority."

Consider here an important distinction that the Founders themselves made between the principles upon which government is based and the actual practices of government. On the one hand, the Declaration of Independence is the organizing, foundational document that gives politics broad guidance, especially about its purposes and ends—government must be based on the principles of equal rights and the consent of the governed, and is to serve the safety and happiness of the citizens—but otherwise specifies no details. A constitution, on the other hand, was needed to create the institutions and practical arrangements by which citizens expressed their consent, assured their safety, secured their rights, and otherwise governed themselves in light of the community's highest purposes, as described in the Declaration of Independence.

It was in this sense that James Madison spoke of two different compacts: one to form a society in the first place around certain core ideas or ends, and another to form an actual government based on those ideas to accomplish its purposes. The first agreement points to—indeed, requires—the second. Even though the Founders were of a common mind about the core principles—stated in the Declaration of Independence—they still needed some solemn and authoritative act of fundamental lawgiving. In order to form a nation based on the principles of liberty, the whole people would need to make a Constitution for themselves.

The Constitutional Convention

In 1785, representatives from Maryland and Virginia, meeting at George Washington's Mount Vernon home to discuss interstate trade, requested a meeting of the states to discuss trade and commerce. The next year, delegates from several states gathered at a conference in Annapolis, Maryland, to discuss commercial issues. James Madison and Alexander Hamilton persuaded that conference to issue a call for a general convention of all the states "to render the constitution of government adequate to the exigencies of the union," in the convention's words. From May 25 to September 17, 1787, delegates met at Philadelphia in the same statehouse from which the Second Continental Congress issued the Declaration of Independence—now called Independence Hall.*

The Constitutional Convention was one of the most remarkable bodies ever assembled. Not only were there leaders in the fight for independence, such as Roger Sherman and John Dickinson, and leading thinkers just coming into prominence, such as James Madison, Alexander Hamilton, and Gouverneur Morris, but also legendary figures, such as Benjamin Franklin and George Washington. Every state was represented, except for Rhode Island. Fearful that a stronger national government would injure its lucrative trade, the state opposed any major change in the Articles of Confederation. Patrick Henry and Samuel Adams, both of whom considered a strong national government antithetical to republican principles, also did not attend the convention.

Notably absent were John Jay, who was then the secretary of foreign affairs, as well as John Adams and Thomas Jefferson, who were both out of the country representing the new nation. Their absence was almost assuredly providential. The attendance of both strong-willed figures might have made it impossible for the convention to make the compromises that proved essential to completion of their work. Nevertheless, Jefferson later described the convention as "an assembly of demigods."

As its first order of business, the delegates unanimously chose Washington as president of the convention. Though he had initially hesitated in attending the convention, Washington pushed the delegates to adopt "no temporizing expedient" and instead to "probe the defects of the Constitution [i.e., the Articles of Confederation] to the bottom, and provide radical cures." While they waited in Philadelphia for a quorum,

---

* Clinton Rossiter's *1787: The Grand Convention* (1966) is very readable and comprehensive, while Catherine Drinker Bowen's *Miracle at Philadelphia: The Story of the Constitutional Convention, May to September 1787* (1966) is more popular and narrative. A more recent work is *The Summer of 1787* (2007) by David O. Stewart.

Washington presided over daily meetings of the Virginia delegation to consider strategy and the set of reform proposals that would become the plan presented at the outset of the convention. Although he contributed to formal debate only once, at the end of the convention, Washington was actively involved throughout the three-and-a-half-month proceedings. "Let us raise a standard to which the wise and honest can repair," he said in his opening remarks. "The event is in the hand of God."

The convention had three basic rules: voting was to be by state, with each state, regardless of size or population, having one vote; proper decorum was to be maintained at all times; and the proceedings were to be strictly secret. To encourage free and open discussion and debate, the convention shifted back and forth between full sessions and meetings of the Committee of the Whole, a parliamentary procedure that allowed informal debate and flexibility in deciding and reconsidering individual issues. Although the convention hired a secretary, the best records of the debate—and thus the most immediate source of their intentions—are the detailed notes written by James Madison, which, in keeping with the pledge of secrecy, were not published until 1840.*

As soon as the convention agreed on its rules, Edmund Randolph, on behalf of the Virginia delegation, presented a set of fifteen resolutions, known as the Virginia Plan, which set aside the Articles of Confederation and created a new national government with separate legislative, executive, and judicial branches. This was largely the work of the brilliant young James Madison, who came to the convention extensively prepared and well-versed in the ancient and modern history of republican government. (He prepared a memorandum on the "Vices of the Political System of the United States.") The delegates generally agreed on the powers that should be lodged in a national bicameral legislature, but disagreed on how the states and popular opinion should be reflected in it. Under the Virginia Plan, population would determine representation in both houses of Congress, giving the advantage to larger, more populous states.

To protect their equal standing, delegates from less-populous states rallied around William Paterson's alternative New Jersey Plan to amend

---

* *The Records of the Federal Convention of 1787* (1986), edited by Max Farrand, gathers into three volumes all the records written by participants of the Constitutional Convention, including the extensive notes taken throughout by James Madison.

the Articles of Confederation, which would preserve each state's equal vote in a one-house Congress with slightly augmented powers. When the delegates rejected the New Jersey Plan, Roger Sherman proffered what is often called "the Great Compromise" (or the Connecticut Compromise, after Sherman's home state), under which a House of Representatives would be apportioned based on population and each state would have an equal vote in a Senate. A special Committee of Eleven (one delegate from each state present at the time) elaborated on the proposal, and then the convention adopted it. As a precaution against having to assume the financial burdens of the smaller states, the larger states exacted an agreement that revenue bills could originate only in the House, where the more populous states would have greater representation.

In late July, a Committee of Detail (composed of John Rutledge of South Carolina, Edmund Randolph of Virginia, Nathaniel Gorham of Massachusetts, Oliver Ellsworth of Connecticut, and James Wilson of Pennsylvania) reworked the resolutions of the amended Virginia Plan into a draft constitution. The text now included a list of the key powers of Congress, a "necessary and proper" clause, and a number of prohibitions on the states. Over most of August and into early September, the convention carefully worked over this draft and then gave it to a Committee of Style (William Johnson of Connecticut, Alexander Hamilton of New York, Gouverneur Morris of Pennsylvania, James Madison of Virginia, and Rufus King of Massachusetts) to polish the language. The literary quality of the Constitution, most prominently the language of the preamble, is due to Morris's work. The delegates continued revising the final draft until September 17 (now celebrated as Constitution Day), when they signed the Constitution and sent it to the Congress of the Confederation, and the convention officially adjourned.

Some of the original fifty-five delegates had returned home over the course of the summer and were not present at the convention's conclusion. Of the forty-one that remained, only three delegates—Edmund Randolph and George Mason of Virginia and Elbridge Gerry of Massachusetts—opposed the Constitution in its completed form and chose not to sign. Randolph (who had introduced the Virginia Plan) thought in the end that the Constitution was not sufficiently republican, and was wary of its single executive. Mason and Gerry (who later supported the Constitution and served in the First Congress) were concerned about the lack of a declaration of specific rights. Despite these objections, George Washington thought that it was "little short of a miracle" that the delegates had agreed on a new constitution.

The Philadelphia convention understood in a profound way that the Constitution needed to be a sovereign act of the whole people, not just of state governments. For this reason, on September 28, according to the rules of the Constitution, Congress sent the document to the states to be ratified not by state legislatures but by conventions that were elected by the people of each state. The first state convention to ratify the Constitution was Delaware's, on December 7, 1787; the last convention of the thirteen original colonies was that of Rhode Island, on May 29, 1790, two-and-a-half years later. Although there was strong opposition in such states as Massachusetts, Virginia, New York, and North Carolina, in the end, no state convention decided against ratifying the new constitution. With the ratification by the ninth state convention—New Hampshire, on June 21, 1788—Congress passed a resolution to make the new constitution operative, and set dates for choosing presidential electors and the opening session of the new Congress.

Those who had concluded that the government under the Articles of Confederation was weak and ineffective, advocated a convention to substantially rework the national government structure, and then supported the new constitution were called "Federalists," while those who opposed changing that structure and then opposed the ratification of the new constitution became known as "Anti-Federalists." Made up of diverse elements and various individuals, the Anti-Federalists initially wrote their criticisms under pseudonyms like "Brutus" (believed to be Robert Yates of New York), "Centinel" (believed to be Samuel Bryan of Pennsylvania), and "Federal Farmer" (the authorship of which is disputed), but found public voice when important revolutionary figures like Patrick Henry came out against the Constitution.

The Anti-Federalists held that the only way to have limited government and self-reliant citizens was through a small republic, and they believed that the Constitution gave too much power to the federal government relative to the states. They were especially suspicious of executive power, fearing that the presidency would devolve into a monarchy over time. At the same time they warned of judicial tyranny stemming from the creation of independent, life-tenured judges. While they failed in preventing the ratification of the Constitution, their efforts—which came to focus on a lack of a federal bill of rights as existed in most state constitutions—led directly to the creation of the first amendments to the U.S. Constitution. Many of their concerns and warnings, whether or not they justified opposition to the Constitution, were prescient in light of modern changes in American constitutionalism.

During the ratification debate in the state of New York, Hamilton, Madison, and John Jay wrote a series of brilliant newspaper essays under the pen name of Publius (a figure from Roman republican history) to refute the arguments of the Anti-Federalists. The eighty-five essays, mostly published between October 1787 and August 1788, were later collected in book form as *The Federalist*. The initial essays (Nos. 2 through 14) stress the weaknesses of the Confederation and the advantages of a strong and permanent national union. The middle essays (Nos. 15 through 36) argue for energetic government, in particular the need for the government to be able to tax and provide for national defense. The last essays (Nos. 37 through 84) describe the branches and powers of the new government and explain the "conformity of the proposed Constitution to the true principles of republican government." In recommending *The Federalist*, George Washington wrote that its authors "have thrown a new light upon the science of government, they have given the rights of man a full and fair discussion, and explained them in so clear and forcible a manner, as cannot fail to make a lasting impression." Thomas Jefferson claimed the work was, simply, "the best commentary on the principles of government which ever was written."[*]

The Momentous Work

When the Philadelphia convention had assembled on the morning of September 17, 1787, the completed document was read aloud to the delegates for one last time. James Madison recorded the moment as the delegates came forward, one at a time, to sign their names to the final document. Benjamin Franklin had noted a sun painted on the back of

---

[*] Of the many editions of *The Federalist Papers*, the Signet Classics edition, edited by the late Clinton Rossiter and updated with an extended introduction and notes by Charles Kesler, is best. A good collection of essays on *The Federalist* is *Saving the Revolution: The Federalist Papers and the American Founding* (1987), edited by Kesler.

the chair from which Washington presided over the convention. "I have often, and often in the course of the Session," he commented, "looked at that behind the President without being able to tell whether it was rising or setting." A fair observation, given the unknown future of the new nation. "But now, at length, I have the happiness to know that it is a rising and not a setting Sun."

The creation of the United States Constitution—John Adams described the Constitutional Convention as "the greatest single effort of national deliberation that the world has ever seen"—was one of the greatest events in the history of human liberty. The result of the convention's work has been the most enduring, successful, enviable, and imitated constitution man has ever known.

"The business being thus closed," George Washington recorded in his diary that evening, the delegates "dined together and took a cordial leave of each other. After which I returned to my lodgings, did some business with and received the papers from the secretary of the Convention, and retired to meditate on the momentous work which had been executed."

6

≈

Constitutionalism in Principle:
The Architecture of Limited Government

The United States Constitution is quite remarkable. A brief document—only some 5,400 words, handwritten on five pieces of parchment paper—it is characterized by straightforward language that is remarkably accessible. At the same time that it addresses timeless ideas and perennial problems of Western political thought and practice, the Constitution's main concepts are readily accessible. They can be understood—and even more readily debated—by the common-sense person, and so the citizen who gives the document its legitimacy and purpose.

"Constitutions are not designed for metaphysical or logical subtleties, for niceties of expression, for critical propriety, for elaborate shades of meaning, or for the exercise of philosophical acuteness or judicial research," wrote Joseph Story in the *Commentaries on the Constitution*. "They are instruments of a practical nature, founded on the common business of human life, adapted to common wants, designed for common use, and fitted for common understandings."

While often overlooked, and likely taken for granted, the Constitution is central to American life. Not simply an organizational structure having to do with narrow legal or governmental matters, it is the arrangement that formally constitutes the American people. It orders our politics, defines our nation, and protects our citizens as a free people. Which is to say that the Constitution is an inherently *political* document, not in the narrow partisan meaning of the word but in the larger sense of shaping the conditions of political self-governance and our way of life.

The challenge for the American Founders in framing the Constitution was to secure the rights and liberties promised in the Declaration of Independence, preserving a republican form of government that reflected the consent of the governed yet avoided despotism and tyranny. The solution was to create a strong and energetic national government of limited powers, along with the institutional arrangements and structural improvements necessary to make the American experiment in republican government work, all carefully enumerated in a written document of fundamental law. The resulting Constitution, concluded Thomas Jefferson, "is unquestionably the wisest ever yet presented to men."

The design, forms, and institutions of the Founders' solution—what is called the *constitutionalism* of the American regime—define the necessary conditions of the rule of law and limited government, and hence liberty. That constitutionalism, made up of the various structural concepts embodied in the Constitution of the United States, is one of our most important first principles—not because these concepts are old, or unique, or exclusively ours for that matter, but because they form the architecture of liberty.

The Constitution of the United States

The Constitution begins with a preamble, or introductory clause, that asserts at the very start the authority—"We the People"—that establishes the document and "ordains" or orders it into effect. This is very different from the opening of the Articles of Confederation, which speaks in the name of individual states, and represents an important shift (hotly opposed by the Anti-Federalists) in the understanding of the constitutional sovereignty underlying the document. The Constitution then proclaims the broad objectives of "We the People," their reasons for constituting a new government, and the ends or purposes for which the Constitution is formed. Of these six reasons, two are immediate requirements of safety and security common to every sovereign nation—"insure domestic tranquility" and "provide for the common defense"—and two look forward to building a particular society that upholds the rule of law and fosters prosperity and well-being for all of its citizens—"establish Justice" and "promote the General Welfare." The other two objectives grandly express the Founders' hopes for their nation's and their people's future: the Constitution is meant to "form a *more perfect* union" and "secure the blessings of liberty to ourselves *and our posterity*." This statement of purpose is as true and valid today as it was in 1787. If it were not, the remainder of the Constitution would be obsolete and mostly irrelevant.

After the preamble, the rest of the Constitution—being a practical document to create a framework of law—describes the powers, procedures, and institutions of government. This is as it should be. "It is a melancholy reflection that liberty should be equally exposed to danger whether the government have too much power or too little power," Madison observed in a letter to Jefferson, "and that the line which divides these extremes should be so inaccurately defined by experience." Liberty is assured not by the anarchy of no government, on the one hand, or the arbitrary rule of unlimited government, on the other, but through a carefully designed and maintained structure of government.

The Constitution is divided into seven parts, or articles, each dealing with a general subject. Each article is further divided into sections and clauses. The first three articles create three distinct branches of government: the legislature, the executive, and the judiciary. The very form of the document separates the branches in accordance with distinct powers, duties, and responsibilities stemming from the primary functions of governing: to make laws, to execute and enforce the laws, and to uphold (judge or adjudicate) the rule of those laws by applying them to particular individuals or cases.*

The Constitution creates three branches of government of equal "rank" in relation to each other. No branch is higher or lower than any other, and no branch controls the others; each has independent authority and unique powers. The order—legislature, executive, judiciary—is important, however, moving from the most to the least "democratic," that is, from the most to the least directly chosen by the people. The legislative branch is the first among equals. Its members "are distributed and dwell among the people at large," wrote Madison in *Federalist* 50.

---

* A clause-by-clause analysis of the document is *The Heritage Guide to the Constitution* (2005), edited by David Forte and Matthew Spalding.

"Their connections of blood, of friendship, and of acquaintance embrace a great proportion of the most influential part of the society." As a result, members of Congress are "more immediately the confidential guardians of their rights and liberties." The Constitution lodges the basic power of government in the legislature not only because it is the branch most directly representative of popular opinion (being the closest to the people) but also because the very essence of governing according to the rule of law is centered on the legitimate authority to make laws.

The Constitution, by its language and nature as a written framework of government, creates a government of *delegated* and *enumerated* powers. Despite the popular term "states' rights," no government (federal, state, county, or local) actually possesses any *rights* at all. Recall from the Declaration of Independence that *persons* are endowed with unalienable rights. Governments only possess *powers*, which in legitimate governments are derived from the consent of the governed. In particular, governments only have those powers that are given (or delegated) to them by the people. Individuals, who possess rights by nature, hold those powers and may grant some of them to the government. This point is implicit throughout the Constitution, but was later stated explicitly in the Tenth Amendment: "The powers not delegated to the United States by the Constitution, nor prohibited by it to the States, are reserved to the States respectively, or to the people."

The concept of enumerated (or listed) powers follows from the concept of delegated powers, as the functional purpose of a constitution is to write down and assign the powers granted to government. The delegation of powers to government along with a written agreement as to the extent (and limits) of those powers are critical (if not necessary) elements of limited constitutional government. The scope of government is determined by the extent of power delegated and then enumerated in the Constitution. And as we shall see, this enumeration applies especially to the powers delegated to Congress.

In many ways, both minor and fundamental, the Constitution does not operate as it was intended and as it did operate for much of our history. There is a vast disjunction between the Founders' Constitution and the "living" Constitution that is today virtually a dead letter. But before we consider those changes, we must first understand the design and form of the original constitutional order.

Article I: The Legislative Power

The first three articles each open with what is called a "vesting clause" that describes the unique powers vested in, or entrusted to, each particular branch of government. The Constitution does not grant any power to the federal government, but only to the institutions created in the three branches of the government. As a result, the differing language of these clauses in each article is very important.

Article I begins: "All legislative powers herein granted shall be vested in a Congress of the United States, which shall consist of a Senate and House of Representatives." This language implies that while there might be other legislative powers, Congress is granted only those "herein" granted, meaning listed in various clauses of the Constitution. The legislative power extends to seventeen topics listed in Article I, Section 8: taxing and borrowing, interstate and foreign commerce, naturalization and bankruptcy, currency and counterfeiting, post offices and post roads, patents and copyrights, federal courts, piracy, the military, and the governance of the national capitol and certain federal enclaves. All told, the powers are not extensive, but they are vital. Apart from some relatively minor matters, the Constitution added to the authority already granted in the Articles of Confederation only the powers to regulate foreign and interstate commerce and to apportion "direct" taxes among the states according to population.

The diverse powers granted to Congress might at first seem rather disorganized, ranging from the clearly momentous (to declare war) to the seemingly minute (to fix weights and measures). But upon reflection, an underlying pattern emerges based on the distinction between key functions assigned to the national government and those left to the state governments. The two most important functions concern the nation's security (such as the powers to maintain national defense) and the national economy (such as the power to tax or to regulate interstate commerce). And as might be expected, many of the powers complement each other in supporting those functions: The power to regulate interstate commerce, for instance, is consistent with the power to control currency, which is supported in turn by the power to punish counterfeiting and to establish standards for weights and measures. How can an economy function without a common currency?

While the federal government's powers are *limited*, the powers granted are *complete*. The objective was to create an energetic government that could effectively accomplish its purposes. The federal government must have all powers needed to do the jobs assigned to it. As such, the granted powers are supported by the auxiliary authority needed to carry out these functions. The central example of this is what is called the "necessary and proper" clause, which empowers Congress to "make all Laws which shall be necessary and proper for carrying into Execution the foregoing Powers, and all other Powers vested by this Constitution in the Government of the United States, or in any Department or Officer thereof." While this language suggests a wide sweep of "implied" powers, it is not a grant to do anything and everything, but only to make those additional laws that are necessary and proper for execution of the powers expressed in the Constitution. Jefferson read this clause extremely narrowly, and Hamilton too broadly. Madison expressed the more balanced view, writing that a necessary and proper law requires "a definite connection between means and ends," in which those means and ends are linked "by some obvious and precise affinity."

"It neither enlarges any power specifically granted; nor is it a grant of any new power to Congress," wrote Joseph Story in his *Commentaries on the Constitution*. "But it is merely a declaration for the removal of all uncertainty, that the means of carrying into execution those, otherwise granted, are included in the grant." While the exact limits of the necessary and proper clause have always been debated, the provision clearly allows Congress to adapt its stated powers to the various crises of the times so that the Constitution can endure. "This provision is made in a Constitution intended to endure for ages to come," John Marshall wrote in *Marbury v. Madison*, "and consequently to be adapted to the various crises of human affairs."

The point is clear: Congress has only the powers delegated to it in the Constitution. The legislature holds the primary position in republican government, being responsible for the core lawmaking function and thus most of the activities of government. As the legislature is also the most popular branch of government—and so the most prone to the temporary passions and narrow interests of democratic majorities—its power must be especially bounded. If Congress could do whatever it wanted, Madison noted in a 1792 letter, then the government is "no longer a limited one, possessing enumerated powers, but an indefinite one, subject to particular exceptions."

To further limit the expansion of legislative power and control the legislative branch in relation to the rest of the government, Article I divides Congress into two chambers (bicameralism) chosen by two different political constituencies and with different terms of office: the House of Representatives, each member being elected by districts every two years, and the Senate, with members (originally) appointed by state legislatures to serve staggered terms of six years each. The House is based on popular representation, and the Senate on equal representation of all of the states. Unlike the House, which is intended to be responsive to the ebb and flow of popular opinion, the Senate—with its longer terms of office and a larger and distinct constituency—was to be more stable, deliberative, and oriented toward long-term state and national concerns. It is because of the nature of the Senate that the chamber is given unique responsibilities concerning the approval of executive appointments (judges, ambassadors, and all other officers of the United States) and treaties with other countries.

Article II: The Executive Power

What to do with executive power proved to be more difficult. The primary reason, of course, was that the Americans had fought a revolution to escape monarchical rule. Through "repeated injuries and usurpations," as it says in the Declaration of Independence, the king of England proved that he was "unfit to be the ruler of a free people." By the time of the Constitutional Convention in 1787, most delegates had become convinced that a strong national executive was necessary but nevertheless remained extremely wary of the dangers (and tendencies) of executive tyranny. Whether caesars, kings, or military dictators, tyranny by executives had been a problem throughout history.

Ultimately, the Constitutional Convention was confident in the creation of the presidency because of the widespread assumption that George Washington would hold the office. The powers of the presidency would not have been left so loosely defined, delegate Pierce Butler of South Carolina observed, "had not many of the members cast their eyes towards General Washington as president; and shaped their ideas of the powers to be given to a president, by their opinions of his virtue." That is, the powers of the presidency were entrusted to the office not on the assumption of executive virtue, but with the knowledge of who would be the first chief executive and who, by the precedents he established, would largely define the newly created office. After that, the executive would be checked by the other branches and through the electoral process.

In Article II, then, "the executive Power shall be vested in a President of the United States of America." The president plays an important role in legislation through the limited veto power (actually assigned in Article I) and the duty to recommend to Congress "such measures as he shall judge necessary and expedient." With the advice and consent of the Senate, the president appoints judges (thus shaping the judiciary) and other federal officers (thus overseeing the executive branch). Reflecting the president's role in directing the nation's foreign affairs, the president also (again with the advice and consent of the Senate) appoints ambassadors and makes treaties with other nations. He also receives ambassadors from other countries and commissions all military officers of the United States.

The president is charged to "take care that the laws be faithfully executed"—a crucial responsibility necessary for the rule of law. The law to be executed is made by Congress, but when Congress creates programs and departments through its lawmaking function, those programs and departments operationally fall under the executive branch. More generally, it means that it is the president's core responsibility to be the nation's chief executive and law-enforcement officer, who is responsible for carrying out and enforcing federal law. Every member of Congress as well as the federal judiciary takes an oath to "support the Constitution," but it is the president's exclusive oath, prescribed in Article II, to "faithfully execute the Office of President of the United States, and . . . preserve, protect and defend the Constitution of the United States."

It is important to note that the president has unique constitutional powers that do not stem from congressional authority. The president is vested directly with power in Article II of the Constitution, not by virtue of Congress' lawmaking power. Article II is a *general* grant of executive power to the president, very different from the "legislative powers, herein granted" to Congress in Article I. The president is granted all the executive powers, except for those specifically granted to Congress (see below). This is especially the case when it comes to war and national security, for the president acts as the commander in chief of the armed forces.

The office of the president is the Constitution's recognition of the basic responsibilities of government (foreign policy, national security, and the common defense) and the practical necessity that the task be directed by one person (rather than 535 members of Congress) with adequate support and competent powers to act with the decisiveness and speed that is often required in times of crisis and conflict. The executive power is not unlimited, though, as the general grant of power is mitigated by the fact that many traditionally executive powers—to coin money, to grant letters of marque and reprisal, to raise and support armies—were given to Congress. The most significant of these limits on the executive is that Congress has the sole power to declare war. Moreover, the president has no power to enforce state laws; presidential executive power is limited to federal matters.

Often misunderstood as undemocratic, Article II also created the unique and important mechanism by which the president and vice president are elected. In the original conception, there were no presidential campaigns, no "tickets" of candidates, and no political parties to support campaigns. Individuals were chosen (the first choice would be president and the second choice would be vice president) by a college of electors from each state. This was designed to encourage the selection of highly respected chief executives with nationwide credentials and with broad and general (rather than regional and narrow) appeal. Today, the electoral college requires presidential candidates to campaign across the country and win electoral votes spread out in states (according to representation in Congress) rather than simply winning the national popular vote. While the Constitution originally allowed a president to be reelected for an unlimited number of four-year terms, it was amended in 1952 (after Franklin Roosevelt was elected four times) to lock in George Washington's tradition of serving only two terms.

Article III: The Judicial Power

Article III, the shortest of the first three articles, vests the judicial power in "one supreme Court and in such inferior Courts as the Congress may from time to time ordain and establish." Justices of the Supreme Court and all federal judges are nominated by the president and confirmed by the Senate; they hold office "during good behavior" and may be impeached by Congress. By the Judiciary Act of 1789, Congress approved a Supreme Court with a chief justice and five associates (changed in 1869 to nine, where it has remained since), and created thirteen district courts, three circuit courts, and the office of the attorney general. Federal trial courts (United States District Courts) have existed in every state since 1789, and intermediate courts of appeal since 1891.

There have been judges and courts throughout history, but the judiciary was not previously understood to be or to require a separate branch of government. The highest court in the British system was the House of Lords, the upper chamber of the legislature. But experience taught, and the American Founders recognized, the importance of an independent judiciary for the rule of law—the need for an impartial body to decide cases of law outside of the lawmaking and law-enforcing elements of government. "The dignity and stability of government in all its branches, the morals of the people, and every blessing of society depend so much upon an upright and skillful administration of justice," John Adams wrote in *Thoughts on Government*, "that the judicial power ought to be distinct from both the legislative and executive, and independent upon both, that so it may be a check upon both, as both should be checks upon that." An independent judiciary is vitally important—not to *make* the law but to *uphold* and *apply* it fairly and impartially in all cases.

Federal judges are vested with *all* of the judicial power, and *only* the judicial power, which is quintessentially the power (and the judiciary's core function) to decide "cases and controversies" that come before the courts by the jurisdiction assigned in the Constitution or as regulated by Congress.

To understand fully the important role of the judiciary, we must look ahead to Article VI, which explains how the Constitution fits into the overall context of constitutional government in the United States. It begins by recognizing the debts that existed prior to the Constitution, which is to say it recognizes that the United States existed before the United States Constitution. Most importantly, it makes the Constitution and the laws and treaties made pursuant to it the "supreme Law of the Land." This means that the United States Constitution is the highest law in the United States and must be followed in all cases. It also means that subsequent laws passed (and treaties approved) by Congress that are consistent with the powers granted to Congress by the U.S. Constitution must be followed in all cases. On the other hand, claims based on state constitutions and state laws that conflict with the U.S. Constitution and laws must be disregarded. Finally, Article VI bans religious tests for office—a key component of religious liberty—and instead binds all federal and state officeholders, by oath, to the Constitution (but not to ordinary laws or treaties). Legal restrictions and political obligations are important but, in the end, political actors within the constitutional order must give complete loyalty to, and solemnly pledge to support, the Constitution of the United States. Article VI makes sure that America's legal system—especially the federal and state courts—is defined and focused on the Constitution.

The Last Articles

The important status of the states is evident throughout the Constitution. While there are some things states explicitly can't do (raise armies or coin money, for instance), their equal representation in the Senate can never be changed, even by constitutional amendment. The states within the constitutional system are dealt with systematically in Article IV, which requires that every state give its "Full Faith and Credit" to the laws and decisions of every other state, and that citizens of each state enjoy all privileges and immunities of citizenship in every other state—both conducive to establishing the rule of law. It also provides for the admission of new states to the union as *states*, not *colonies*, on an equal footing with the original thirteen—an exceedingly important distinction that made for America's successful growth as a nation of states, rather than a colonial empire. Lastly, Article IV stipulates that the United States will guarantee to each state a republican form of government, and protect the states from invasion and, upon request, domestic violence.

The process for amending the Constitution is provided for in Article V. Here we see the rule of law concept that the Constitution is fundamental law that can be changed—thus allowing for constitutional reform and adaptation—but only by a popular decision-making process and not by ordinary legislation or judicial decree. "As the people are the only legitimate fountain of power and it is from them that the constitutional charter, under which the several branches of government hold their power, is derived," James Madison wrote in *Federalist* 49, "it seems strictly consonant to the republican theory, to recur to the same original authority" to alter the Constitution. Neither an exclusively federal nor an exclusively state action, the amendment process is a shared responsibility of both Congress and the states representing the American people. To succeed, an amendment proposed by Congress must have the votes of two-thirds each of the House of Representatives and the Senate, or two-thirds of the states must call for a constitutional convention to propose amendments (a method that has never successfully been employed); in either case the proposal must then be ratified by three-quarters of the states.

Changing the document too often would weaken the Constitution, and cause it to be treated as an ordinary statute, which can be altered by the passions of the moment. As "every appeal to the people would carry an implication of some defect in the government," Madison notes, so frequent appeals would "deprive the government of that veneration which time bestows on every thing, and without which perhaps the wisest and freest governments would not possess the requisite stability." Regardless, "a constitutional road to the decision of the people ought to be marked out and kept open, for certain great and extraordinary occasions."

Article V has the double effect of affirming the Constitution's foundation in republican self-government, yet making the amending task sufficiently difficult and broad-based to protect the document and elevate it to the status of higher law. This forces the development of overwhelming and long-term majorities, and is intended to assure that constitutional amendments will be rare and pursued only after careful and serious consideration, when it is necessary to address an issue of great national magnitude, consistent with the deeper principles of American constitutionalism, and when there is a broad-based consensus among the American people, throughout the states.

Article VII provides that the Constitution shall be ratified by state conventions rather than state legislatures, again pointing to the document's legitimacy as an act of the sovereignty of the whole people. It also dates the Constitution in "the Year of our Lord" 1787 and "of the Independence of the United States of America the twelfth," thereby locating the document in time according to the two most important dates in human history, one following the religious traditions of Western civilization and the other pointing twelve years earlier to the birth of the United States as proclaimed in the Declaration of Independence.

A Bill of Rights

The Bill of Rights is a distinctive and impressive mark of our liberty. Unlike the citizens of many other countries, Americans are protected from their government in the exercise of fundamental equal rights.

Many speak of the Bill of Rights as if it is the whole Constitution, but that is not correct. These amendments to the Constitution have taken on a very different meaning than what was envisioned. The Constitutional Convention considered and unanimously rejected a motion to draw up such a bill of rights for the constitution its delegates were framing. Why did they deny this added protection? For one thing, the Constitution already contained several related provisions, such as the clauses against ex post facto laws, religious tests, and the impairment of contracts. In creating a limited government by which rights were to be secured and the people free to govern themselves, the Constitution, as Hamilton insisted, is itself a bill of rights.

The more important reason had to do with the difference between the state and federal constitutions. As states had broader reserved powers, bills of rights in state constitutions made sense: They were necessary to guard individual rights against very powerful state governments. But the federal government only possessed those limited powers that were delegated to it in the Constitution. As such, the federal government did not possess the power to address basic individual rights, so there was no need for a federal bill of rights—indeed, one might be dangerous. Such a bill of rights, Hamilton argued in *Federalist* 84, "would contain various exceptions to powers which are not granted; and on this very account, would afford a colourable pretext to claim more than were granted. For why declare that things shall not be done which there is no power to do?"

Put another way, why state in a bill of rights that Congress shall make no law abridging free speech if Congress in the Constitution has no power to do so in the first place? And does forbidding the federal government in a bill of rights from acting in certain areas imply that the government has the power to act in other areas? If that were the case, as Madison earlier warned, then the government was "no longer a limited one, possessing enumerated powers, but an indefinite one, subject to particular exceptions."

Nevertheless, the lack of a bill of rights similar to those found in most state constitutions became an important rallying cry for the Anti-Federalists during the ratification debate, compelling the advocates of the Constitution to agree to add one in the first session of Congress.

When the first Congress convened in March 1789, Representative James Madison took charge of the process. Only eighteen months before, as a member of the Philadelphia convention, Madison had opposed a bill of rights. But he wanted above all for the new constitution to be ratified and, if possible, have the widest possible popular support. If that meant adding a bill of rights, then Madison would draft the language himself to make sure these early amendments did not impair the Constitution's original design.*

Based largely on George Mason's Declaration of Rights written for the Virginia Constitution of 1776, seventeen amendments were quickly introduced. Congress adopted twelve, and President Washington sent them to the states for ratification. By December 15, 1791, three-fourths of the states had ratified the ten amendments (the first two proposed amendments, concerning the number of constituents for each representative and the compensation of congressmen, were not ratified), now known collectively as the Bill of Rights.

The First Amendment guarantees *substantive* political rights involving religion, speech, press, assembly, and petition, recognizing certain areas that are to be free from federal government interference. Likewise, the Second Amendment guarantees an individual right to keep and bear arms. The next six amendments deal with more *procedural* political rights, mostly restraints on criminal procedure (warrants must be based on probable cause, no person shall be tried twice for the same offense or be forced to testify against himself, accused criminals have a right to a speedy and public trial and the assistance of counsel, the right to a trial

---

* The story of the creation of the Bill of Rights is told in Robert Goldwin's *From Parchment to Power: How James Madison Used the Bill of Rights to Save the Constitution* (1997).

by jury shall be preserved) that regulate the exercise of government's law enforcement so that it is not arbitrary or excessive.

The Bill of Rights also includes important property protections. The Second Amendment prohibits confiscation of arms, and the Third Amendment the lodging of troops in any home. The Fourth Amendment prohibits unreasonable searches and seizures of persons, homes, papers, and effects, and the Eighth Amendment prohibits excessive bail and fines, as well as cruel and unusual punishment, an additional protection of property in one's person. Most significantly, of course, the Fifth Amendment says that no person shall "be deprived of life, liberty, or property, without due process of law; nor shall private property be taken for public use, without just compensation." In this sense, the protection of property is both a substantive and a procedural right guaranteed by the Constitution.

The Ninth and Tenth Amendments briefly encapsulate the twofold theory of the Constitution: The purpose of the Constitution is to protect *rights* that stem not from the government but from the people themselves, and the *powers* of the national government are limited to those delegated to it by the people in the Constitution. They also address the confusion (which was Madison's concern) that may arise in misreading the other amendments to imply unlimited federal powers. While the Ninth Amendment notes that the listing of rights in the Constitution does not deny or disparage others retained by the people, the Tenth Amendment states explicitly that all government powers except for those specific powers that are granted by the Constitution to the federal government belong to the states or the people.

The purpose of the Bill of Rights—stated by both the Federalists and the Anti-Federalists—was to limit the federal government, not the states. This is underscored by the first words of the First Amendment: "Congress shall make no law . . ." John Marshall confirmed this when he wrote in *Barron v. Baltimore* (1833) that these amendments "could never have occurred to any human being, as a mode of doing that which might be effected by the state itself." Congress was not empowered to act in "the extraordinary occupation of improving the constitutions of the several states, by affording the people additional protection from the exercise of power by their own governments, in matters which concerned themselves alone."

For much of our history, the Bill of Rights played virtually no role in the Supreme Court's jurisprudence. It was only in 1925 that the court began to "incorporate" the Bill of Rights into the provisions of the Fourteenth Amendment (which had been adopted in 1868). As the Fourteenth Amendment applies to the states, this meant applying the provisions of the Bill of Rights against the states as well. This process proceeded by fits and starts over the course of the twentieth century. Today, the Bill of Rights mainly serves to secure rights *against* the state governments—the exact reverse of the role these amendments were intended to play in our constitutional system.

Amendments to the Constitution

Although more than five thousand bills proposing to amend the Constitution have been introduced in Congress since 1789, there have been only seventeen additional amendments to the Constitution besides the Bill of Rights. A disputed Supreme Court decision (*Chisholm v. Georgia*) led to the enactment of the Eleventh Amendment (1795), limiting the jurisdiction of the federal judiciary with regard to suits against states. The election of 1800, which was decided by the House of Representatives because of an electoral-vote tie, led to the enactment of the Twelfth Amendment (1804), which provided for separate balloting for president and vice-president. The Civil War was followed by the enactment of the Thirteenth, Fourteenth, and Fifteenth Amendments (ratified in 1865, 1868, and 1870, respectively), which abolished slavery; conferred citizenship on all persons born or naturalized in the United States and established the rule that a state cannot "deprive any person of life, liberty, or property, without due process of law"; and made clear that the right of citizens to vote cannot be denied or abridged on account of race, color, or previous condition of servitude.

There were four amendments during the Progressive era, at the beginning of the twentieth century. The Sixteenth Amendment (1913) gave Congress the power to levy taxes on incomes, from any source, without apportionment among the several states, and so was born the modern income tax. The Seventeenth Amendment (1913) provided for the direct election of senators by popular vote, a devastating defeat for federalism. The Eighteenth Amendment (1919), the so-called prohibition amendment, prohibited the manufacture, sale, or transportation of intoxicating liquors. (This failed experiment in social reform was repealed by the Twenty-First Amendment in 1933). The Nineteenth Amendment (1920), completing a political movement that had started much earlier, extended to women the right to vote.

The remaining amendments have dealt with the executive and elections. The Twentieth Amendment (1933) cut in half the "lame-duck" period between presidential elections and the inauguration of the new executive; the Twenty-Second Amendment (1951), following in the wake of Franklin Roosevelt's four terms, limited presidents to two terms (the tradition up to that point); the Twenty-Third Amendment (1961) gave the District of Columbia electors in the electoral college system; the Twenty-Fourth Amendment (1964) abolished poll taxes, which were used to deny persons the right to vote in presidential and congressional primaries and elections; and the Twenty-Fifth Amendment (1967) established the procedure (following in the wake of the Kennedy assassination) for presidential succession. With the military draft of eighteen-year-old males during the Vietnam conflict, the Twenty-Sixth Amendment (1971) lowered the voting age to eighteen, and the most recent change was the Twenty-Seventh Amendment, which provided that any pay raise Congress votes itself would not take effect until after an intervening congressional election. It was ratified finally in 1992, 203 years after James Madison wrote and proposed it as part of the original Bill of Rights.

Our Sacred Constitution

While there is no pattern for the seventeen amendments ratified after the Bill of Rights, each successful amendment represents the codification of a national consensus that was able to cross the hurdles set out in Article V to assure that that consensus was deliberative, reasonable, and legitimate.

By cultivating and allowing the deliberative, popular will to assert, by constitutional means, its sovereign authority over government, the amending process affirms the rule of law and links our highest law back to the republican idea that government ultimately derives its just powers and legitimate authority from the consent of the governed, and that the governed can alter their government to affect their safety and happiness.

At key moments, under unusual circumstances, the amendment process expands our constitutional discourse beyond the courts and our political institutions to engage the American people in national deliberations about core principles and fundamental questions, and in so doing invokes their sovereign authority, through the extraordinary process of constitutional lawmaking, to settle the issue at hand.

"The basis of our political systems is the right of the people to make and to alter their Constitutions of Government," George Washington wrote in his Farewell Address of 1796. "But the Constitution which at any time exists," he reminded us, "'till changed by an explicit and authentic act of the whole People, is sacredly obligatory upon all."

7

Constitutionalism in Practice:
The Workings of Ordered Liberty

It is important to understand how the workings of the Constitution relate to the principles underlying it, and so the project of establishing a regime of liberty.

"A dependence on the people is, no doubt, the primary control on the government," Madison noted in *Federalist* 51, "but experience has taught mankind the necessity of auxiliary precautions." The Founders believed that citizen virtue was crucial for the success of republican government, but they knew nevertheless that passion and interest were permanent parts of human nature and could not be controlled by parchment barriers alone. Rather than relying on a predominance of virtue and civic responsibility in all cases, a dangerous assumption for constitution-makers, the Founders designed a system that would harness man's competing interests—not to lower politics to questions of narrow self-interest but to provide what they called "the defect of better motives."

The two great problems of republican government are democratic or majority tyranny, on the one hand, and democratic ineptitude on the other. The first was the problem of majority faction, the abuse of minority or individual rights by an "interested and overbearing" majority. The second was the problem of making a democratic form of government, which is naturally weak and divided, energetic and effective enough to defend itself and serve its purposes without becoming despotic.

So in addition to the formal provisions of the document, three important but unstated mechanisms at work in the Constitution demand our attention: the extended republic, the separation of powers, and federalism. These "auxiliary precautions" constitute improvements in the science of politics developed by the Founders and form the basis of what they considered "a republican remedy for the diseases most incident to republican government." They are crucial to the operational success of our constitutional system.

Two other monumental issues of constitutional meaning—both of which are widely misunderstood today—are crucial to understanding the principles of constitutionalism in practice: who in the end says what the Constitution means? And how are we to understand the Constitution's compromises in the beginning with slavery? The answers to these questions, as well as the extent to which the workings of the constitutional government are consistent with the principles of liberty, will go far in establishing our fidelity to the American Constitution.

Representation and the Extended Republic

In the American theory of constitutional government, sovereignty exists in the people, who in turn delegate certain powers to the government. Government, in order to be legitimate, must reflect the consent of the governed. In this sense, the United States is a *popular* form of government. But popular governments can vary as to the way in which they reflect democratic opinion. Strictly speaking, a pure democracy is a system by which the people rule directly, voting on each law and policy. In a representative democracy like the United States, lawmaking is done not by the people themselves, but by individuals they have chosen to represent them in the government.

The American Founders were wary of the passions of democracy, and wanted to encourage a politics of settled and thoughtful public opinion. They designed a form of popular government in which the people govern—equal rights means popular consent—but their consent is reflected through a representative process, under rules and regulations set down by a written constitution, which allows for majority rule at the same time that it protects minority rights. The United States is a *representative democracy*, or better yet, a *republic*. The distinction is not unimportant.

The consequence of representation—of individual citizens being represented in government rather than ruling through direct participatory democracy—is to filter democratic opinion so that "the cool and deliberate sense of the community" (*Federalist* 63) rules rather than "every sudden breeze of passion" (*Federalist* 71) that might come over the popular will. The effect of representation—of slowing the passions and emphasizing deliberation—is to "refine and enlarge the public views" (*Federalist* 10).

The Founders sought to correct the historic problem of majority tyranny while remaining true to the principle of popular government. Giving up on democratic liberty would be a solution worse than the problem. There was no talk of turning government over to monarchs, dictators, or other nonpopular forms of rule. But it would be just as self-defeating (not to say tyrannical) in a free society to try to make everyone have the same opinions, passions, and interests. The solution of the men who wrote the Constitution, famously laid out in *The Federalist*, was to control the political effects of these differences and thwart the formation of unjust majorities while celebrating the natural diversity inherent in human liberty.

Reversing the prevailing assumption that republican government could work only in small nation-states, the Americans argued that the key to making this view of representation work was to "extend the sphere" and "expand the orbit." That is, they argued that representation would work better in a larger and more expansive nation. As a small government is more easily dominated by a majority faction (usually based on class distinctions), increasing the size of the nation would take in a greater number and variety of opinions, including many more "fit characters" to serve in public office, making it harder for a majority to form on narrow interests. The majority that did develop in such a nation would, by necessity, encompass a wider array of opinions and represent a stronger consensus grounded in the common good.

The Separation of Powers

Old-fashioned tyranny was also a problem. The Founders knew—as Lord Acton later famously quipped—that power corrupts and absolute power corrupts absolutely. "The accumulation of all powers," Madison explains in *Federalist* 47, "legislative, executive, and judiciary, in the same hands, whether of one, a few, or many, and whether hereditary, self-appointed, or elective, may justly be pronounced the very definition of tyranny." Keeping the powers of government divided in distinct branches is "admitted on all hands to be essential to the preservation of liberty." Here the Founders were following the writings of Montesquieu, who made a strong case for such a division.

But it was not enough to divide power and hope that it remained nicely confined within the written barriers of the Constitution. This was especially the case with the legislature: The "parchment barriers" of early state constitutions had proven an inadequate defense against a legislative proclivity toward "everywhere extending the sphere of its activity and drawing all power into its impetuous vortex." It is with this proclivity in mind that the Constitution grants powers to three separate and distinct branches of government, yielding the concept of the separation of powers. Each branch has only those powers granted to it, and can do only what its particular grant of power authorizes it to do.

The full meaning of the separation of powers, however, goes beyond this parchment distinction. "In framing a government which is to be administered by men over men, the great difficulty lies in this," Madison wrote in *Federalist* 51. "You must first enable the government to controul the governed; and in the next place oblige it to controul itself." That meant that, in addition to performing its proper constitutional functions (lawmaking, executing and adjudicating the law), there needed to be an internal check to further limit the powers of government. Rather than create another coercive authority for that purpose (a dubious proposition to say the least), the Founders not only divided power but also set it against itself. This separation of powers, along with the further provisions for checks and balances, creates a dynamism within the workings of government that uses the interests and incentives of those in government to enforce constitutional limits beyond their mere statement.

The Constitution creates three branches of government, and each is vested with independent powers and responsibilities. Each also has its own basis of authority and serves different terms of office. No member of one branch can at the same time serve in another branch. But their powers aren't separated completely: In order to protect themselves and guard against encroachment, each department shares overlapping powers with the others. Before it becomes law, congressional legislation, for instance, must be approved by the executive—who also has a check against Congress in the form of the qualified veto, which the legislature in turn can override by two-thirds votes in the House and the Senate. The president is commander in chief but the House has the power to declare war, and it is up to Congress to fund executive activities, including war-making. Treaties and judicial appointments are made by the executive but only with the advice and consent of the Senate. The Supreme Court can strike down executive or legislative actions that come up in cases before it as unconstitutional, but Congress has the power to reenact or modify overturned laws, strip the court's jurisdiction in many cases, and impeach federal judges.

The solution is found in structuring government such that "its several constituent parts may, by their mutual relations, be the means of keeping each other in their proper places," as Madison explained in *Federalist* 51. In other words, government is structured so that each branch has an interest in keeping an eye on the others, checking powers while jealously protecting its own. By giving each department an incentive to check the other—with overlapping functions and contending ambitions—the Founders devised a system that recognized and took advantage of man's natural political motivations to both use power for the common good and to keep power within constitutional boundaries. Or as Madison put it, the "interest of the man [becomes] connected with the constitutional rights of the place."

The separation of powers and the introduction of legislative balances and checks, according to Hamilton in *Federalist* 9, are "means, and powerful means, by which the excellencies of republican government may be retained and its imperfections lessened or avoided." They discourage the concentration of power and frustrate tyranny. At the same time, they require the branches of government to collaborate and cooperate in doing their work, limiting conflict and strengthening consensus. But these means also have the powerful effect of focusing individual actors on protecting their constitutional powers and carrying out their constitutional duties and functions—and that fact transforms the separation of powers from a mere negative concept to a positive and important contributor to limited government and constitutional fidelity.*

---

* See *What Separation of Powers Means for Constitutional Government* (Heritage First

Jefferson called the "republican form and principles of our Constitution" and "the salutary distribution of powers" in the Constitution the "two sheet anchors of our union." "If driven from either," he predicted, "we shall be in danger of foundering."

Federalism: A Nation of States

While everyone knows that this is a nation of states, few seem to think that this division is more than a quirk of history. Yet federalism is a crucial component of our system of government and part of the very infrastructure that makes our political liberty possible.

At the Constitutional Convention, despite a clear recognition of the need for additional national authority in the wake of the Articles of Confederation, there was great concern that an overreaction might produce an all-powerful national government. While they harbored no doctrinaire aversion to government as such, the Founders remained distrustful of government, especially a centralized national government that resembled the British rule they had revolted against. The solution was a unique American innovation: a *federal* government with strong but limited national powers that respected and protected the vitality of states. Half a century later, Alexis de Tocqueville would celebrate democracy in America as precisely the result of the political life supported and encouraged by this decentralized structure. *

Keep in mind that the United States Constitution is but one aspect of constitutional government in the United States. There are fifty state governments, each with their own constitutions, and they are key components of our "compound republic." Although national powers were clearly enhanced by the Constitution, the federal government was to exercise only delegated powers, the remainder being reserved to the people or the states as defined in their constitutions. The federal government was not supposed to not hold all, or even most, power.

The distinction between national and state government is inherent throughout the Constitution. The government created by the Constitution, Madison explains in *Federalist* 39, is "partly national and partly

---

Principles Essay #17) by Charles R. Kesler.

* A brief history and defense of federalism is *Why States? The Case for Federalism* (Heritage First Principles Monograph) by Eugene Hickok.

federal." The House of Representatives is elected directly by the people, but to give states more leverage within the national government, equal state representation in the Senate was blended into the national legislature (and permanently guaranteed in Article V). The executive is the most national of the branches, yet the electoral college process by which the president is elected is based on states. It is striking that in this powerful national government, there is not a single official chosen by a national constituency. The process by which the Constitution is amended is ultimately based on state approval. The document was ratified by the states.

To the extent that the United States government acts on individuals it is national, but in the extent of its powers it is limited to certain national functions. "Since its jurisdiction extends to certain enumerated objects only," Madison concludes, it "leaves to the several States a residuary and inviolable sovereignty over all other objects." Here is how Madison described this in *Federalist* 45:

> The powers delegated by the proposed Constitution to the federal government are few and defined. Those which are to remain in the State governments are numerous and indefinite. The former will be exercised principally on external objects, as war, peace, negotiation, and foreign commerce; with which last the power of taxation will, for the most part, be connected. The powers reserved to the several states will extend to all the objects which, in the ordinary course of affairs, concern the lives, liberties, and properties of the people, and the internal order, improvement and prosperity of the States.

In the same way that the separation of powers works *within* the federal and state constitutions, federalism is the basic operational structure of American constitutional government as a whole and provides the process by which the two levels of government check each other. "In the compound republic of America, the power surrendered by the people is first divided between two distinct governments, and then the portion allotted to each subdivided among distinct and separate departments," wrote Madison in *Federalist* 51. "The different governments will control each other; at the same time that each will be controlled by itself."

"This balance between the National and State governments ought to be dwelt on with peculiar attention, as it is of the utmost importance," Hamilton argued at the New York state ratifying convention. "It forms a double security to the people. If one encroaches on their rights they will find a powerful protection in the other. Indeed, they will both be prevented from overpassing their constitutional limits by a certain rivalship, which will ever subsist between them."

Although federalism was a practical invention of the Constitutional Convention, the idea of maintaining strong state governments was nothing new. The general notion that political authority and decision making should be kept as decentralized and close to home as possible was a well-established theme of the Anti-Federalists. The view of those who doubted the political efficacy of the new Constitution was that good popular government depended as much, if not more, upon a political community that would promote civic or public virtue as on a set of institutional devices designed to check the selfish impulses of the majority. But the structure of federalism is not only an "auxiliary precaution." By keeping authority and functions divided between two levels of government, federalism recognizes legitimate national power at the same time that it protects a sphere of state autonomy and local self-government.

Judicial Review

As with the auxiliary precautions, the power of federal courts to declare laws unconstitutional is not stipulated in the Constitution. While it is sometimes disputed, "judicial review" is a fundamental component of judicial power and was clearly understood to be logically implicit in the judicial function as judges consider individual cases or disputes, since a party may claim that an ordinary law and the Constitution are in conflict in the particular case before them. "The Constitution ought to be the standard of construction for the laws, and that wherever there is an evident opposition, the laws ought to give place to the Constitution," wrote Hamilton in *Federalist* 81. "But this doctrine is not deducible from any circumstance peculiar to the plan of convention, but from the general theory of a limited Constitution."

The unprecedented judicial power to declare laws "unconstitutional" is a logical consequence of having a supreme written Constitution which divides government into separate and coequal branches. The case for judicial review is made by Alexander Hamilton in *Federalist* 78:

> The interpretation of the laws is the proper and peculiar province of the courts. A constitution is, in fact, and must be regarded by the judges, as a fundamental law. It therefore belongs to them to ascertain its meaning, as well as the meaning of any particular act proceeding from the legislative body. If there should happen to be an irreconcilable variance between the two, that which has the superior obligation and validity ought, of course, to be preferred; or, in other words, the Constitution ought to be preferred to the statute, the intention of the people to the intention of their agents.

In short, when there is a conflict between ordinary law and the Constitution in a case before them, courts are obligated to take the side of the Constitution. This is no different than saying the Congress, in considering legislation, and the president, in considering signing legislation into law, must do so only if consistent with the Constitution.

The practice of judicial review is justified—and, importantly, controlled—by the idea of the Constitution as the fundamental law that limits government. Hamilton concludes: "Limitations of this kind can be preserved in practice no other way than through the medium of courts of justice, whose duty it must be to declare all acts contrary to the manifest tenor of the Constitution void. Without this, all the reservations of particular rights or privileges would amount to nothing." That is, without judicial review, constitutional limitations on government power would be virtually meaningless.

John Marshall makes the same point in *Marbury v. Madison*, the first Supreme Court case of judicial review in 1803:

> It is emphatically the province and duty of the Judicial Department to say what the law is. Those who apply the rule to particular cases must, of necessity, expound and interpret that rule. If two laws conflict with each other, the Courts must decide on the operation of each. So, if a law be in opposition to the Constitution, if both the law and the Constitution apply to a particular case, so that the Court must either decide that case conformably

to the law, disregarding the Constitution, or conformably to the Constitution, disregarding the law, the Court must determine which of these conflicting rules governs the case. This is of the very essence of judicial duty. If, then, the Courts are to regard the Constitution, and the Constitution is superior to any ordinary act of the Legislature, the Constitution, and not such ordinary act, must govern the case to which they both apply.

It is sometimes presumed that judicial review gives the Supreme Court the final say in all constitutional matters, but this does not follow from the explanations of Hamilton or Marshall. "To consider the judges as the ultimate arbiters of all constitutional questions," as Jefferson put it in 1820, "would place us under the despotism of an oligarchy." Judicial review arises from (and is confined by) the need for impartial legal decisions concerning the protection of the rights of individuals in particular cases—the very reason for an independent judiciary. But the judicial power does not extend to questions of a political nature—that is, concerning public policy and the public good. The courts have no authority to substitute their own preferences for laws enacted by lawmakers. "The province of the Court is solely to decide on the rights of individuals," Marshall wrote in the *Marbury* decision. "Questions, in their nature political or which are, by the Constitution and laws, submitted to the Executive, can never be made in this court."

Congress, not courts, has the power to make laws. Presidents, not judges, have the power to veto laws. Just as particular cases are to be judged by impartial and independent bodies, so questions that are inherently public or general can only be decided by representatives elected by the people. While the Constitution required the doctrine of judicial review to protect itself from legislative assault, the rule of law and the principles of republican government mean that in cases where there is not a clear constitutional question at issue (that is, in cases dealing with the policy preferences of elected representatives) the judiciary should defer to the lawmaking branch of government.

Who Says What the Constitution Means?

Who, then, does have the final say as to the meaning of the Constitution? Strictly speaking, the Constitution is silent on the matter. For sure, the Supreme Court has the say in particular cases and controversies before it, and no lower level federal or state court can reverse a Supreme Court decision. But it is not the same with the general judgments of the court. These judgments, or "holdings," are the written opinions of the justices that go beyond the particulars of the case. They are important in guiding other judges, officials. and the public as to how the Supreme Court will decide similar cases that might come before it. They track the Supreme Court's jurisprudence over time, creating stability and setting precedents for future courts to consider—a crucially important aspect of the rule of law. But the judgments of the Supreme Court beyond the decision between the parties in the immediate case or controversy are always provisional, and never *final*.

In practice, either by its own reconsideration or as retiring judges are replaced by new appointees, the Supreme Court has often revised or even reversed its earlier decisions. (Over the long run, the court has reversed itself on average more than once every term.) Beyond that, Congress could withdraw the court's appellate jurisdiction, or remove original jurisdiction from the lower federal courts, leaving certain issues to state courts. Ultimately, a Supreme Court decision could be overturned by a constitutional amendment, as has happened on a few occasions. It has not been unknown for presidents to refuse to enforce the court's holdings or general judgments, the most famous example being Lincoln's refusal to uphold the *Dred Scott* decision beyond the immediate parties to the case. That said, these last few actions, taken by institutions other than the court itself, have proven to be rare. In the overwhelming number of cases, the Supreme Court's rulings stand and take root, giving the appearance of finality. Regardless, it is important to recognize that the Constitution is not merely whatever the Supreme Court says it is. The decisions of the Supreme Court, no matter how benighted or controversial, never replace the Constitution.

Just as the Supreme Court is not the *final* interpreter, nor is it the *exclusive* interpreter of the Constitution either. Judges, congressmen, and presidents all take an oath to the Constitution, which means, as

Madison put it, that "each must in the exercise of its functions be guided by the text of the Constitution according to its own interpretation of it." After all, it is the Constitution—and not the legislature, the executive, or the courts—that is the supreme law of the land.

And just as the Supreme Court must take the side of the Constitution in interpreting the laws in cases before it (judicial review), so Congress in making laws and the president in signing and then executing laws are required—by the very nature of delegated powers in a written constitution, as well as their solemn oath of office—to do the same in the exercise of their functions. Here is how Jefferson described "coordinate branch construction" in an 1804 letter:

> [N]othing in the Constitution has given [the judiciary] a right to decide for the Executive, more than to the executive to decide for them. Both magistracies are equally independent in the sphere of action assigned to them. . . . [The Constitution] meant that its coordinate branches should be checks on each other. But the opinion which gives to the judges the right to decide what laws are constitutional, and what are not, not only for themselves in their own sphere of action, but for the Legislature & Executive also, in their spheres, would make the judiciary a despotic branch.

Neither the legislative nor the executive can check and balance the other branches of government—and neither can stand up to the judiciary—unless they take seriously their responsibility to act according to their interpretation of the Constitution. For the elected branches of government to turn this authority over to the courts is an abdication of both constitutional responsibility and popular consent. Lincoln put it this way in his First Inaugural, having in mind the Supreme Court's *Dred Scott* decision: "If the policy of the Government upon vital questions, affecting the whole people, is to be irrevocably fixed by decisions of the Supreme Court, the instant they are made, in ordinary litigation between parties in personal actions, the people will have ceased to be their own rulers, having to that extent practically resigned their Government into the hands of that eminent tribunal."

Regarding the question of how to read the Constitution, there have long been certain common-sense rules for interpreting legal documents.

These rules, having grown out of British constitutional thought, were well known and widely accepted at the time of the American Founding, even if they are less so today. These rules are ultimately rooted in principles of justice, reflecting the idea that all man-made law is based on a higher or permanent unwritten law. "The first and governing maxim in the interpretation of a statute is to discover the meaning of those who made it," wrote James Wilson in his famed *Lectures on Law*. This is because the Constitution was adopted by a sovereign act of the people, precisely for the purpose of creating a fundamental law above ordinary legislation and the political winds of the times. Joseph Story agreed in his *Commentaries on the Constitution*:

> Temporary delusions, prejudices, excitements, and objects have irresistible influence in mere questions of policy. And the policy of one age may ill suit the wishes or the policy of another. The constitution is not subject to such fluctuations. It is to have a fixed, uniform, permanent construction. It should be, so far at least as human infirmity will allow, not dependent upon the passions or parties of particular times, but the same yesterday, today, and for ever.

A proper constitutional jurisprudence, then, requires those who make, interpret, and enforce the law to be guided by the Constitution— the supreme law of the land—according to the original meaning and intent of the people who adopted it. "On every question of construction, we should carry ourselves back to the time when the Constitution was adopted, recollect the spirit manifested in the debates, and instead of trying what meaning may be squeezed out of the text, or invented against it, conform to the probable one in which it was passed," wrote Jefferson. Such a jurisprudence is the only approach that comports with a written constitution of fundamental law based on unchanging principles of justice. "Our peculiar security is in the possession of a written Constitution," Jefferson wrote on another occasion. "Let us not make it a blank paper by construction."

While there have always been debates over the details of *what* was intended in the Constitution—for instance, between a "strict" and "loose" interpretation of its clauses—there should be no question over *whether* the original meaning of the Constitution should be the ultimate guide for constitutional interpretation. "I entirely concur in the propriety of resorting to the sense in which the Constitution was accepted and ratified by the nation," wrote James Madison. "In that sense alone it is the legitimate Constitution. And if that be not the guide in expounding it, there can be no security for a consistent and stable, more than a faithful exercise of its powers." If the Constitution is to be taken seriously, the place to start is to understand and respect its original meaning.*

A Bundle of Compromises: Slavery Revisited

It is often said that the Constitution is "a bundle of compromises," implying that those who wrote the document abandoned principle in favor of cutting eighteenth-century backroom deals whenever possible to protect their own interests.

Not only the "Grand Compromise" between the large and the small states concerning representation in Congress, but federalism in general, the electoral college, and many other smaller details were the result of compromise. But the presence of compromise—often simply splitting the difference—does not necessarily prove that the principle was thrown by the wayside. Underlying agreement on core principles—such as the need of republican institutions based on consent—made possible such key compromises as each state having two senators while representation in the House is based on population. This compromise allowed large states more representation in the House of Representatives and small states a guarantee of representation in the Senate, thus surmounting a stumbling block at the Constitutional Convention.

In some cases, accepting compromise might be the wise course in order to preserve principles that might be fully achieved only with the passage of time. Which is to say that any compromise must be understood in light of the larger principles at issue. The most difficult and controversial compromise of the Constitution concerned the question of slavery. Keep in mind that the objective of the Founders was to establish a regime of equal rights and human liberty. We discussed earlier how slavery was understood as a violation of these principles. How the Con-

---

* See *How to Read the Constitution: Self-Government and the Jurisprudence of Originalism* (Heritage First Principles Essay #5) by Keith E. Whittington.

stitutional Convention dealt with slavery, in light of this violation and consistent with its ultimate objective, illustrates the point.

When the delegates met in Philadelphia, strong sectional interests supported the maintenance of slavery and the slave trade. "The *real* difference of interests," Madison noted, "lay not between large and small states but between the Northern and Southern states. The institution of slavery and its consequences formed a line of discrimination." In order to get the unified support needed for the Constitution's ratification and successful establishment, the framers made several concessions to the proslavery interests. The compromises they agreed to, however, were designed to tolerate or limit slavery where it currently existed, not to endorse or advance the institution, let alone grant that slavery was acceptable under or consistent with the foundational principles of the American Founders.

Consider the three compromises made by the Constitutional Convention delegates and approved as part of the final text. The first is the so-called "Three-Fifths Clause." Article I, Section 2 says that apportionment for representatives and taxation purposes would be determined by the number of free persons and three-fifths "of all other Persons." This clause does not apply to blacks (as free blacks were understood to be free persons) but to all unfree persons. The proslavery delegates wanted their slaves counted as whole persons, thereby according their states more representation in Congress. It was the antislavery delegates who wanted to count slaves as less—not to dehumanize them but to penalize slaveholders and give them less power in government to determine future policy matters. Antislavery delegate James Wilson of Pennsylvania proposed the three-fifths compromise, and it was seconded by Charles Pinckney of South Carolina, suggesting that a deal had already been struck. Nor was this compromise unprecedented: It was debated (and similar language proposed) in drafting the Articles of Confederation and adopted in 1783 to apportion requisitions among the states.

The second clause concerned the slave trade: Congress by the Constitution was prohibited from blocking the migration and importation "of such Persons as any of the states now existing shall think proper to admit" prior to 1808 (Article I, Section 9). Although protection of the slave trade was a major concession demanded by proslavery delegates, the final clause was only a temporary exemption (for twenty years) for states existing at the time from a federal power to prohibit the trade. Moreover, it did not prevent states from restricting or outlawing the slave trade themselves, which many had already done. "If there was no other lovely feature in the Constitution but this one," James Wilson observed, "it would diffuse a beauty over its whole countenance. Yet the lapse of a few years, and Congress will have power to exterminate slavery from within our borders." By granting the power to outlaw the slave trade at a future date, the Constitution held out to Congress a powerful weapon against domestic slavery. Congress passed, and President Jefferson signed into law, a national prohibition of the slave trade effective January 1, 1808.

The third clause deals with the return of fugitive slaves: The Privileges and Immunities Clause (Article IV, Section 2) guaranteed the return upon claim of any "Person held to Service or Labour" in one state who had escaped to another state. At the last minute, the phrase "Person *legally* held to Service or Labour in one state" was amended to read, "Person held to Service or Labour in one state, *under the Laws thereof.*" Note the critical change in language, from "legally held" to "held to Service" in a state "under the laws thereof." This revision emphasized that slaves were held according to the laws of individual states, making it clear that the Constitution itself did not sanction the legality of slavery.

None of the three clauses recognized slavery as having any legitimacy from the point of view of federal law. Beyond these clauses, the Constitution (until amended) granted no authority to the federal government to prevent (or advance) slavery in the several states.

It is very significant that the words "slave" and "slavery" were not used in the Constitution. Madison recorded in his notes that the delegates "thought it wrong to admit in the Constitution the idea that there could be property in men." This seemingly minor point of insisting on the use of the word "person" rather than "slave" was not a clever euphemism to hide the hypocrisy of slavery but was of the utmost importance, establishing in the Constitution that slaves were, indeed, human persons rather than property. The implication of this is that slaves had equal natural rights just as their masters, even though those rights were not being secured or enforced by government. Madison explained in *Federalist* 54:

> But we must deny the fact, that slaves are considered merely as property, and in no respect whatever as persons. The true state of

the case is, that they partake of both these qualities: being considered by our laws, in some respects, as persons, and in other respects as property. In being compelled to labor, not for himself, but for a master; in being vendible by one master to another master; and in being subject at all times to be restrained in his liberty and chastised in his body, by the capricious will of another— the slave *may appear* to be degraded from the human rank, and classed with those irrational animals which fall under the legal denomination of property. In being protected, on the other hand, in his life and in his limbs, against the violence of all others, even the master of his labor and his liberty; and in being punishable himself for all violence committed against others—the slave is no less evidently regarded by the law as a member of the society, not as a part of the irrational creation; *as a moral person, not as a mere article of property.*

While it was not realized immediately, the premise laid down in the Constitution is that those held in servitude were to be regarded by the law as persons. This further shapes how the three clauses concerning slavery are to be read. All else being equal, the language of the Constitution sets the institution of slavery, as Lincoln put it, on the course of ultimate extinction. "In the way our Fathers originally left the slavery question, the institution was in the course of ultimate extinction, and the public mind rested in the belief that it was *in the course of ultimate extinction*," Abraham Lincoln observed in 1858. "All I have asked or desired anywhere, is that it should be placed back again upon the basis that the Fathers of our government originally placed it upon."

Frederick Douglass had been born a slave in Maryland, but escaped and eventually became a prominent spokesman for free blacks in the abolitionist movement. He believed that the government created by the Constitution "was never, in its essence, anything but an anti-slavery government." "Abolish slavery tomorrow, and not a sentence or syllable of the Constitution need be altered," he wrote in 1864. "It was purposely so framed as to give no claim, no sanction to the claim, of property in man. If in its origin slavery had any relation to the government, it was only as the scaffolding to the magnificent structure, to be removed as soon as the building was completed." This point is underscored by the fact that, although slavery was abolished by constitutional amendment, not one word of the original text had to be amended or deleted.

The slavery compromises included in the Constitution can only be understood—that is, can only be understood to be prudent compromises rather than a surrender of principle—in light of the Founders' proposition that all men are created equal. It took a bloody civil war to reconcile the protections of the Constitution with that proposition and to attest that this nation, so conceived and dedicated, would endure.

Constitutional Fidelity

In its simplest meaning, the United States Constitution establishes in writing a government, by the legitimate authority of the sovereign people, designed to secure the rights and liberties necessary for their safety and happiness—safety being the floor and happiness being the ceiling, if you will, of America's national purpose. As the act constituting government, the Constitution lays out the structure of powers and gives instructions as to the limits and extent of those powers. Individuals who exercise constitutional powers—the president, members of Congress, and judges—are bound and obligated to regard those instructions, as long as and until the sovereign people alter them, as fundamental and permanent.

"What is a Constitution?" asked Justice William Paterson in a 1795 case before the Supreme Court. "It is the form of government, delineated by the mighty hand of the people, in which certain first principles of fundamental law are established. The Constitution is fixed and certain; it contains the permanent will of the people, and is the supreme law of the land; it is paramount to the power of the Legislature, and can be revoked or altered only by the authority that made it."

The principles established by the Constitution of the United States are deemed fundamental and designed to be permanent. As such, constitutional government requires a commitment to the procedures and institutions established by the Constitution. But it also requires fidelity to the principles and purposes which are the substance of the Constitution—or more precisely, a faithfulness to *this* Constitution, ordained and established by the American people, to form "a more perfect union" and "secure the Blessings of Liberty for ourselves and our posterity."

8

The Virtues of Self-Government:
Building Community, Forming Character,
and Making Citizens

Levi Preston of Danvers, Massachusetts, was in his early twenties in the spring of 1775 when he fought at the Battle of Concord, at the opening of the American Revolution.

Many years later, Captain Preston was asked why he went to fight that day. Was it the intolerable oppressions of British colonial policy, or the Stamp Act? "I never saw any stamps." What about the tax on tea? "I never drank a drop of the stuff; the boys threw it all overboard." It must have been all your reading of Harrington, Sidney, and Locke on the principles of liberty? "Never heard of 'em. We read only the Bible, the catechism, Watt's *Psalms and Hymns*, and the *Almanack*." Well, what was it? asked the interviewer. What made you take up arms against the British? "Young man, what we meant in going for those redcoats was this: we always had governed ourselves, and we always meant to. They didn't mean we should."

Today when we think of self-government, we usually have in mind the various forms of political participation, like voting in elections or serving on a jury, associated with the democratic process. These activities are a very important aspect of the concept. But in addition to these practices, the Founders meant the preconditions that were required for the success of that process and that fulfilled man's higher purpose beyond the limited ends of government.

The Founders understood self-government in the twofold sense of *political* self-government, in which we govern ourselves as a political community, and of *moral* self-government, according to which each individual is responsible for governing himself. They believed that the success of the former required a flourishing of the latter. Individuals could not govern themselves as a body politic unless they were each first capable of governing themselves as individuals, families, and communities. The Founders were deeply concerned not only with the structures of limited constitutional government but also with the public virtues and civic habits needed to maintain the capacity for political self-government. This constant challenge is the reason that American constitutionalism was from the beginning, and will always remain, an experiment.

The purpose of limiting government, assuring rights, and guaranteeing the consent of the governed is to protect a vast realm of human freedom. That freedom creates a great space for the primary institutions of civil society—family, school, church, and private associations—to flourish, forming the habits and virtues required for liberty. The American Founders also knew that it was through these institutions, through the enjoyment of family, faith, and community life, that man secured, as it says in the Constitution, "the blessings of liberty"—that liberty which is truly a blessing. Moral self-government both precedes and completes political self-government, and thus political freedom. It is in this sense that the primary as well as the culminating first principle of American liberty is self-government.

The Challenge of Self-Government

Liberty is the great theme of America. It was the objective of the American Revolution and the overarching purpose of the founding. But virtue was never far behind.

Some think that it is contradictory to favor individual rights and promote public virtue at the same time. Historians debate the emphasis in the founding on rights and freedoms, on the one hand, and classical republican concepts of virtue and character, on the other. But the Founders made both of these arguments with equal fervor. There are important tensions between rights and responsibilities, for sure, but far from being contradictory, the concepts are necessarily intertwined.

Rights were understood to be compatible with moral character, and virtue to be complementary to individual rights.

The Founders never thought liberty to be an open-ended right to do whatever one wanted. They were careful to distinguish "the spirit of liberty from that of licentiousness, cherishing the first, avoiding the last," as George Washington once phrased it. The right to human liberty necessarily had a sense of self-control about it, as liberty was understood to mean that liberty which was appropriate for the nature of man. And while human nature made men prone to their passions, that did not mean that liberty was the liberation of the passions to overrule the human mind, like an animal following its instinct. Liberty, properly understood, was an expression of man's higher nature—of reason over passion, and virtue over vice—the triumph of the "better angels of our nature," as Lincoln later wrote. In this sense, the Founders' concept of liberty aligns itself with traditional moral philosophy and theology.

"The most perfect freedom consists in obeying the dictates of right reason, and submitting to natural law," said the influential clergyman Samuel West in an Election Day address to the Massachusetts legislature in 1776. "When a man goes beyond or contrary to the law of nature and reason, he becomes the slave of base passions and vile lusts; he introduces confusion and disorder into society, and brings misery and destruction upon himself. This, therefore, cannot be called a state of freedom, but a state of the vilest slavery and the most dreadful bondage." Such license was not at all what the Founders meant by liberty. "Where licentiousness begins," concluded West, "liberty ends."

This distinction is implied in the very terms that they used. Just as they took the philosophical ground of rights seriously, so too did they take seriously the basis of moral character. And here again, as with rights, the dual foundation is philosophical reasoning and biblical revelation. It is significant that the Founders always spoke of virtue and vice (as opposed to the more modern language of "personal values"), as these are the terms of classical thought and Christian theology. Recall the language of Washington's First Inaugural, where the president asserted that "there exists in the economy and course of nature, an indissoluble union between virtue and happiness," and that no nation can prosper that "disregards the external rules of order and right, which Heaven itself has ordained." This is not the language of moral relativism.

Virtue, it is fair to say, was a primary concern of the Anti-Federalists, the critics of the Constitution who feared that the national government would overwhelm liberty, and who demanded the addition of a Bill of Rights to protect constitutional freedoms. They believed that moral corruption was inevitable and that, as a result, a virtuous people could be fostered only in a small republic of homogenous and mostly agrarian citizens. "The experience of every age," argued an anonymous Anti-Federalist writer in the *Virginia Independent Chronicle*, "evinces that arguments drawn from the native charms of moral rectitude, and its necessary connection with the happiness and welfare of states, are too feeble to ensure the requisite practice of virtue when opposed to the allurements of self-interest and self-gratification."

But the federalist advocates of the Constitution were equally concerned about the maintenance of citizen virtue, and shared a realistic assessment of the weaknesses of human nature. The difference is that they not only recognized man's natural interests and weaknesses but also designed institutions of government to account and compensate for those flaws. They emphasized the structural framework of government and called for an expansive republic to supply "the defect of better motives." This was not because virtue was unimportant or unnecessary—that was not at all their view—but because they knew that virtue alone could not be relied on to provide the foundation for limited constitutionalism. John Adams captured the problem: "We must not then depend alone upon the love of liberty in the soul of man for its preservation."

In *Federalist* 51, Madison observed that "experience has taught mankind the necessity of auxiliary precautions." He prefaced it, though, by noting that "a dependence on the people is, no doubt, the primary control on the government." No matter how effective, expanded representation, the separation of powers, and the structural mechanisms of government do not override a primary dependence on the people, and that requires a self-governing citizenry.

As a whole, the Founders recognized that citizen virtue was necessary for the success of republican government, and that limited government was possible only if citizens were able first to govern themselves by ruling their own passions. In this, they followed Montesquieu in concluding that, while fear is the basis of despotism, and nobility characterizes monarchies, "virtue is the principle of republican government."

Samuel Williams made this point in 1775: "In a despotic government, the only principle by which the tyrant who is to move the whole machine means to regulate and manage the people is fear, by the servile dread of his power. But a free government, which of all others is far the most preferable, cannot be supported without virtue."

"As there is a degree of depravity in mankind which requires a certain degree of circumspection and distrust, so there are other qualities in human nature which justify a certain portion of esteem and confidence," Madison wrote in *Federalist* 55. "Republican government presupposes the existence of these qualities in a higher degree than any other form." If the assessment of man's depravity were as bad as some claimed, Madison continued, "the inference would be that there is not sufficient virtue among men for self-government." If that were so, republican government would not be viable and the American experiment would be destined from the start for failure. If men were incapable of any moral restraint, Madison concluded, then "nothing less than the chains of despotism can restrain them from destroying and devouring one another." The very possibility of liberty and limited government depends on man's capacity for virtue and moral character.

Just as liberty requires limited constitutional government focused on securing the rights to life, liberty, and the pursuit of happiness, so it also requires a certain type of citizen, with characteristics appropriate for republican government. Here is how John Adams made the point: "We have no government armed with power capable of contending with human passions unbridled by morality and religion. Avarice, ambition, revenge, or gallantry, would break the strongest cords of our Constitution as a whale goes through a net. Our Constitution was made only for a moral and religious people. It is wholly inadequate to the government of any other."

American Virtues

What were the public qualities the Founders thought especially important for Americans, as a self-governing people, to acquire and practice? Their writings emphasize four key categories of civic virtue.

First, in order to be free, citizens had to possess the virtue of self-reliance. A primary moral quality of independent personal character is to take primary responsibility for the well-being of one's life, family, and neighbors. Hard work, whether physical labor such as farming and crafts, or mental work needed for commercial enterprise, was encouraged. By contrast, in Europe, work, especially physical labor and commerce, was looked down upon. The social ideal in Europe had been the leisured life of the refined gentleman of wealth, whose ancestors acquired estate and power as rewards for fighting for kings and aristocrats. The Founders' ideal American citizen was to be very different.

Independent character includes a feeling of embarrassment at receiving welfare from others, and although assistance in times of need should be offered and could be accepted, good character demands that the recipient quickly return to employment and restore the goods and favors he received. Moreover, that kind of character was formed within the personal context of family, church, and community, where government welfare at the local level was itself a last resort only for those few persons who had no personal relationships. The thought of formal welfare programs organized at the remote national level was unimaginable.

On the other hand, the kind of moral qualities the Founders inculcated were opposed to a cold indifference to suffering and misfortune. Both God and country demanded unselfishness and charity, and disregard for one's fellow man was inconsistent with "the Laws of Nature and of Nature's God." What was not tolerable to the founding generation was laziness, refusal to work, or permanently living off of others. "I am for doing good to the poor, but I differ in opinion of the means," wrote Franklin. "I think the best way of doing good to the poor, is not making them easy *in* poverty, but leading or driving them *out* of it." The notion of a "right to welfare" was the very type of dependency that undermined self-government.

Second, the Founders valued those qualities that made for an assertive and spirited citizenry, possessing what Madison in *Federalist* 57 described as that "vigilant and manly spirit which actuates the people of America, a spirit which nourishes freedom, and in return is nourished by it." Strong character included the virtues of courage, risk-taking, and competitiveness. Courage is required so that citizens are willing to fight for the freedom and independence of their community and their country when necessary. During times of peace, the courage of self-governing citizens strengthens their resistance to government encroachment on their rights, whether property or civil rights. While people who are excessively dependent easily invade the property and civil rights of others, a spirited people have the pride and courage to resist and reject the advance of despotism.

At the same time, the Founders did not want America to fall into the harsh, cruel, militaristic courage of some ancient societies. Americans' courage would be channeled into and tempered by commercial life. Commercial people earn wealth and resources by the peaceful means of manufacturing and trade, not by war and imperialism. Central to the moral vision of the Founders were the qualities appropriate to commerce: a willingness to take risks for the sake of reward, discipline and skill in work and craft, the practical wisdom to meet the needs of neighborhood and market that must be satisfied by successful enterprise, a sense of justice that comes from respecting contracts and agreements, and the hope of future rewards for self-improvement and family that lengthens the individual's time horizon and encourages saving and investment.

Third, the Founders knew that a free people must possess and maintain a keen knowledge of the rights and responsibilities of citizenship. Americans must know about the nature of free government and the requirements of liberty. A good synopsis of this type of knowledge is found in George Washington's First Annual Message to Congress:

> Knowledge is in every country the surest basis of public happiness. In one in which the measures of Government receive their impression so immediately from the sense of the Community as in ours it is proportionably essential. To the security of a free Constitution it contributes in various ways: By convincing those who are intrusted with the public administration, that every valuable end of Government is best answered by the enlightened confidence of the people: and by teaching the people themselves to know and to value their own rights; to discern and provide against invasions of them; to distinguish between oppression and the necessary exercise of lawful authority; between burthens proceeding from a disregard to their convenience and those resulting from the inevitable exigencies of Society; to discriminate the spirit of Liberty from that of licentiousness—cherishing the first, avoiding the last, and uniting a speedy, but temperate vigilance against encroachments, with an inviolable respect to the Laws.

This means that among the virtues to be cultivated for free government was knowledge of the first principles of liberty. Citizens must know that legitimate government is grounded in the protection of equal natural rights and the consent of the governed—the principles of the Declaration of Independence—and understand and appreciate how the Constitution and our institutions of limited government work to protect liberty and the rule of law. They must also have the capacity to make moral distinctions and possess a certain spirit of vigilance in actively protecting their freedom.

And fourth, implied in Washington's call for the people "to discriminate the spirit of Liberty from that of licentiousness," a self-governing people must possess great self-restraint and a strong sense of personal and public moderation. They must be able to control their own passions, in order not only to rule themselves as individuals and as a people, but also to respect the rights of others. Citizens must respect lawful authority and obey the legitimate processes of constitutional government. In short, they must abide by the rule of law—including majority decision-making—rather than be tempted to pursue or follow the arbitrary rule of men, whether through the exercise of their own will or by enabling others.

In general, the Founders drew on the chief virtues inculcated by the long Western tradition of faith and reason: prudence, justice, moderation, courage, hope, and charity. Thinkers and writers in the Western tradition dreamed of a society made up of a people of good character. The American Founders sought to establish the constitutional basis for a society that could inspire these moral qualities in the American character, strengthened by the religious faith held by nearly all Americans. They also understood that the practice of these virtues was the essence of self-government in the individual and the firmest foundation for an independent, self-governed society.

The Founders knew that civic virtues were instilled through proper habits of mind and practice. How were these habits to be established and inculcated? They looked to the character-forming role of law, education, and the institutions of civil society, especially religious institutions and the family.

Constitutional Morality

"[T]he first transactions of a nation, like those of an individual upon his first entrance into life," Washington wrote at the time of the ratification of the Constitution, "make the deepest impression, and are to form the leading traits in its character." We cannot overlook the fact that government plays a role in forming the virtues of self-government.

Under the Articles of Confederation, the individual states had become hotbeds of political corruption and poor management, mired in their own local concerns and prejudices. By nourishing petty politics, speculation, and special interests, and in general aiding narrow political passions, government invited and encouraged a jealous and petty spirit in the people. As a result, the common interests of America were moldering and sinking into ruin. The resulting breakdowns of political and economic order, Washington lamented, "afford too many melancholy proofs of the decay of public virtue." Government structured to appeal to the passions was not good for civic character.

The American Founders saw the establishment of the Constitution as a necessary step in the moral reform of American politics. That is, they believed that good laws—and especially a good constitution— would have critical and salutary effects on political choices and the habits of government. A well-constructed and limited national government would itself encourage self-government, thereby contributing to the establishment of a national character.

Good opinions held by the people, and good government, would have complementary effects on politics. The legislative, executive, and judicial processes, under the supremacy of the Constitution, vindicate the rule of law over the decrees of men. The separation of powers and the system of checks and balances thwart governmental despotism and encourage responsibility in public representatives. A responsible government, in turn, bolsters a responsible people. The legitimate constitutional amendment process allows basic reform at the same time that it elevates the fundamental law of the nation above the popular passions of the moment, thereby encouraging deliberation and patience in the people.

Laws, by permitting or restraining certain behaviors, cannot help but shape habits and form the character of citizens. The Founders did not think such a concept at all improper. The Northwest Ordinance of 1787 (the organic law governing the federal territories, passed by the Congress of the Confederation and then again by the new Congress) is the best example of this view at the national level: "Religion, morality, and knowledge, being necessary to good government and the happiness of mankind, schools and the means of education shall forever be encouraged." Under the law, land in each township established in the Northwest Territory was set aside for schools and for purposes of religion. (Similar language exists in a number of state constitutions.)

But there was a limit to what could be done directly at the *national* level to shape morality without trampling on the very liberty the Founders sought to establish. The federal government is confined to those powers delegated to it by the Constitution. It could support moral virtue through example (as in opening sessions of Congress with prayer), exhortation (as in presidential addresses), and encouragement (as in a general, nonsectarian support of religion). But the federal government, by intention and design, plays only a limited role in the task of forming moral character.

To the extent that government was to nourish virtues and regulate civic morality, it was primarily the responsibility of state and local government. That states took these matters seriously, and devoted considerable attention to questions of citizen virtue, is evident from early state constitutions. The Virginia Constitution (1776) states, "That no free government, or the blessings of liberty, can be preserved to any people, but by a firm adherence to justice, moderation, temperance, frugality, and virtue, and by frequent recurrence to fundamental principles." The Constitution of Pennsylvania (1776) instructs that "[l]aws for the encouragement of virtue, and prevention of vice and immorality, shall be made and constantly kept in force, and provision shall be made for their due execution." The Constitution of the Commonwealth of Massachusetts (1780) affirms that "[w]isdom, and knowledge, as well as virtue, diffused generally among the body of the people, being necessary for the preservation of their rights and liberties," it is the duty of legislators and magistrates "to countenance and inculcate the principles of humanity and general benevolence, public and private charity, industry and frugality, honesty and punctuality in their dealings; sincerity, good humor, and all social affections, and generous sentiments among the people."

It is important to understand that state constitutions (and hence legitimate state lawmaking authority) are very different from the federal constitution. The federal government is one of delegated and enumerated powers. States, however, traditionally had authority to exercise what are called police powers—sometimes called reserved powers, as these powers are "reserved" to the states or to the people in the federal constitution—which, in addition to law enforcement, include legislating for the health, safety, welfare, education, and morals of state residents. States pass laws concerning educational standards, the use of alcohol, the conditions of marriage, and the age of consent, for instance. The states also have greater involvement with religion than the federal government is permitted under the First Amendment. (Recall that some states had establishments of religion under the federal constitution.) The two levels of government had very different responsibilities and duties. While the national government was to do a few very important functions well, the bulk of government powers by design remained at the state and local level, where it could have more discretion and responsibility to, among other things, shape and form civic character through the sanction of civil and criminal law. The powers of the federal government are "few and defined," as Madison wrote in *Federalist* 45, but "the powers reserved to the several states will extend to all the objects which, in the ordinary course of affairs, concern the lives, liberties, and properties of the people, and the internal order, improvement and prosperity of the States."

In *Democracy in America*, Tocqueville describes this situation by distinguishing between government, by which he means the tasks assigned to the central or national government, and administration, meaning the general and ordinary responsibilities exercised by state and local government, such as building roads, providing police and fire protection, and generally exercising the police powers. The United States was intended to have a strong national government, but most governing—the day-to-day governing that touches the lives of citizens and communities—was to be done by the decentralized administration of state and local government.

State and local governments are better able to decide and take responsibility for issues of state and local import that do not involve the federal government or other communities. Consider this from Jefferson's *Autobiography* in 1821:

[I]t is not by the consolidation, or concentration of powers, but by their distribution, that good government is effected. Were not this great country already divided into states, that division must be made, that each might do for itself what concerns itself directly, and what it can so much better do than a distant authority. Every state again is divided into counties, each to take care of what lies within its local bounds; each county again into townships or wards, to manage minuter details; and every ward into farms, to be governed each by its individual proprietor. Were we directed from Washington when to sow, & when to reap, we should soon want bread. It is by this partition of cares, descending in gradation from general to particular, that the mass of human affairs may be best managed for the good and prosperity of all.

All government is constitutionally limited, and states are still subject to constitutional oversight by courts of law, but while the federal government is limited to certain core functions—national defense and foreign affairs, protecting rights of citizens, regulating interstate commerce—state governments historically had much more extensive authority over Americans' daily lives. State government does not merely play a role in negative liberty—that is, protecting against violations of liberty—but along with local subunits of government plays a positive role in shaping the conditions of self-government. It is at the state level, then, that can be seen the more meaningful and robust role of government alluded to in the earlier discussion of federalism.

Liberty and Learning

"Knowledge will forever govern ignorance: and a people who mean to be their own governors, must arm themselves with the power which knowledge gives," James Madison once observed. "What spectacle can be more edifying or more seasonable, than that of Liberty and Learning, each leaning on the other for their mutual and surest support?"

Education was the mechanism for the general diffusion of knowledge, and the Founders believed that widespread popular education was the ultimate check on tyranny. When it came to republican government, built on popular opinion, education was an absolutely necessary component of liberty. "Promote, then, as an object of primary importance, institutions for the general diffusion of knowledge," Washington wrote in his Farewell Address. "In proportion as the structure of a government gives force to public opinion, it is essential that public opinion should be enlightened." After all, as Jefferson put it, "Knowledge is power."

The Founders also believed that education was a leading instrument for teaching virtue, shaping character, and molding citizens. The "best means of forming a manly, virtuous and happy people, will be found in the right education of youth," Washington wrote in 1784. "Without this foundation, every other means, in my opinion, must fail." Moral education began when the first habits and manners were established. This formation started and was mostly defined at an early age by parents, who had the primary responsibility for the upbringing of their children. As well, the nature of early learning explains why elementary education should be controlled at the local level, where the habits and good character of parents, family, and local community can have their full formative effect on children.

For these reasons, the Founders proposed and strongly supported a system of general public education. As a practical matter, this meant establishing throughout the nation public or common schools at the state and local level, a process that had already begun in the New England states. "Children should be educated and instructed in the principles of freedom," John Adams wrote his 1787 work, *A Defence of the Constitutions of Government of the United States of America*. "The education here intended is not merely that of the children of the rich and noble, but of every rank and class of people, down to the lowest and poorest. It is not too much to say that schools for the education of all should be placed at convenient distances, and maintained at the public expense."

As commissioners for the University of Virginia, Thomas Jefferson and James Madison wrote a report describing the civic purpose of schools. Primary education was to focus on the rudimentary elements of knowledge, teaching reading, writing, arithmetic, geography, and history, but a key object was "to instruct the mass of our citizens in these, their rights, interests and duties, as men and citizens." As for "the higher branches of education"—that is, education taught at the private and public colleges scattered around the country—its civic purposes were "to develop the reasoning faculties of our youth, enlarge their minds, cultivate their morals, and instill into them the precepts of virtue and order," "to form them to habits of reflection and correct action, rendering them examples of virtue to others, and of happiness within themselves," and "to form the statesmen, legislators and judges, on whom public prosperity and individual happiness are so much to depend."

Jefferson and Madison also designed the curriculum for teaching the principles of government at the University of Virginia's law school, where many of those who would be responsible for upholding the rule of law were to be educated. Their proposed course of study is highly instructive and applies generally to the teaching of American political principles. With "especial attention to the principles of government which shall be inculcated therein" and "to point out specifically where these principles are to be found legitimately developed," they recommended that

> as to the general principles of liberty and the rights of man in nature and in society, the doctrines of Locke, in his "Essay concerning the true original extent and end of civil government," and of Sidney in his "Discourses on government," may be considered as those generally approved by our fellow-citizens of this, and of the US. and that on the distinctive principles of the government of our own state, and of that of the US. the best guides are to be found in 1. the Declaration of Independence, as the fundamental act of union of these states. 2. the book known by the title of "The Federalist," being an authority to which appeal is habitually made by all, and rarely declined or denied by any as evidence of the general opinion of those who framed, and of those who accepted the Constitution of the US. on questions as to its genuine meaning. 3. the Resolutions of the General assembly of Virginia in 1799 on the subject of the Alien and Sedition laws, which appeared to accord with the predominant sense of the people of the US. 4. the Valedictory address of President Washington, as conveying political lessons of peculiar value.

In addition to knowing the Constitution and constitutional history, students were to read John Locke and Algernon Sidney about the principles of liberty and natural rights, and study in particular the core documents of the American Founding.

The purpose of education was to spread useful knowledge (such as mathematics and science) and a higher knowledge of literature, philosophy, history, language, and the arts—but also to teach of the rights and responsibilities of citizenship. A good education in "reading, writing and common arithmatick," wrote Jefferson in 1779, followed by the study of "Graecian [Greek], Roman, English and American history," would render Americans "worthy to receive, and able to guard the sacred deposit of the rights and liberties of their fellow citizens."

Enlightened Patriotism

A primary objective of education in a democratic republic is to teach citizens the first principles of republican government. One characteristic to be encouraged in the schoolroom is patriotism or love of country. That is, educational institutions—and the family again begins this formative process—should teach not only the principles and practices of liberty, but also an appreciation of the country that upholds and protects those principles and that liberty. At younger ages, this was especially to be done by teaching American history. History fosters attachment, and attachment—a necessary precondition to sustained civic engagement— fosters patriotism. As constitutional signer James Wilson reminds us in his 1790 textbook, "Law and liberty cannot rationally become the objects of our *love*, unless they first become the objects of our *knowledge*."

Noah Webster understood the necessity and the potential of public education in American society. He wrote the nation's first textbooks to advance national identity, and published a distinctive American dictionary to maintain the common language needed for popular deliberation and self-government. "Every child in America should be acquainted with his own country," he wrote in 1788. "He should read books that furnish him with ideas that will be useful to him in life and practice. As soon as he opens his lips, he should rehearse the history of his own country; he should lisp the praise of liberty, and of those illustrious heroes and statesmen, who have wrought a revolution in her favor." The objective of an education oriented toward a life of citizenship is to "implant in the minds of the American youth the principles of virtue and of liberty and inspire them with just and liberal ideas of government and with an inviolable attachment to their own country." Webster's blue-backed spellers sold in the tens of millions in the early republic, only to be surpassed in popularity and influence by William McGuffey's readers, which sold more than 120 million copies between 1836 and 1920. McGuffey's lessons were grounded in religious instruction but also told stories of George Washington and other American heroes.*

In forming citizens, the Founders were concerned not only about the upbringing of America's youth, but also the education of those coming from other nations to become Americans. Naturalization—the idea of an immigrant becoming an equal citizen *as if by nature*, based on reciprocal and voluntary consent of the immigrant and the citizens of the welcoming nation—is entirely consistent with and follows logically from the political theory of the American Founding. Individual transformation from any ethnic heritage or racial background to American citizenship is possible in the United States because the very openness of liberty to diverse heritages and backgrounds stems from political principles of free government that can be held by all people regardless of individual background. But that transformation or assimilation did not occur of its own accord. It required a robust process of assimilation by which immigrants maintained their ethnic backgrounds but also developed certain similarities of habit and mind.

In his *Notes on the State of Virginia*, Jefferson worried that immigrants would "bring with them the principles of the governments they leave, imbibed in their early youth; or, if able to throw them off, it will be in exchange for an unbounded licentiousness, passing, as is usual, from one extreme to another. It would be a miracle were they to stop precisely at the point of temperate liberty." Hamilton held similar opinions:

> The safety of a republic depends essentially on the energy of a common national sentiment; on a uniformity of principles and habits; on the exemption of the citizens from foreign bias and prejudice; and on that love of country which will almost invariably be found to be closely connected with birth, education, and family. The opinion advanced in *Notes on Virginia* is undoubtedly correct, that foreigners will generally be apt to bring with them attachments to the persons they have left behind; to the

---

* See Walter Berns's *Making Patriots* (2001).

country of their nativity; and to its particular customs and manners. They will also entertain opinions on government congenial with those under which they have lived; or if they should be led hither from a preference to ours, how extremely unlikely is it that they will bring with them that temperate love of liberty, so essential to real republicanism?

While recognizing the inevitable, and desirable, diversity of opinion that would result from immigration, the Founders understood that there needed to be a certain uniformity of opinion about America and the fundamental principles of the revolution. As Hamilton put it, immigration policy should strive "to enable aliens to get rid of foreign and acquire American attachments; to learn the principles and imbibe the spirit of our government; and to admit of a philosophy at least, of their feeling a real interest in our affairs."

This is why immigrants, without the natural advantage of having been born and raised in this country, must be given a specific education in the history, political ideas, and institutions of the United States. They must know who we are and what we believe as a people and a nation. They must speak our common language, reflect a republican character, and draw their primary national identity from the United States. In this way, as Washington predicted, immigrants "get assimilated to our customs, measures and laws: in a word, soon become one people."*

The Institutions of Civil Society

A good constitution was necessary but not sufficient to define and maintain self-government, as it could neither remove the need for nor create of its own accord good citizens. Recall John Adams's observation: "We have no government armed with power capable of contending with human passions unbridled by morality and religion. Avarice, ambition, revenge, or gallantry, would break the strongest cords of our Constitution as a whale goes through a net. Our Constitution was made only for a moral and religious people. It is wholly inadequate to the government of any other." Without a virtuous people, all the best constitutional struc-

---

* See *Making Citizens: The Case for Patriotic Assimilation* (Heritage First Principles Essay #3) by Matthew Spalding.

tures and provisions, no matter how well constructed, would be unable to perpetuate republican government.

George Washington pointedly recognized this fact in the draft of his First Inaugural. When political leaders "incited by the lust of power" and prompted by popular passions overstep constitutional barriers and violate "the unalienable rights of humanity," it would be yet another proof that no mere contract among men is perpetual or sacrosanct, and that "no Wall of words, that no mound of parchment can be so formed as to stand against the sweeping torrent of boundless ambition on the one side, aided by the sapping current of corrupted morals on the other."

In the inaugural address he delivered to Congress on April 30, 1789, Washington indicated the solution. He spoke of "the talents, the rectitude, and the patriotism" of those that were to "devise and adopt" the laws. While institutional arrangements were critical for checking power and upholding constitutional government, Washington ultimately saw the "surest pledges" of wise policy in the character of the individual lawmakers. This would not only ensure that petty interests and partisan passions would not detract from their higher responsibility to their country but also prove that "the foundation of our national policy will be laid in the pure and immutable principles of private morality." Only if our representatives can govern themselves—restraining individual wants and passions—can they be capable of devising and adopting good laws while avoiding the temptation of tyranny.

Some maintain that morality is a private concern that should have no bearing on public matters, a personal value of no political importance. The Founders, however, held that in republican government *public* policy ultimately depended on the prevalence of *private* morality. But to say that private morality is a public concern does not mean that it is to be addressed directly by public means—that is, government.

America's Founders did not think that law alone—even state and local law close to the people—could (or should) shape morality without the active engagement of character-forming institutions outside of government. The teaching and transmission of morality, in the context of a limited government securing rights and protecting individual liberty, was primarily the job of the civilizing element of society that was separate and independent of the government. Put another way, what gave the Founders confidence in limited government were the nongovernmental institutions that filled the space and served the *functional* role of government where *formal* government had no authority and business operating. This "civil society" is home to the small groupings—family, church, schools, voluntary associations, and charitable organizations—that make up the informal social networks of ordinary American life.

The institutions of civil society, as well as their activities and purposes, are rooted in family life and religious community, and are naturally suited and uniquely responsible for the formation and development of moral character. Civil society helps transform self-interested and solitary individuals into morally responsible citizens, elevating the purpose of political liberty and bolstering republican government—all without being part of government.

Civil society provided the practical, personal connections and interactions of daily life, and was responsible for performing and providing most of the assistance and charity to meet the social problems of the day. Government in the early republic provided a minimal safety net but otherwise did not do much when it came to such activities. In early welfare laws, for instance, state and local government assumed responsibility for the deserving poor—those truly unable to care for themselves and who lacked family or other interpersonal forms of support—but otherwise required the able-bodied to work and take responsibility for their own welfare. Benjamin Franklin wrote that "the best way of doing good to the poor, is not making them easy in poverty, but leading or driving them out of it," and that "the more public provisions were made for the poor, the less they provided for themselves, and of course became poorer." Expansive welfare systems removed "the greatest of all inducements to industry, frugality, and sobriety." The solution to poverty and its attendant social problems was to be found in education, work, religious practice, and marriage—and that meant the active involvement of civil society. Likewise, while local government did help those who could not help themselves, state laws encouraged (and some like Franklin were actively involved in the formation of) private associations to promote mutual aid and assistance for the less fortunate.*

This is the self-governing nation celebrated by Tocqueville in *Democracy in America*. "Americans of all ages, all conditions, all minds, con-

---

* Thomas G. West discusses this subject in *Vindicating the Founders: Race, Sex, Class, and Justice in the Origins of America* (1997).

stantly unite," he wrote. A limited national government was designed to assure the decentralized politics and local governance necessary to encourage a flourishing of civil society's institutions and associations. Decentralized political life was necessary "to multiply infinitely the occasions for citizens to act together and to make them feel every day that they depend on one another."

Liberty ultimately depends on a whole host of forces that are not the making of government, and indeed, are prepolitical institutions that have a dignity and authority of their own.*

Religion and Republican Government

Civil society, growing out of the personal relationships and public associations that define and express man's deepest convictions, is especially the realm of faith and family. The centrality of religion to the Founders' project bears repeating. Tocqueville commented extensively on this in *Democracy in America* as well. "Freedom sees in religion the companion of its struggles and its triumphs, the cradle of its infancy, the divine source of its rights," he observed. "It considers religion as the safeguard of mores; and mores as the guarantee of laws and the pledge of its duration." Far from being its enemy, religion in America is liberty's greatest ally.

The Founders held to this simple syllogism: morality is necessary for republican government; religion is necessary for morality; therefore, religion is necessary for republican government. "Of all the dispositions and habits which lead to political prosperity," Washington wrote in his Farewell Address, "Religion and morality are indispensable supports. In vain would that man claim the tribute of Patriotism who should labor to subvert these great Pillars of human happiness—these firmest props of the duties of Men and citizens." These two sentences are very illuminating. Religion and morality, Washington says, are the props of duty, the indispensable supports of the dispositions and habits that lead to political prosperity, and the great pillars of human happiness. They aid good government by teaching men their obligations and shaping the moral parameters for a decent and civil politics.

---

* A more recent but classic work on this question is Robert Nisbet's *The Quest for Community: A Study in the Ethics of Order and Freedom* (1953). See also *The Tragedy of American Compassion* (1992) by Marvin Olasky.

And while there might be a few individuals whose morality is so firmly held that it does not depend on religion, this can never be the case for the nation as a whole. "Let us with caution indulge the supposition that morality can be maintained without religion," Washington warned. "Whatever may be conceded to the influence of refined education on minds of peculiar structure, reason and experience both forbid us to expect that national morality can prevail in exclusion of religious principle."

"Piety, religion, and morality are intimately connected with the well being of the state, and indispensable to the administration of civil justice," Joseph Story wrote in his *Commentaries on the Constitution*. And because it teaches beliefs and cultivates virtues conducive to ordered liberty—piety and morality chief among them—religion and religious practice is generally to be encouraged as a matter "wholly distinct" from the concerns of religious liberty. So important are the doctrines of religion to liberty that government has a duty "to foster and encourage it among all the citizens." Wrote Story:

> The promulgation of the great doctrines of religion, the being, and attributes, and providence of one Almighty God; the responsibility to him for all our actions, founded upon moral freedom and accountability; a future state of rewards and punishments; the cultivation of all the personal, social, and benevolent virtues;—these never can be a matter of indifference in any well ordered community. It is, indeed, difficult to conceive, how any civilized society can well exist without them.

At the time of the founding, schooling in America was mostly religious or at least rooted in religious faith. In his essay *Of the Mode of Education Proper for a Republic*, Benjamin Rush notes that in a self-governing republic, educators have the added responsibility for "laying the foundations for nurseries of wise and good men" and so must adapt their "modes of teaching to the peculiar form of our government." Students must be taught republican principles, and learn to "cherish with a more intense and peculiar affection" their fellow citizens and country. But in order to form the moral character required for self-government, education must be grounded in religion. "The only foundation for a useful education in a republic is to be laid in Religion," he wrote. "Without this there can be no virtue, and without virtue there can be no liberty, and liberty is the object and life of all republican governments." Such is Rush's respect for "every religion that reveals the attributes of the Deity, or a future state of rewards and punishments."

Family and the Founders

Since education and religious formation begin in early childhood, the association that exists for the purpose of such formation—the family built on the intimate and natural bond of husband and wife, and parent and child—is the first of the prepolitical institutions of civil society. The family is the critical link between the private moral and religious instruction that restrains the passions and nourishes good character, on the one hand, and the inculcation of the public virtue required for republican government, on the other. By creating and maintaining a safe and unique learning environment for children, the family, more than anything else, makes the immature child into the self-governing citizen.

The Founders did not write much about the family; it is not mentioned in the Constitution or other core documents of the era. That is because the family was the universally acknowledged cornerstone of society, and its centrality could be taken for granted. What they did have to say makes their sentiments clear. "The foundation of our national policy will be laid in the pure and immutable principles of private morality," as Washington affirmed in his First Inaugural, but they also knew that "the foundation of national morality must be laid in private families," as John Adams further noted. "How is it possible that Children can have any just Sense of the sacred Obligations of Morality or Religion if, from their earliest Infancy, they learn their Mothers live in habitual Infidelity to their fathers, and their fathers in as constant Infidelity to their Mothers?"

Family, by being the earliest teacher of virtues and character, as well as the primary educator of citizens, was often referred to as the "seminary of the republic," a popular translation of Cicero's reference to the family as the "nursery of the commonwealth." Referring to "that important and respectable, though small and sometimes neglected establishment, which is denominated the family," James Wilson writes in his *Lectures on Law* that the family is "the principle of the community; it is that seminary, on which the commonwealth, for its manners as well as its numbers, must ultimately depend. As its establishment is the source, so its happiness is the end, of every institution of government, which is wise and good." Joseph Story used the analogy in describing marriage as the center for the family. "Marriage is treated by all civilized societies as a peculiar and favored contract. It is in its origin a contract of natural law," he wrote in his *Commentaries on the Conflict of Laws*. "It is the parent, and not the child of society; the source of civility and a sort of seminary of the republic."

That most of the discussion of the family—and marriage—is found in commentaries on law (as opposed to more popular writings) should not be surprising. State and local laws recognized and supported marriage, family, and the authority of parents in the upbringing and education of children. "The most important consequence of marriage is, that the husband and the wife become in law only one person," wrote Wilson in his *Lectures on Law*. "Upon this principle of union, almost all the other legal consequences of marriage depend." And again: "It is the duty of parents to maintain their children decently, and according to their circumstances to protect them according to the dictates of prudence; and to educate them according to the suggestions of a judicious and zealous regard for their usefulness, their respectability and happiness."

Marriage and family are also discussed in various writings having to do with natural law and human nature. Consider this written by Samuel Williams, a Congregationalist minister and professor of mathematics and natural philosophy at Harvard College, in 1794:

> Every thing useful and beneficial to man, seems to be connected with obedience to the laws of his nature: And where the state of society coincides with the laws of nature, the inclinations, the duties and the happiness of individuals resolve themselves into customs and habits favorable, in the highest degree, to society. In no case is this more apparent, than in the customs of nations respecting marriage.

In unsigned article on "Natural Law" that appeared in the *Encyclopedia Americana* of 1836, Joseph Story (then an associate justice of the Supreme Court) eloquently conveys how marriage and family were understood not only to derive from nature but also to provide great societal and civic benefits:

Marriage is an institution, which may properly be deemed to arise from the law of nature. It promotes the private comfort of both parties, and especially of the female sex. It tends to the procreation of the greatest number of healthy citizens, and to their proper maintenance and education. It secures the peace of society, by cutting off a great source of contention, by assigning to one man the exclusive right to one woman. It promotes the cause of sound morals, by cultivating domestic affections and virtues. It distributes the whole of society into families, and creates a permanent union of interests, and a mutual guardianship of the same. It binds children by indissoluble ties, and adds new securities to the good order of society, by connecting the happiness of the whole family with the good behavior of all. It furnishes additional motives for honest industry and economy in private life, and for a deeper love of the country of our birth.

For most of America's history, federal courts assumed that the legal protection of marriage and family was legitimate and important for the sake of inculcating moral character and undergirding civil society, and thus liberty. In an 1823 court decision, John Marshall spoke of "the sacredness of the connection between husband and wife," and noted, "All know that the sweetness of social intercourse, the harmony of society, the happiness of families, depend on that mutual partiality which they feel, or that delicate forbearance which they manifest towards each other." As late as 1885, Justice Stephen J. Field declared for the Supreme Court:

No legislation can be supposed more wholesome and necessary in the founding of a free, self-governing commonwealth . . . than that which seeks to establish it on the basis of the idea of the family, as consisting in and springing from the union for life of one man and one woman in the holy estate of matrimony; the sure foundation of all that is stable and noble in our civilization; the best guarantee of that reverent morality which is the source of all beneficent progress in social and political improvement.

A Republic, If You Can Keep It

The Founders knew full well that it would always be up to the people—and future generations—to make successful what they had created. The viability of the American experiment in self-government, despite their work in forming the Constitution, ultimately depended not on the precision of the laws, the strength of the nation's economy, or the extent of its military power, but on the character of the citizenry. What did they give us? "A republic," was Benjamin Franklin's response, "*if you can keep it.*"

At the end of the American Revolution, James Madison wrote for Congress an address to the states which concludes with a warning that still rings true:

> [T]he citizens of the United States are responsible for the greatest trust ever confided to a political society. If justice, good faith, honor, gratitude and all the other qualities which ennoble the character of a nation and fulfill the ends of government be the fruits of our establishments, the cause of liberty will acquire a dignity and lustre, which it has never yet enjoyed, and an example will be set, which cannot but have the most favourable influence on the rights of Mankind. If on the other side, our governments should be unfortunately blotted with the reverse of these cardinal virtues, the great cause which we have engaged to vindicate, will be dishonored and betrayed; the last and fairest experiment in favor of the rights of human nature will be turned against them; and their patrons and friends exposed to be insulted and silenced by the votaries of tyranny and usurpation.

Self-government is possible only if citizens acquire and practice the moral qualities that help them remain free, independent, and responsible, not only in the political sense but also in the personal sense of not being dependent on others, whether the government or the wealthy and powerful for their well-being. "Dependence begets subservience and venality, suffocates the germ of virtue, and prepares fit tools for the designs of ambition," wrote Jefferson in his *Notes on the State of Virginia*. A free government could not be maintained if the people themselves were enslaved to small passions and disordered appetites and desires.

So in their project of creating a self-governing constitution, it was paramount that the people also be able to govern themselves.

9

⌇⌇⌇

The Command of Our Fortunes:
Sovereign Independence and
America's Role in the World

Independence was the clarion call of the American Revolution.
"Yesterday the greatest question was decided which ever was debated in America, and a greater, perhaps, never was or will be decided among men," John Adams wrote to Abigail on July 3, 1776. "You will see in a few days a Declaration setting forth the causes which have impelled us to this mighty revolution, and the reasons which will justify it in the sight of God and man." Later that same day he wrote again of the momentous decision:

> I am apt to believe it will be celebrated, by succeeding Generations, as the great anniversary Festival. It ought to be commemorated, as the Day of Deliverance by solemn Acts of Devotion to God Almighty. It ought to be solemnized with Pomp and Parade, with Shows, Games, Sports, Guns, Bells, Bonfires and Illuminations from one End of this Continent to the other from this Time forward forever more.

Adams was wrong about the date—he thought the July 2 action would be celebrated rather than the issuance of the Declaration of Independence two days later—but he was right that the event would become our country's anniversary.

Independence Day is our greatest national celebration, with barbecues, parades, speeches, and fireworks all across the country. And although there seem to be fewer grand commemorations these days, historically the Fourth of July has been the occasion for solemn ceremonies and great speeches about the meaning and purpose of America. That's because, while we tend to think of independence mainly as an important historic event that marks our separation from Great Britain, the Founders and subsequent generations had a larger understanding of what was signified by the national independence they were celebrating.

Americans sought independence not only from Great Britain, after all, but also from military occupation, royal overseers, arbitrary laws, taxation without representation, and—as it says in the Declaration of Independence—everything that "evinces a design to reduce them under absolute Despotism." But in doing so they also were declaring their unity—or interdependence—as a people, a compact of states, and a new nation. Independence implied at the same time *separation* as well as the creation of a new and independent country, living and governing by its own means and according to its own ways.

The concept of independence—that is, what we mean when we speak of American independence—has profound implications for how we understand and govern ourselves as a nation, and how we justify and defend ourselves as an independent actor on the world stage. Properly understood, independence takes on a much more compelling meaning, then and now, and is a first principle of American liberty.

A Separate and Equal Station

What does it mean to be independent? Literally, the word means "not dependent," which comes from the Latin for "hang down" or "suspended from"—as in a pendant hanging from a necklace. In practical terms, something that is dependent hangs on, or is reliant on, something else. A person who is dependent is less free. The American Founders deplored this idea, following Blackstone's definition: "Dependence is very little else but an obligation to conform to the will or law of that superior person or state upon which the inferior depends."

To be independent, when it comes to men and nations, is to be not only physically detached, but also fundamentally self-governing. This dual meaning of independence—technical separation from another ruling nation as well as political self-government—can be seen in our own Declaration of Independence. Indeed, this deeper sense of independence explains why we celebrate Independence Day—not the dates of the end of the Revolutionary War or even the completion of the Constitution—as our nation's birthday.

From its opening words, the Declaration of Independence expresses certain assumptions about independent nationhood. The document begins by presupposing a crucial aspect of nationhood: that the Americans are or are becoming "one people," and that it has become necessary for that one people to dissolve the political bands that had connected it to another people—the British. This people is entitled (has a right) to "assume among the powers of the earth" a "station," or status that is "separate and equal" to that of other nations and peoples. This status is due to them not from their English charters or British constitutional law, but by virtue of "the Laws of Nature and of Nature's God."

To claim a separate and equal status among nations is to make a claim of "sovereignty" in the context of international law. A nation is sovereign if it is independent of rule by other nations, controlling its own affairs and dealing with other nations as coequals in rank. Nations are of course not equal in regard to their size, wealth, power, and traditions. Separateness and equality are the key characteristics of what it means to be a sovereign nation.[*]

The document concludes by declaring that "these Colonies are, and of Right ought to be Free and Independent States . . . [that] have full Power to levy War, conclude Peace, contract Alliances, establish Commerce, and to do all other Acts and Things which Independent States may of right do." Those same "Laws of Nature and Nature's God" imply that nations are independent, self-governing entities when it comes to the core functions of nationhood. So it was that at the same time the Continental Congress declared independence it also called for a plan of unity and confederation to confirm this equal status and create a new government to exercise sovereign powers.

---

* See Jeremy Rabkin, *The Case for Sovereignty* (2006), as well as his *The Meaning of Sovereignty: What Our Founding Fathers Could Tell Us About Current Events* (Heritage First Principles Essay #10).

The immediate purpose of the Declaration of Independence was to announce and defend before "the opinions of mankind" the American separation from Great Britain. The document was also intended to make the case to other nations that this separation justified America's right to seek formal diplomatic relations and military alliances. In short, the Declaration proclaimed to the world that the united colonies—having become a people—were now separate, sovereign, and by international law equal to Great Britain and all other nations.

The Declaration of Independence also describes the enduring principles by which this nation claims a right to be an independent sovereign people. Certain foundational principles instruct not only our own political structure but also our concept of legitimacy in the world. For example, the principle of consent—that government derives its just powers from the consent of the governed—also makes legitimate a particular claim to a separate and equal rank among nations. National sovereignty in the world, based on popular sovereignty at home, underscores the primary responsibility of the national government—to defend and provide for the freedom and well-being of the people who authorized this government. Republican government means a government that expresses and represents the consent of the governed, and defends American society both at home and in the world.

Lastly, the Declaration commits this nation to universal ideas— human equality, natural rights, consent of the governed, the rule of law—that have profound consequences. The Declaration of Independence submits its facts to "a candid world," but the decision to become independent is not left to the international community, which cannot have moral authority in this matter. Instead, the Declaration asserts independence by appealing "to the Supreme Judge of the World for the rectitude of our intentions." That is, it appeals to a higher standard to which all other laws are answerable—a universal standard above all communities, against which all other nations should be measured as well. The document makes all-important distinctions, for instance, between "civilization" on the one hand, and "barbarism" or "savagery" on the other. By that standard, the object of British rule was to establish an absolute tyranny over the colonies, and it was the Americans' right and duty—after suffering a "long train of abuses"—to free themselves of that colonial rule: "A Prince, whose character is thus marked by every act which may define a Tyrant, is unfit to be the ruler of a free people."

America is a unique nation in that it is founded on *universal* principles. It justified its independence on, and then formed a nation around, principles understood to be true not just for Americans but for everyone everywhere. But the United States is also a *particular* nation, with a particular history and a particular people. This combination of universal and particular helps explain why our foreign policy, in the broadest sense, strives to relate these noble principles to the real-world challenges and requirements of international politics. This is far from saying that American foreign policy has always been true to these principles. But rightly understood, America's national self-interest in the international order is inseparable from the interest and well-being of freedom everywhere.

Prudence and Foreign Affairs

Foreign affairs, that field of politics dealing with the outside world, is inherently different from domestic affairs. At home, we have our own laws and share a constitutional framework for deciding and enforcing the rules within a common legal framework. We are one people "among the powers of the earth." In the world, by contrast, there is no common political community, thus no international consent of the governed.

Throughout history, different groups of peoples have banded together to form political communities—states, confederations, commonwealths, nations—based on different historical and geographic conditions and interests, resulting in different opinions about man, government, and justice. It is because of the nature and requirements of government, of communities of people uniting as a nation for common purposes, that the measure of international affairs will always be sovereign countries and national interests as each nation conceives them. The interaction of nations can be peaceful but often leads to competition and conflict. Nations are never completely free from the demands of necessity—above all, national survival and self-preservation.

Foreign policy choices are often presented as alternatives between two abstract categories: "idealism," meaning that nations should be motivated by ideals to the exclusion of practical concerns and self-interests, and "realism," meaning that nations are primarily motivated by the desire for more military and economic power or security rather than by principles. The distinction is false and misleading. The concept of idealism rejects the practical reality of particular national interests in favor of a dogmatic moralism, while the concept of realism suggests a narrow, cynical view that completely excludes moral considerations in dealing with other nations.

These two approaches share the assumption that principle and power are opposites and contradictory, and that a nation pursuing its interests is by definition selfish and immoral, while principle is inherently dogmatic and inflexible and can only be followed when absolutely separated from concern about interest and power. But an allegiance to principle and a clear recognition of the requirements of international security can be complementary. When rightly understood, they are inseparable—at least, this is what the American Founders thought. Neither idealism nor realism satisfies an integrated worldview that is consistent with a true understanding of the nature of international politics.

A better approach, understood by the Founders and consistent with the common sense of foreign affairs, relates principles and practice through the gauge of practical wisdom or prudence. Foreign affairs—dealing with friends and enemies in a constantly changing and often unstable world—is especially the realm of prudence. For one thing, it is impossible to predetermine the extent, priority, and immediacy of the nation's security requirements, which shift with the balance of world forces, and over which one nation has little, if any, control. Likewise, it is impossible to predetermine the challenges and opportunities for furthering principles and long-term objectives in the world. So it is impossible to know beforehand what prudence will dictate at any particular time and place.

A great example of the Founders' prudence is their early foreign policy. It is often said that the American Founders were isolationists—and that the principle of their foreign policy was to withdraw from the world in favor of focusing solely on the home front. This fails to distinguish between a particular policy conditioned on the times and the permanent principles which underlie the policy and inform changing circumstances.

At the time of its founding, the United States was a weak and fledgling nation, unique in claiming its republican institutions, extremely vulnerable to the great powers that dominated the world. Its objectives were to strengthen its constitutional government, build an adequate military capacity to defend itself, and, if possible, remove European influence from the North American continent. If America failed in this, Alexander Hamilton warned in *Federalist* 11, it would become "the instrument of European greatness." But if it succeeded, it would be "superior to the control of all transatlantic force or influence and be able to dictate the terms of the connection between the old and the new world."

The Founders had few choices. They were active in some areas of the world—especially concerning international trade, as well as some matters of national security—but generally constrained by the circumstances in which they found themselves. American weakness, in order to avoid getting caught up and destroyed in the competition of European powers, dictated a policy of neutrality in Europe's wars. At the same time, the geopolitical situation that caused this policy also provided an advantage that offset American weakness—distance from Europe and the time to gain strength. It was in America's interest to take advantage of the European balance of power, exploiting Old World rivalries to prevent any one power from dominating Europe and threatening American independence. A policy of "global noninvolvement" would be as prudent for a weak nation as it would be foolish for a strong one.

The Founders were neither utopian idealists—they strongly disagreed with the "visionary, or designing men, who stand ready to advocate the paradox of perpetual peace" and hoped to "soften the manners of men," as Hamilton put it in *Federalist* 6—nor vulgar realists, relegating justice to the whims of the strongest. Theirs was a worldview that was both principled *and* practical, where the preeminent virtue of statesmanship was prudence, the practical wisdom and ability to relate universal principles to particular circumstances.

By implication, the Founders rejected modern approaches in American foreign policy represented in what today is called power politics, isolationism, and crusading internationalism. Instead, they designed a truly American foreign policy—fundamentally shaped by our principles but neither driven by nor ignorant of the place of necessity in international relations.

The Command of Our Own Fortunes

The American Founders were deeply divided over the appropriate poli-cies in foreign affairs during the early years of the republic. Alexander Hamilton thought America should build a stronger military and side more with the British, while Thomas Jefferson preferred diplomacy and favored the French. Divisions on foreign policy were the catalyst that led to the establishment of the first political parties. That said, there was a core agreement about the nature of America and its national interest in liberty. Taking a broader view, it is possible to develop an underlying consensus view of the Founders' framework for thinking about Ameri-can foreign policy.

The classic statement of the Founders' understanding of the rela-tionship between domestic and foreign policy is George Washington's Farewell Address of 1796. Its immediate purpose was to announce Washington's decision to retire from public life and not seek a third term as president, but the larger objective was to give advice and warnings about the long-term safety and happiness of the American people. It is all the more significant since Washington was assisted in its drafting by Alexander Hamilton and James Madison, who later became political enemies over foreign policy. Madison described Washington's essay as one of "the best guides to the distinctive principles" of American gov-ernment.*

The Farewell Address presents Washington's advice concerning the Constitution and the rule of law, political parties, religion and morality, foreign influence in domestic affairs, international relations, and com-mercial policy. While it is often remembered for its recommendations concerning American involvement in international affairs and Wash-ington's defense of his debated policy of neutrality in the wars of the French Revolution, the overarching argument of the Farewell Address transcends the requirements of the moment in favor of maintaining America's national independence. Washington argues that the United States should take advantage of its peculiar geographic and political situation—a physical separation from Europe and the opportunity to remain aloof from its quarrels—to pursue a long-term strategy of

---

* On the Farewell Address, see *A Sacred Union of Citizens: George Washington's Farewell Address and the American Character* (1996) by Matthew Spalding and Patrick Garrity.

defying external threats and choosing its own course as a nation. As described by Washington, early policy was designed "to gain time for our country to settle and mature its recent institutions, and to progress, without interruption, to that degree of strength and consistency, which is necessary to *give it, humanly speaking, command of its own fortunes*."

Samuel Flagg Bemis, the great twentieth-century diplomatic historian, interpreted this to mean "strategic independence," or freedom of action in international affairs.* A better way to understand fully what Washington meant is to recall the older term used to encompass the goal for a political community: self-sufficiency. Certainly, strategic independence requires taking care of the nation's security and material interests. But self-sufficiency is not exclusively or even primarily material. It comprehends a larger sense of moral purpose, well-being, and completeness that needs no outside support or guidance for its existence or perpetuation.

Self-sufficiency means sovereignty in the fullest sense. Or as the Declaration of Independence says: "to assume among the powers of the earth, the separate and equal station to which the Laws of Nature and Nature's God entitle them," and obtain the full power to do the "Acts and Things which Independent States may of right do." Rather than a *permanent* condition of detachment from the world, the Founders advocated a *flexible* policy aimed at achieving and thereafter permanently maintaining the sovereign independence for Americans to determine their own fate.

A self-sufficient America could freely choose its own leaders, establish its own laws, and set up a government that ensured its own safety and happiness and could reach its full potential as a republican political community. In *Common Sense*, Thomas Paine wrote that independence "means no more than whether we shall make our own laws, or, whether the king, the greatest enemy this continent hath, or can have, shall tell us 'there shall be no laws but such as I like.'" If a foreign power can tell America "what we shall do, and what we shall not do," Washington once told Hamilton, "we have Independence yet to seek, and have contended hitherto for very little."

True independence, then, is not only the absence of physical restraint and control, but also the flourishing of an autonomous and

---

* Much of the best work of Samuel Flagg Bemis on the founding era is collected in *American Foreign Policy and the Blessings of Liberty* (1962).

free character. This requires freedom of action and independent think-ing—an important theme of the Farewell Address. Americans must be free from hatreds and irrational attachments to foreign nations if they are to become partisans of their own. Preconceived positions restrict policy options and prevent the nation from responsibly choosing its own course. When these attachments dominate the public mind, they not only lead the nation away from its duty and interest, but also make the supposedly free nation "in some degree a slave" to the other. "Against the insidious wiles of foreign influence," Washington warned, "the jeal-ousy of a free people ought to be *constantly* awake."

As America's fate is necessarily tied to its principles, the key to American self-sufficiency was to find the political ground on which the requirements of independence could be reconciled with those principles at home and in our relations with other nations. How is this to be done? Here is Washington's answer:

> If we remain one people, under an efficient government, the period is not far off when we may defy injury from external annoyance; when we may take such an attitude as will cause the neutrality we may at any time resolve upon to be scrupulously respected; when belligerent nations, under the impossibility of making acquisitions upon us, will not lightly hazard the giving us provocation; when we may choose peace or war, as *our interest guided by justice shall counsel.*

While appreciating the difficulties, prejudices, and self-interested character of politics, the Founders sought to elevate American foreign policy by the guidance of higher and nobler principles. In order to command our own fortunes in the world we must first provide for the nation's security and serve its interests, but our actions must always be enlightened by fundamental and universal principles at the heart of our national identity.

Safety and Happiness

Security, whether for an individual or for a nation, is the first require-ment of self-sufficiency. "Security against foreign danger is one of the primitive objects of civil society," Madison observed in *Federalist* 41. "It is an avowed and essential object of the American Union." Without providing for our own security, we could never hope to control our own destiny or command our own fortunes.

All political communities need to defend themselves and acquire those things they need to survive. Governments are instituted among men to secure their rights—which are insecure without government—and that includes a general right to liberty free from violence (hence the rule of law) and external threats.

Collective defense against external threats is the primary reason why the colonies banded together in the first place. A key weakness of the Articles of Confederation was that it did not create sufficient capacity for security, and a central purpose of the Constitution is "to provide for the common defense." Congress and the president are given the power to provide for defense, and the president, also commander in chief of the military forces, is constitutionally and morally obligated to "preserve, protect, and defend the Constitution of the United States."

The Founders often spoke of national security in terms of "safety." In the Declaration of Independence, the right of the people to institute government was said to mean "laying its foundations on such principles and organizing its powers in such form, as to them shall seem most likely to effect their *safety* and *happiness.*" The pursuit of happiness is a natural right of liberty, but safety is the initial requirement of the pursuit. "Among the many objects to which a wise and free people find it necessary to direct their attention, that of providing for their safety seems to be first," John Jay wrote in *Federalist* 2. "Nations, as well as men, are taught by the law of nature, gracious in its precepts, to consider their happiness as the great end of their existence," James Wilson wrote in his *Lectures on Law*. "But without existence there can be no happiness: the means, therefore, must be secured, in order to secure the end."

In defending the new constitution against the Articles, Hamilton in *Federalist* 43 appealed "to the absolute necessity of the case; to the great principle of self-preservation; to the transcendent law of nature and of nature's God, which declares that the safety and happiness of society are the objects at which all political institutions aim." That is, necessity and self-preservation, the most basic requirements of safety, must be given their due before the higher claims of the happiness of society can be attended to.

National security is challenging in an often competitive, and sometimes hostile, international environment. The most prominent instrument of national security is military power and the potential use of force against powers and persons who threaten America and its citizens. But there are many other instruments of national security as well, including diplomacy and foreign relations, commerce with and aid to other nations, participation in alliances, foreign intelligence, and the exchange of ambassadors.

The requirements of security are dictated by the challenges and threats we face in the world. "How could a readiness for war in time of peace be safely prohibited, unless we could prohibit, in like manner, the preparations and establishments of every hostile nation?" Madison asked in *Federalist* 41. "The means of security can only be regulated by the means and the danger of attack. They will, in fact, be ever determined by these rules, and by no others. . . . If one nation maintains constantly a disciplined army, ready for the service of ambition or revenge, it obliges the most pacific nations who may be within the reach of its enterprises to take corresponding precautions." And in the passions of human nature were to be found the dangerous ambitions of power. "To judge from the history of mankind," Hamilton wrote in *Federalist* 34, "we shall be compelled to conclude that the fiery and destructive passions of war reign in the human breast with much more powerful sway than the mild and beneficent sentiments of peace; and that to model our political systems upon speculations of lasting tranquility, is to calculate on the weaker springs of the human character."

Necessity dictates that the United States must be ready to fight wars and use force to protect the nation and the American people. Washington often liked to use the old Roman maxim, "To be prepared for war is one of the most effectual means of promoting peace." At the time, such preparations included the creation of a well-organized militia, development of a naval force sufficient to vindicate American commerce from insult or aggression, the promotion of a manufacturing base that would render the United States independent of others for essential military supplies, the provision of military stores, arsenals, and dockyards, and the establishment of a military academy. There was disagreement over the particulars necessary for national defense, but the policy objective was broadly supported. Washington was anxious that the country, as he once described it in an Annual Message to Congress, "leave nothing to the uncertainty of procuring a warlike apparatus at the moment of public danger." It is imprudent to wait until it's too late.

The right of a sovereign nation to preserve itself is not merely passive or defensive. Sovereignty also entails a proactive right to eliminate threats. "When a nation has a right, and is under an obligation to preserve itself and its members; it has, by a necessary consequence, a right to do every thing, which, without injuring others, it can do, in order to accomplish and secure those objects," wrote Wilson in his *Lectures on Law*. "The same principles, which evince the right of a nation to do every thing, which it may lawfully do, for the preservation of itself and its members, evince its right, also, *to avoid and prevent*, as much as it lawfully may, every thing which would load it with injuries, or threaten it with danger." The American Revolution, after all, was a preemptive military action. Over the course of "a long train of abuses," the Americans had become convinced that British policy amounted to the establishment of a tyranny over the American colonies, and they acted to prevent this outcome.

National security is a challenge for all nations, but particularly for democratic political systems dedicated to the limitation of power. "Safety from external danger is the most powerful director of national conduct," Hamilton noted in *Federalist* 8. "Even the ardent love of liberty will, after a time, give way to its dictates." Those dictates can rub up against liberty, as many actions necessary for security employ the use of force and proceed in ways that are often secretive and less open than democracy prefers. Likewise, national security sometimes requires restrictions and sacrifices that would be inimical to personal liberty were it not for significant threats to the nation. The solution to this dilemma is not to deny the use of force or to make it so onerous as to be ineffective. Rather, it is to establish a well-constructed constitution that focuses powers on legitimate purposes and then divides that power so that it does not go unchecked, preserving liberty while providing for a nation that can—and will—defend its liberty.

Nevertheless, the nature of international affairs demands different processes and institutional arrangements for dealing with foreign challenges, which is why the Constitution grants the national government rather than the states extensive powers in the realm of national security and foreign affairs. This is especially the case when it comes to the president's power as commander in chief of the armed forces. Consider this from *Federalist* 23:

> The authorities essential to the common defense are these: to raise armies; to build and equip fleets; to prescribe rules for the government of both; to direct their operations; to provide for their support. These powers ought to exist without limitation, because it is impossible to foresee or define the extent and variety of national exigencies, and the correspondent extent and variety of the means which may be necessary to satisfy them. The circumstances that endanger the safety of nations are infinite, and for this reason no constitutional shackles can wisely be imposed on the power to which the care of it is committed.

The extent of this authority, then and now, has always been a point of contention. Alexander Hamilton and James Madison debated executive authority in a famous series of essays called the Pacificus-Helvidius debates. Hamilton (Pacificus) argued that the executive had broad constitutional power in foreign affairs, while Madison (Helvidius) argued in favor of strong legislative authority over foreign affairs in all areas except those specifically granted to the executive in the Constitution.

Obviously not every action we take in the world involves threats to national security. Nevertheless, whatever the United States does in the international arena must be guided by the duty of a constitutional government based on consent to guarantee the nation's security and safety.

National Interests, Guided by Justice

Independence, to have substantive meaning, must first and foremost remain an internal concern about how we govern ourselves within the confines of our own nation. For the United States to exist as a cohesive, self-governing political community—in command of its own fortunes—it must begin with a fundamental, and entirely proper, distinction between this nation and its national interests, on the one hand, and other nations and their interests, on the other. All political communities need to defend themselves and to acquire what they need to survive and prosper, and that means that nations have distinct interests in the context of world politics. Foreign policy must protect the nation's security, interests, and goals in a world where different nations with different national interests—not bound by the laws of our political system—may be competitive, threatening, or hostile.

The concept of national interest follows from the primary obligation to the community that constitutes the nation in the first place. "Under every form of government rulers are only trustees for the happiness and interest of their nation," Hamilton wrote in the Pacificus essays, "and cannot, consistently with their trust, follow the suggestions of kindness or humanity toward others, to the prejudice of their constituents." This is especially the case in a representative democracy, in which the elected leaders have an obligation to act in the best interests of the people they represent and on whose behalf they exercise power. The first obligation of government is to the particular community it governs.

Independence means that it is always in our interest to prevent the United States from becoming subservient to the interests of another nation. "Europe has a set of primary interests which to us have none; or a very remote relation," Washington warned. "[I]t must be unwise in us to implicate ourselves, by artificial ties, in the ordinary vicissitudes of *her* politics, or the ordinary combinations and collisions of *her* friendships or enmities." We have our own interests to protect, and we must not leave our destiny to be determined "in the toils of European ambition, rivalship, interest, humor or caprice."

National interest is a matter of the greatest prudence. Some interests are immediate and others long term; some are absolutely vital, some important, others minor and marginal. And in general, interests change according to changing circumstances—other nations' actions, new threats, technological advances—in the world. While America had, for instance, an immediate interest at the time of the founding in preventing entanglement in Europe's wars, and has a permanent interest in not becoming embroiled in other nation's political quarrels, the country has always had a paramount interest in preventing (and a willingness to ally with other nations to prevent) a hostile power from dominating the European continent, since such a power would potentially threaten the freedom and very existence of the United States as an independent nation—as when Nazi Germany was conquering Europe, or Soviet Russia threatened to do so.

The Constitution and the union were the vehicles by which the national interest with respect to foreign powers, as well as the interests of individuals and sections, could best be realized. The American people would achieve the material requirements necessary to command their own fortunes by remaining united rather than divided. The greater strength and greater resources provided by the Constitution were essential for security against external danger. Combining resources and enterprises would bring great prosperity to the nation, which in turn would provide important advantages in foreign commerce.

The point is that interest, properly understood, represents an entirely legitimate feature of moral principle in foreign affairs. The Founders never wavered from the view, expressed in the Farewell Address, that it was "the universal experience of mankind, that no nation is to be trusted farther than it is bound by its interest; and no prudent statesman or politician will venture to depart from it." Washington insisted that "there can be no greater error than to expect, or calculate upon real favours from Nations." A nation relying on the altruism of others would "pay with a portion of its Independence" for that conceit.

This recognition of interest does not diminish the importance of justice in American foreign policy. The Founders argued that it was in the true interest of America to act with justice toward other peoples. Jefferson put it this way in his Second Inaugural: "We are firmly convinced, and we act on that conviction, that with nations, as with individuals, our interests, soundly calculated, will ever be found inseparable from our moral duties."

Commerce, Not Conquest

We can begin to understand this clearly in the Founders' emphasis on the development of international commerce. An important argument for ratifying the Constitution was that it would create a commercial republic appropriate for the entrepreneurial character of the American people. America's "unequaled spirit of enterprise" makes for "an inexhaustible mine of national wealth," Hamilton argued in *Federalist* 11. He worried that if the states failed to unite under the Constitution, commerce "would be stifled and lost, and poverty and disgrace would overspread a country which, with wisdom, might make herself the admiration and envy of the world."

In the Farewell Address, Washington warned the United States against entering into binding political agreements with other countries or into permanent alliances that would not account for changing national interests. But while he opposed *political* connections and *permanent* alliances (recognizing the need for temporary alliances for extraordinary emergencies, such as fighting a war or defending against a mutual threat), he recommended that the United States pursue commercial relations with other countries and supported commercial agreements with willing nations. In general, Washington favored harmony and liberal intercourse with all nations as recommended by "policy, humanity and interest."

A foreign policy of interest, guided by justice, implies that commerce, not military conquest or intimidation, should be the primary method of acquiring and trading goods, the preferred means of securing the necessities for national life that the United States did not possess within its territory and the general means of dealing with the other nations of the world.

It was in the commercial realm that depends so completely on contracts and negotiations—and where America had an interest in prosperity—that justice could most clearly be defined, rendered, and exacted. To foster peaceful commercial relations with other nations—and to create an interest in living in peace and friendship—American commercial policy, according to the Farewell Address, "should hold an equal and impartial hand, neither seeking nor granting exclusive favours or preferences; consulting the natural course of things; diffusing and diversifying by gentle means the streams of Commerce, but forcing nothing."

The Founders appreciated the importance of foreign commerce to the long-term interests of the United States. Placed in the proper channels, the American genius for commerce could be an enormous boon: "A people however, who are possessed of the spirit of commerce, who see, and who will pursue their advantage, may achieve almost anything," Washington wrote in 1784. They also subscribed, though with reservations, to the view that the development of international commerce was one of the best policies available to ameliorate conflict among nations.

They were not so naïve as to suppose that the spread of commerce and republican government would abolish conflict between nations. It was, noted Hamilton in *Federalist* 6, "time to awake from the deceitful dream of a golden age, and to adopt as a practical maxim for the direction of our political conduct that we, as well as the other inhabitants of the globe, are yet remote from the happy empire of perfect wisdom and perfect virtue."

Nevertheless, the possibility of transforming international relations by encouraging peaceful commercial relations, and the proper and necessary role that the United States should play in that transformation, remained an inseparable part of the Founders' thinking. The American character in the world was to be defined generally by commercial pursuits, and the Founders expressed hope, within limits, that commerce might temper international relations.

Justice and Benevolence

Washington began his Farewell Address by asserting that the success of the American experiment—to bring about the happiness of the American people under the auspices of liberty—would give the United States the glory of recommending the American model "to the applause, the affection, and the adoption of every nation which is yet a stranger to it." The transcendent theme of the founding, elevating it beyond the action of merely one country, was for Americans to demonstrate the viability of self-government not only for themselves, but for the imitation of mankind everywhere.

The process of calmly deliberating, creating, ratifying, and implementing a self-governing constitution through democratic means—demonstrating that reflection and choice, not accident and force, could govern men—was the example that would give America moral authority in the world. As James Wilson had remarked, "The United States now exhibit to the world, the first instance, as far as we can learn, of a nation, unattacked by external force, unconvulsed by domestic insurrections, assembling voluntarily, deliberating fully, and deciding calmly, concerning that system of government, under which they would wish that they and their posterity should live."

The Farewell Address introduced a matching American ambition in foreign policy: "It will be worthy of a free, enlightened, and, at no distant period, a great Nation, to give mankind the too novel example of a People always guided by an exalted justice and benevolence." Independence would allow the United States to follow a more enlightened approach to the world, and give America the freedom to choose a course in accord with a larger sense of justice and commitment to universal principles of liberty. "Religion and morality enjoin this conduct," Washington wrote, "and can it be that good policy does not equally enjoin it?" This standard of morality should characterize America, abroad as well as at home. This was the higher aim that ultimately defined the American purpose in the world. "Can it be, that Providence has not connected the permanent felicity of a Nation with its virtue?" Washington asked in the Farewell Address. "The experiment, at least, is recommended by every sentiment which ennobles human nature. Alas! is it rendered impossible by its vices?"

What does it mean to be "guided by an exalted justice and benevolence" in foreign affairs?

First, it means respecting other nations. Our claim to a separate and equal status implies that others, too, have a rightful claim to that same status. Each people have a sovereign right to determine the government that seems to them to serve their own safety and happiness. That doesn't mean that the United States must recognize or treat repugnant regimes in the world as legitimate nation-states, but it does mean that we have a general obligation to respect other nations' sovereignty and not intervene in their affairs when our security or vital interests are not involved. "A nation has a right to manage its own concerns as it thinks fit," Hamilton wrote, and it "ought to have a right to provide for its own happiness." The "self-evident right" of a nation to determine its own affairs, Madison wrote, "can be denied to no independent nation."

Second, it means observing good faith and justice toward other nations. Having recognized other nations' right to manage their own affairs, this country should approach and treat other nations as befits separate and equal sovereign nations. In general, the United States should act honestly and fairly in dealing with other countries, fulfill its contractual obligations, and keep its word. Relations among nations should be matter-of-fact and openly diplomatic rather than based on cynicism or an assumption of disinterested friendship. It is "the universal experience of mankind, that no nation is to be trusted farther than it is bound by its interest; and no prudent statesman or politician will venture to depart from it," Washington observed. Because all nations are limited by their own interests, the best way to make and keep obligations is through agreements that define the obligations of each party. Despite the Founders' aversion to permanent political alliances, our security and our respect for the sovereignty of other nations suggest that alliances are the appropriate ways of securing relationships with nations that have common economic or security interests.

Third, it means cultivating peaceful relations with other nations. The guidelines of usage and right reason, represented by the law of nature and nations, determine the boundaries of justice in foreign affairs. To be sure, the specific requirements of the law of nations are often controversial and ill-defined, but it indicates principles and practices that conform to natural justice. The Farewell Address identified the foremost of these principles as "the obligation which justice and humanity impose on every Nation, in cases in which it is free to act, to maintain inviolate the relations of Peace and amity toward other nations." The important qualification "in cases in which it is free to act" represented a positive injunction not merely to avoid unnecessary war, but also to prevent being forced in to war through our own weakness or the actions of others. As Hamilton wrote in the *Federalist* 11: "The rights of neutrality will only be respected when they are defended by adequate power. A nation, despicable by its weakness, forfeits even the privilege of being neutral." John Jay added that the American people ought to support steps that would "put and keep them in *such a situation* as, instead of *inviting* war, will tend to repress and discourage it."

By establishing a well-administered union that observed justice and good faith in international relations, the United States might create an international environment in which other nations would lack the incentive or opportunity to become America's enemy. The interests of the United States and other nations were not static or immutable; America, within the limits of what is humanly possible, could help shape in a positive fashion a world where a general amity among nations—or at least between the United States and the rest of the world—could be sustained. We should hold other nations, as the Declaration of Independence says of Great Britain, "Enemies in War, in Peace Friends."

Lastly, it means not only defending but promoting the cause of liberty in the world. Other nations have the same sovereign right as we do to choose governments they believe will best serve their safety and happiness. But that has never meant that the United States is indifferent to the choice between liberty and tyranny. America's principles compel this country to advocate freedom in the world.

The Cause of Liberty in the World

The Declaration of Independence holds that all men—not just Americans—are endowed with a right to liberty. That liberty is an aspect of human nature everywhere is central to understanding America's first principles. This is why the promotion of freedom in the world has been and should always be a predominant theme of American foreign policy. Washington put it this way in his First Inaugural Address: "The preservation of the sacred fire of liberty and the destiny of the republican model of government are justly considered as *deeply*, perhaps as *finally*, staked on the experiment entrusted to the hands of the American people."

The question, then, is not *whether* but *how* to advance liberty, and this is a preeminent question of prudence and statecraft, relating principles and practice. The Founders framed the question with three important caveats.

First, they understood that America, though dedicated to a universal principle, is a particular nation. The United States must always keep in mind its own sovereign obligations and be careful not to risk its capacity to perform the vital task of defending itself, its people, and its interests.

Second, the Founders understood that America acted within the possibilities of the real world. And in a world of limited resources, the nation must not forget its limits. Moreover, no matter how passionate we are to expand free government, it is not in our hands to dictate the final outcome. Making the right to liberty into an enduring principle of a nation's political order can be fully accomplished only by the people of that nation.

And third, and most importantly, the Founders were acutely aware of the difficulties involved in advancing the cause of liberty. They based their hopes, as James Madison wrote in *Federalist* 39, on "that honorable determination which animates every votary of freedom to rest all our political experiments on the capacity of mankind for self-government." Liberty is not just about holding an election now and again; it is also about establishing stable constitutional government and the rule of law, upholding majority rule, and securing civil and religious liberty. There is a great distance between the natural *right* to liberty and the *capacity* of particular peoples and nations for self-government. Although every human being has a desire to be free, by no means are all willing to fight (and perhaps die) for it, or to acknowledge the political forms necessary to establish and preserve it for themselves or for others. The Founders' own experience—breaking with a sovereign power, fighting a war for independence, creating constitutional forms and institutions, building on extensive experience in self-government and deep constitutional traditions inherited from their mother country—proves the case.

This is not to say the Founders thought establishing republican government unlikely or impossible—or that they were opposed in all cases to intervention on behalf of liberty and the republican cause. That would make a mockery of their own call for foreign support in the Declaration of Independence.

The French Revolution is an instructive example. Americans were optimistic about the influence that their principles would have on the cause of liberty elsewhere and initially welcomed the possibility of an American-inspired revolution in France, replacing its monarchy with a constitutional republic like their own. But as events developed, they were increasingly concerned about the disorder and violence that seemed to stem from deliberate policies of the revolutionary French leadership. Although there was great debate over how to interpret these events—Hamilton saw violent social upheaval where Jefferson saw the chaotic advance of liberty—the Washington administration (which included Hamilton and Jefferson) ultimately concluded that the French Revolution threatened to spread violence throughout Europe, drawing other nations—perhaps including America—into a worldwide war. While there was disagreement about implementing the policy, there was wide agreement that the United States should stay out of the conflict.

Alexander Hamilton made an important distinction between a nation that had "come to a resolution to throw off a yoke, under which it may have groaned" and "is in the act of liberating itself" on the one hand, and the policy of the French Revolution on the other, which held out "a general invitation to insurrection and revolution" in all countries, and had declared it would "treat as enemies the people who, refusing or renouncing liberty and equality, are desirous of preserving their prince and privileged castes." In the former case, it would be "justifiable and meritorious" for another nation to offer assistance (as France had supported the American cause), but the latter situation amounted to a declaration of war against all opponents and all nations.

Likewise, Washington made important distinctions when it came to the French Revolution. He stirringly proclaimed to the French minister in 1796 that "my anxious recollections, my sympathetic feelings, and my best wishes are irresistibly excited, whensoever in any country, I see an oppressed nation unfurl the banners of Freedom." But in praising the cause of freedom in France, Washington made explicit the grounds on which Americans would evaluate the true merits of the French Revolution: "I rejoice that liberty . . . now finds an asylum in the bosom of a *regularly organized government*; a government, which, being formed to secure the happiness of the French people, corresponds with the ardent wishes of my heart, while it gratifies the pride of every citizen of the United States, *by its resemblance to their own*." It is one thing to unfurl the banners of freedom, but quite another to actually establish constitutional government.

The Founders fervently welcomed opportunities to promote liberty in the world. But they judged those opportunities in light of America's legitimate national interests and obligations, and recognized that the success of liberty ultimately required stable institutions of constitutional government—what today we often refer to broadly as liberal democracy. Likewise, while it is important to understand the universal and even revolutionary implications of our principles, as a nation with sovereign responsibilities it is not our objective—or our responsibility—to intervene in every case when our principles are invoked or to impose liberal democratic forms on the rest of the world. When opportunities for advancing liberty arise, the United States is entitled (even obligated) to make prudent distinctions about commitments (such as cost, time, and manpower) relative to our interests and sovereign responsibilities, including the larger cause of liberal democracy. The principal duty this nation has toward the world is to remain strong and independent, so that the United States can maintain the freedom to advance and, when necessary, defend freedom in the world.

The Founders sought to advance liberty not *directly* by imperial expansion or by using force to change other nations, but *indirectly*—even secondarily to our primary obligations and interests as a nation. America should promote and assist democracies, and even prevent others from intervening with or imposing nondemocratic governments (implied in the Monroe Doctrine, when the United States agreed not to intervene in Europe in exchange for Europe's not establishing European-backed monarchical regimes in South America). But otherwise—with strong encouragement and general support for the spread of liberal democracy—it should let particular peoples determine their own fate. This approach reflects our historical understanding of how best to uphold and vindicate the universal principle of human liberty.

This is the meaning of John Quincy Adams's famous speech delivered to Congress on July 4, 1821. The son of President John Adams, he was at the time secretary of state (and would help author the Monroe Doctrine), and would be president of the United States in less than four years. The address is a wonderful statement of American principles and history, focusing on America and the world. Consider this key passage:

> Wherever the standard of freedom and independence has been or shall be unfurled, there will her heart, her benedictions and her prayers be. But she goes not abroad, in search of monsters to destroy. She is the well-wisher to the freedom and independence of all. She is the champion and vindicator only of her own. She will recommend the general cause by the countenance of her voice, and the benignant sympathy of her example. She well knows that by once enlisting under other banners than her own, were they even the banners of foreign independence, she would involve herself, beyond the power of extrication, in all the wars of interest and intrigue, of individual avarice, envy, and ambition, which assume the colors and usurp the standard of freedom. The fundamental maxims of her policy would insensibly change from liberty to force.

Adams concludes, in speaking of the United States: "Her glory is not *dominion*, but *liberty*. Her march is the march of the mind. She has a spear and a shield: but the motto upon her shield is *Freedom, Independence, Peace*. This has been her declaration: this has been, as far as her necessary intercourse with the rest of mankind would permit, her practice." America is an empire, but not of servitude or mastery. As Jefferson once said, it is "an empire of liberty."

The Founders believed that whatever temporary advantages might be lost by following a foreign policy of interest guided by justice would be richly repaid over the course of time. The practices of other nations, following America's example in foreign as well as domestic affairs, would lead to a structure of international relations that might achieve America's interests in security and prosperity more surely than one in which nations act unjustly in an international system marked by the pursuit of narrow self-interests. America could provide for its security and realize its interests—in short, command its own fortunes—better in a peaceful and prosperous world than in a world torn by constant avarice and strife.

To be sure, the Founders did not think that a peaceful and prosperous world was around the corner, any more than they believed that self-government would soon become the norm. America would do its part in leading by example in both foreign and domestic affairs. The great American experiment would further ennoble the American character, giving moral content to American interests in relation to other nations and peoples.

Independence Forever

The Founders sought to create an independent, self-sufficient American political community, in the form of a large commercial republic, able to control its destiny through a foreign policy that pursued American interests guided by justice.

The American political community and the national character depended on establishing in the mind of the people the proper relationship, and distinction, between America and other nations and peoples. Above all, the American character was to be republican. America would be founded and sustained not merely for narrow interests of a particular people in a particular place, but for the sake of that people's commitment to achieving civil and religious liberty for all under the rule of law.

America's Founders sought to define a national good that transcended local interests and prejudices. The national good included the common benefits of self-defense and prosperity that all Americans would realize by participating in a large, commercial nation able to hold its own in an often hostile world. But it was only with the constitutional rule of law that the higher purpose, or true national interest, of America could be realized. That purpose was to demonstrate to all mankind the feasibility of self-government and the suitability of justice as the proper and sustainable ground for relations among nations and peoples.

The honor of striving for domestic and international justice would give moral purpose to the American character. The United States would support, defend, and advance the cause of freedom everywhere. It would be a refuge for the sober, industrious, and virtuous of the world, as well as for victims of persecution. By sympathy and appropriate action, Americans would show themselves to be true friends of humanity.

July 4, 1826, marked the fiftieth anniversary of the Declaration of Independence. It was the great jubilee of American national independence. As if to give new significance to the important date, both Thomas Jefferson and John Adams—the author of the Declaration of Independence and the man mostly responsible for getting the Declaration through the Continental Congress—died on that day. Many saw this coincidence as not only a sign of providence but also a reminder of America's principled foundation. Jefferson's final words were, "Is it the Fourth?"

Before the jubilee, Adams had been asked to sum up the moment in a celebratory address. A grand speech, suitable for the occasion, was undoubtedly expected. Yet for a man of so many words, his response was remarkably brief. In two words, Adams conveyed everything that needed saying, then as well as now: "Independence forever."

10

≈

A New Republic:
The Progressive Assault on
the Founders' Principles

The year 1987 marked the two hundredth anniversary of the United States Constitution. The Commission on the Bicentennial, headed by Chief Justice Warren Burger, regarded the anniversary as "an historic opportunity for all Americans to learn about and recall the achievements of our Founders and the knowledge and experience that inspired them, the nature of the government they established, its origins, its character, and its ends, and the rights and privileges of citizenship, as well as its attendant responsibilities." The commission invited "every state, city, town and hamlet, every organization and institution, and every family and individual" to celebrate the great occasion with fitting ceremonies, both solemn and festive.

Not everyone agreed. "I cannot accept this invitation," wrote Associate Justice Thurgood Marshall, "for I do not believe that the meaning of the Constitution was forever 'fixed' at the Philadelphia Convention." Not only is the Constitution merely "a product of its times," Marshall wrote, but it also "was defective from the start." All of the patriotic celebrations marking the grand event, "prompting proud proclamations of the wisdom, foresight, and sense of justice shared by the Framers and reflected in a written document now yellowed with age," Marshall argued, amounted to "little more than a blind pilgrimage to the shrine of the original document now stored in a vault in the National Archives." Meaningless homage to faded documents enshrined in glass cases. Mere words, handwritten on a few sheets of parchment.

In many circles, especially among our intellectual, cultural, and political elites, the principles of America's Founding have been largely abandoned because they are seen as either outdated or defective, the product of wealthy, undemocratic slaveowners bent on erecting barriers to change and progress. The American Founders are more to be departed from than looked up to as a guide for today. America's great founding documents still exist, but they must be disentangled from that past and continually adapted to the future.

How—and why—did this come to be? The answer is to be found in profound changes over the course of the twentieth century in how we think of ourselves, our past, and the underlying principles of our nation.

What began a hundred years ago as an intellectual project made up mostly of academics and independent writers became a popular reform effort under the banner of progressivism. It informed the large-scale political movement of modern liberalism that came to dominate the politics of the twentieth century. It continues to shape our politics and confuse the public mind.

If we wish to regain our bearings, we need to understand and come to grips with these changes. If we are to reorient our nation to its first principles, we must understand how deeply these changes have transformed our politics and society—and where, unchecked, they are taking our country.

The American Consensus

The great challenge of free government, as the Founders understood it, was to restrict and structure the powers of government in order to secure the rights articulated in the Declaration of Independence, preventing tyranny while preserving liberty. The solution was to create a strong, energetic government of limited authority, its powers enumerated in a written constitution, separated into different functions and responsibilities, and further divided between the national and the state governments in a system of federalism. The result is a framework of limited government and a vast sphere of human freedom, leaving ample room for republican self-government.

A general agreement on these core principles—equal rights grounded in a permanent human nature, constitutionalism and the rule of law, republican self-government—formed the underlying consensus of the American political tradition, underscored by the experience of American political life. Despite their various (and sometimes significant) disagreements and the eventual divisions among them that led to the establishment of the first political parties in the United States, Washington, Madison, Hamilton, Jefferson, Adams, and the other leading Founders all agreed when it came to the foundational concepts behind the American idea of liberty and constitutionalism. This principled consensus—transcending important differences of practical application and party competition— generally held from the time of the founding to the end of the nineteenth century, through the decline of the Federalists to the rise of the Democratic-Republicans, from the Jacksonians to the development of the slavery controversy and the outbreak of the Civil War.

The one great exception proves the rule. That a nation is based on principles does not always mean a complete agreement on the meaning of those principles. With the expansion of slavery in the decades after the American Founding, and the challenges it presented to the ideas as well as the institutions of constitutional government, it became increasingly imperative to resolve finally the question of slavery consistent with America's foundational principles. Does the institution of slavery violate those principles? Can a territory decide by majority vote to be a slave state? Can the Supreme Court decide that black persons are property? Are all men really created equal?

The Civil War of 1861–65 represented a profound disagreement over the most basic meaning of America's foundational principles. Eleven southern slave states declared their secession from the United States and sought to form the Confederate States of America, while the remaining free states and the five border slave states remained loyal to the union under President Abraham Lincoln. Some, like Senator John C. Calhoun of South Carolina, had denied the principle of human equality and gone so far as to embrace slavery as a "positive good." Alexander Stephens, the vice president of the Confederacy, argued that slavery would be the cornerstone of their new nation. Chief Justice Roger B. Taney argued for the Supreme Court in *Dred Scott v. Sanford* that slaves were property and "had no rights which the white man was bound to respect." Senator

Stephen Douglas of Illinois hoped to solve the problem by turning to "popular sovereignty" and allowing territories and new states to decide for themselves whether to endorse slavery or not. It didn't matter what they decided as long as a majority consented.

Abraham Lincoln rejected these views. He held that slavery violated the Declaration of Independence and recalled the nation to the Founders' constitution and the principles it enshrined in order to place slavery once again on "the road to ultimate extinction."

Lincoln exemplified the older understanding of a formal constitutionalism built on the foundations of permanent principles. He once explained the relationship between the Declaration of Independence and the Constitution by reference to Proverbs 25:11: "A word fitly spoken is like apples of gold in a setting of silver." While he revered the Constitution, and was a great defender of the union, he knew that the word "fitly spoken"—the apple of gold—was the assertion of principle in the Declaration of Independence. "The *Union*, and the *Constitution*, are the *picture of silver*, subsequently framed around it," Lincoln wrote. "The *picture* was made *for* the apple—*not* the apple for the picture." He maintained that the Constitution was made to secure the principles proclaimed in the Declaration of Independence, and that those principles and the Constitution, properly understood, were perfectly compatible. His great achievement, in probably the most trying epoch of our history, was to preserve our constitutional republic while restoring its dedication to the timeless principles of liberty, "applicable to all men and all times," that form the central idea of America.*

America's principles, severely tested by the deadliest war in the United States' history, were ultimately vindicated, constitutional government was upheld, and the American consensus was restored on the grounds defined by the American Founding. The question of slavery was settled partially with the Emancipation Proclamation in 1863, and then finally with the Thirteenth and Fourteenth Amendments, abolishing slavery and extending citizenship and the protection of fundamental civil rights to the newly freed slaves. The Fifteenth Amendment secured

---

* The classic work on Lincoln's political thought is *Crisis of the House Divided: An Interpretation of the Issues in the Lincoln-Douglas Debates* (1959), and its companion volume, *A New Birth of Freedom: Abraham Lincoln and the Coming of the Civil War* (2000), both by Harry V. Jaffa.

voting rights to the former slaves and their descendants. In assuring that no state shall abridge the privileges or immunities of *any* citizen, deprive *any* person of due process of law, or deny to *any* person within its jurisdiction the equal protection of the law, these amendments resolved the question of slavery and can be said to have completed the constitutional design of the American Founding.

A New Republic

In the years after the Civil War, as the nation began to reunite and rebuild, American society rebounded, the economy expanded, and the United States prospered. Never before had there been such a vibrant, diverse, and strong democratic nation. Many thought that with the conflict over and changes abounding, America was becoming a new nation.

The unleashing of the industrial revolution, the expansion of urban society, and the development of the United States as a modern world power—not to mention the large-scale challenges and opportunities that resulted from these changes—led to widespread calls for rethinking and reform in virtually every aspect of American life. The intellectual and programmatic response to this overwhelming sense of change was called *progressivism*, and the period between 1890 and 1920 is generally called the Progressive Era. While it was pervasive, progressivism was not all of one piece. There were many different manifestations: the muckraking novels of Upton Sinclair, the architecture of Frank Lloyd Wright, the revisionist history of Charles Beard, the progressive educational theories of John Dewey. There were extensive reform efforts throughout society—ranging from the establishment of new disciplines in the social sciences to the theological project known as the Social Gospel movement—and progressive political candidates and legislation at the local, state, and federal levels of government.

A number of leading political thinkers came to believe that the Founders' political science could not adequately address the emerging character of society. Concluding that the old constitutional system had failed (indeed, its insistence on principles of natural equality and constitutional government could be blamed for bringing the Civil War upon the nation), they argued that America needed a new way of thinking appropriate for the modern age. And so it was that they looked for new foundational ideas and other models of governance outside of the United States, in what were perceived to be more modern nations like England, France, and especially Germany. Based on the new concepts they learned there, these thinkers sought to build a new consensus and a new politics in the United States. What resulted was a broad intellectual, social, and political movement that for the first time self-consciously aimed at fundamentally transforming the principles and practices of American constitutionalism.

New (Anti-) Foundational Principles

The American concept of liberty stems from certain foundational ideas about man and nature, equal rights, and the consent of the governed, from which follow other principles, from religious liberty and economic freedom to self-government and independence.

The new progressive thinking was profoundly shaped by two revolutionary, *anti*-foundational concepts.

First, the progressive view rejected outright the very idea, at the heart of the Founders' way of thinking, of political thought and practice being guided by permanent principles. Deeply skeptical about any philosophical ideas that claimed to be true beyond their particular situation, the progressives held that there were no fixed truths—certainly no objective or unchanging standards of right to guide politics. All truth claims are contingent, merely personal "values" relative to other equally valid claims. It made no sense to say anything was a "self-evident" truth. This was a faulty assumption, they argued, and assuredly the wrong starting point for establishing a political system, especially one meant to be responsive to changing circumstances. As the prominent progressive historian Carl Becker put it in 1922, "To ask whether the natural rights philosophy of the Declaration of Independence is true or false, is essentially a meaningless question." This relativist view renders meaningless the whole American political tradition.

By this argument, any concepts of natural right or natural law—that is, ideas of right and law grounded in a fixed or enduring nature—had to be rejected. "The idea that men possess inherent and inalienable rights of a political or quasi-political character which are independent of the state, has been generally given up," the prominent progressive scholar

Charles Merriam wrote in his 1920 book *American Political Ideas*. "The present tendency, then, in American political theory is to disregard the once dominant ideas of natural rights and the social contract, although it must be admitted that the political scientists are more agreed upon this point than is the general public." Notions of a natural moral order, of standards that can and should guide man and politics, were considered naïve and akin to mythology. "No man who is as well abreast of modern science as the Fathers were of eighteenth century science, believes any longer in unchanging human nature," wrote the historian Richard Hofstader. "Modern humanistic thinkers who seek for a means by which society may transcend eternal conflict and rigid adherence to property rights as its integrating principles can expect no answer in the philosophy of balanced government as it was set down by the Constitution-makers of 1787."

The second anti-foundational concept is called "historicism." According to this view, not only are ideas relative to each other but all ideas and their meaning (and status) are relative to their moment in time. As such, ideas are relative to the era in which they are constructed, and must constantly be adapted to various historical developments. This means that ideas of the past are relevant only to the past. What might have been suitable for one century inevitably becomes outdated in another, making the past inferior to the present and the present but a step on the way to the future. The problem with the American Founders, the new thinkers argued, is that they did not understand and account for this lack of permanence and the constant flux and change in all things. Consider this from John Dewey, the progressive father of modern education theory:

> Liberalism is committed to the idea of historic relativity. It knows that the content of the individual and freedom change with time; that this is as true of social change as it is of individual development from infancy to maturity. The positive counterpart of opposition to doctrinal absolutism is experimentalism. The connection between historic relativity and experimental method is intrinsic. Time signifies change. The significance of individuality with respect to social policies alters with change of the conditions in which individuals live. The earlier liberalism [of the Founders] in being absolute was also unhistoric.

Experimenting with and learning new ideas inevitably leads to change, moving toward ever increasing improvement and perfectibility of man and society. This movement is captured in the wonderfully indefinite concept of "Progress." The American Founders themselves believed in progress, of course. "The science of politics has received great improvement," Hamilton wrote in *Federalist* 9. Many of the Founders' innovations were "wholly new discoveries, or have made their principal progress towards perfection in modern times." Washington in his Circular Address of 1783 noted that the foundations of America were "not laid in the gloomy age of Ignorance and Superstition, but at an Epocha when the rights of mankind were better understood and more clearly defined, than at any former period." For the Founders, though, progress was understood to be change in light of unchanging standards. Improvement implies the ability to progress toward what is better, in light of what is good or bad. But for the progressive thinkers, everything was subject to Progress with a capital P—not just science and technology or even man's understanding of natural rights, but the very foundational principles and the standards of society changed as well. Change becomes an end in itself.

The great optimism among the new thinkers about the possibility of progress was based largely on their faith in the advance of modern science. Just as science brought technological changes and new methods of study to the physical world, so that same approach, if it were applied to man and society, would bring great change and improvement not only to society but also to man himself. Human nature was no longer fixed but was now seen as an evolving product of changing conditions and social structures, to be formed rather than taken as a given. Here one can see the wide influence of Charles Darwin, whose work and assumptions concerning the scientific theory of the origin and evolution of animals and man—of a changing nature in animals and man—spilled over to areas of study outside of science. (This can also be seen in the racist ideas of some progressive thinkers, who maintained the superiority of the Germanic peoples and the inferiority of all other races—hence their widespread support of eugenics.) Liberty was no longer a condition consistent with human nature and an exercise of God-given natural rights but an evolving concept to be achieved and socially constructed.

As one might imagine, these two concepts—that there are no fixed truths and that all ideas change and evolve with time—led to a serious

reassessment of American political thought and practice. These new thinkers did not understand themselves to be rejecting the American Founding
outright, but correcting the Founders' mistaken assumptions and updat-
ing their flawed handiwork to reflect the newly discovered concepts of
relativism and historicism. If there are no permanent truths, then politics could not—and should not—be guided by claims of fixed principles
or self-evident truths. If all ideas change and evolve, then the American
political order, both in principle and form, would have to be updated continually in order to allow and bring about historical progress.

One can see these new theories reflected in the many thinkers and
writers of the day—academics especially, but political leaders as well.
Progressive opinions took hold in both political parties, initially among
the Republicans, one of the first enthusiasts being Vice President (and
later president) Theodore Roosevelt. "I do not for one moment believe
that the Americanism of today should be a mere submission to the American ideals of the period of the Declaration of Independence," Roosevelt
wrote in 1916. "Such action would be not only to stand still, but to go
back. American democracy, of course, must mean an opportunity for
everyone to contribute his own ideas to the working out of the future.
But I will go further than you have done. I have actively fought in favor
of grafting on our social life, no less than our industrial life, many of the
German ideals."

Perhaps the clearest example of what this means for American politics and political thought comes from Woodrow Wilson, whose successful campaign for president of the United States in 1912 was premised on
this new concept of progress. "Some citizens of this country have never
got beyond the Declaration of Independence," the former Princeton
University president argued (in a speech titled "What Is Progress?"), but
that document "did not mention the questions of our day" and "is of no
consequence to us" unless it can be turned into a program of government action for modern circumstances. Consider how he describes the
new idea of government and its relationship to the Constitution:

> Government is not a machine, but a living thing. It falls, not under
> the theory of the universe, but under the theory of organic life.
> It is accountable to Darwin, not to Newton. It is modified by its
> environment, necessitated by its tasks, shaped to its functions by

the sheer pressure of life. No living thing can have its organs off-set against each other, as checks, and live. On the contrary, its life is dependent upon their quick cooperation, their ready response to the commands of instinct or intelligence, their amicable community of purpose. . . . There can be no successful government without the intimate, instinctive coordination of the organs of life and action. This is not theory, but fact, and displays its force as fact, whatever theories may be thrown across its track. Living political constitutions must be Darwinian in structure and in practice. Society is a living organism and must obey the laws of life, not of mechanics; it must develop.

All that progressives ask or desire is permission—in an era when "development," "evolution," is the scientific word—to interpret the Constitution according to the Darwinian principle; all they ask is recognition of the fact that a nation is a living thing and not a machine.

Government must develop consistent with the evolutionary theory of Charles Darwin. It must grow and change in order to keep fit and survive. It must be understood as a living organism, adapting to its environment. And so too must the Constitution be understood.

In the minds of the new thinkers, this "refounding" marked the end of the old order and the birth of a new republic—based on a new theory of the state, a new understanding of rights, a new concept of national community, and a new doctrine of the "living" Constitution.

A New Theory of Unlimited Government

According to the Founders' view, the purpose of government is to secure fundamental natural rights within a rule of law framework of constitutional government. The ends of government were limited to certain core functions assigned to it in the Constitution. The new end of government, by contrast, was to bring about "Progress." And since progress had not yet been achieved (really, can never be fully achieved, given that there is always more progress to be made in the future), there needed to be a new form of government that was not restricted to securing a few rights or exercising certain limited powers but broadened to achieve the more ambitious objective of bringing about more and more progress and social change.

In this view, government must always evolve and expand, and be ever more actively involved in day to day American life. Given the unlimited goal, government by definition must itself be unlimited. How could there be any limit? "It is denied that any limit can be set to governmental activity," wrote Charles Merriam.

> The exigencies of modern industrial and urban life have forced the state to intervene at so many points where an immediate individual interest is difficult to show, that the old doctrine has been given up for the theory that the state acts for the general welfare. It is not admitted that there are no limits to the action of the state, but on the other hand it is fully conceded that there are no natural rights which bar the way. The question is now one of expediency rather than of principle.

There was no longer any principle—whether natural rights or constitutional government derived from those rights—that limited the action of the state. The extent of government activity was only a matter of convenience; what is beyond the scope of government today would be fair game tomorrow.

Given this new understanding of government, it is no surprise that the progressives viewed the Constitution as an eighteenth-century plan unsuited for the modern day. Its basic mechanisms of the separation of powers and federalism were considered obsolete and inefficient, slowing political change and, by encouraging the levels of government and the branches within government to check each other, making it harder to get things done. It was seen as a reactionary document designed to stifle progress. As a result, the old limited constitutional system had to be transformed into a dynamic, evolving state that would be a genuine instrument of democratic change. Recall Woodrow Wilson's description of government: the state must be Darwinian (evolutionary) rather than Newtonian (static), a living thing that grows and adapts with the times.

The new task of government was to be the principal voice and instigator of change. The progressives advocated more democracy and populist reform to open up the system and make it more responsive, hence the open primary, the initiative process, and the referendum. They also advocated the direct elections of senators, which significantly weakened federalism by making senators elected by popular vote rather than appointed by (and so responsible to) state legislatures, an arrangement that had respected states as entities in the structure of the federal government.

Progressives also insisted that change had to be directed according to new scientific methods of politics. In order to reconcile these seemingly contradictory objectives—allowing more democratic opinion and at the same time directing and managing that change—the progressives posited a sharp distinction between popular politics and what they called "administration." Politics would remain the realm of expressing popular opinions (hence the need for democratic reforms to better reflect those opinions), but the real decisions and details of governing would be handled by administrators, separated and immune from the influence of opinion and partisan politics.

These administrators would be in charge of running a new form of government, designed to keep up with the expanding ends of government, called "the administrative state." Where the Founders went to great lengths to moderate democracy and limit government, the progressives believed that barriers to change had to be removed or circumvented to speed popular change and grow government. Likewise, emphasis would be placed not on a *separation* of powers (which divided and checked government power) but rather a *combination* of powers (which would concentrate and direct government power) in order to bring about reform, consistent with the popular will.*

The particulars of accomplishing the broad objectives of reform—the details of regulation and many rule-making functions previously left to legislatures—were given over to a permanent class of government bureaucrats trained in the new science of progressive ideas. This ruling class of bureaucrats would reside in the recesses of endless agencies like the FCC (Federal Communications Commission), the SEC (Securities and Exchange Commission), the CPSC (Consumer Product Safety Commission), or OSHA (Occupational Safety and Health Administration). Their decisions, mostly unseen and beyond public scrutiny, were to be based on scientific facts rather than political opinions. The theory was

---

* See *The Birth of the Administrative State: Where it Came From and What it Means for Limited Government* (Heritage First Principles Essay #16) by Ronald J. Pestritto.

that, as "objective" and "neutral" experts, these administrators would act above petty partisanship and faction to responsibly serve the long-term objectives of the nation's social programs.

The result is that many of the actual decisions of lawmaking and public policy—decisions previously the constitutional responsibility of elected legislators—are delegated to unaccountable bureaucrats in administrative agencies. While these agencies call their laws "rules," there is no doubt that they have the full force and effect of law as if they were passed by Congress. Today, when Congress writes legislation, it uses very broad language that essentially turns legislative power over to agencies, which are also given the authority of executing and adjudicating violations of their regulations in particular cases. In sum, while seemingly advocating more *democracy*, in practice progressive liberalism wants the opposite: more centralized government *authority* exercised by government bureaucrats.

The constantly changing structure of the administrative state requires dynamic management to keep it moving forward, of course, and so the new thinkers developed their own concept of "leadership" to complete their theory of government. If the times are constantly changing, and the constitutional system must always move to adapt to that change, there must be a role for those who have the foresight and ability to lead the nation in the new directions of history, keeping ahead of popular opinion and always pointing the nation toward its future development. This clarity of vision and unity of direction—of rhetorical inspiration combined with strong political management—is to be provided especially by vigorous presidential leadership.

In this new conception of the state, government is *unlimited*, subject only to the perceived wants of the popular will, under the forward-looking guidance of progressive leadership. Its form is administrative and bureaucratic, run more and more by government experts and bureaucrats not subject to popular consent. The objective of this new theory is to turn government into a dynamic, evolving rational state, constantly changing and growing to achieve more Progress.

A New Theory of Rights

The American Founding was grounded in the concept of certain unalienable rights, held equally by every person. These rights are unchanging and fundamental, since they stem from human nature, and so pre-exist the institution of government. Legitimate governments, deriving their just powers from the consent of the governed, were to secure these fundamental rights. The progressive idea, based on the concept that all things change, was the very opposite: Rights are created by government in order to address current problems and new conditions. "In speaking of natural rights, therefore, it is essential to remember that these alleged rights have no political force whatsoever, unless recognized and enforced by the state," wrote Charles Merriam. "Rights are considered to have their source not in nature, but in law."

Notice how this reverses the relationship between the individual (who previously possessed rights by nature) and government, which was to secure those rights by exercising certain powers delegated to it by the people. Now the state defines, creates, and expands rights and gives them to individuals in order to bring about social change. It was not enough to recognize and secure certain rights inherent in the human person. There are no longer timeless rights with which man is endowed by "the Laws of Nature and Nature's God," as the Declaration of Independence puts it, but instead evolving historical rights to be discovered and granted by government.

A clear example of this sense of expanding rights (further justifying an expanding government) can be seen in Franklin Delano Roosevelt's Annual Message to Congress of January 1944. Coming later in Roosevelt's presidency, after his New Deal programs had been mostly established, this speech argues that the ideas of the Founders are outdated and need to be replaced by an evolving idea of rights and government.

> This Republic had its beginning, and grew to its present strength, under the protection of certain inalienable political rights—among them the right of free speech, free press, free worship, trial by jury, freedom from unreasonable searches and seizures. They were our rights to life and liberty.
>
> As our Nation has grown in size and stature, however—as

our industrial economy expanded—these political rights proved inadequate to assure us equality in the pursuit of happiness.

We have come to a clear realization of the fact that true individual freedom cannot exist without economic security and independence. "Necessitous men are not free men." People who are hungry and out of a job are the stuff of which dictatorships are made.

In our day these economic truths have become accepted as self-evident. We have accepted, so to speak, a second Bill of Rights under which a new basis of security and prosperity can be established for all regardless of station, race, or creed.

The next day, an editorial in the *Wall Street Journal* noted that President Roosevelt spoke of the original Bill of Rights in the past tense— "They *were* our rights to life and liberty," said Roosevelt—and corrected him: "*Are*, not *were*, Mr. President." But that was exactly what Roosevelt meant. The old concept of natural rights—those associated with the Declaration of Independence, the Constitution, and the original Bill of Rights—was increasingly limited because it didn't guarantee economic and social equality. Roosevelt's "Second Bill of Rights" was intended to do just that—"to assure us equality in the pursuit of happiness."

True independence cannot exist without economic security, according to Roosevelt. What good is the *right* to property unless one *possesses* sufficient property to enjoy the right? From the Founders' perspective, dependence was a problematic reliance on government or others for economic and social security, threatening one's independence and liberty. Government was to break down barriers to opportunity so that individuals could provide for themselves. The new view is just the opposite: The primary task of modern government, often called the "welfare state," is to alleviate economic want by assuming responsibility for guaranteeing the economic security of its citizens. The implications of this redefinition are vast, as the list of such economic "rights" is unlimited, requiring more and more social programs and government regulation of the economy in order to achieve new and higher goals of human happiness and well-being.

Here is Roosevelt's catalog of the rights (at least as of 1944) that government was to guarantee for everyone:

The right to a useful and remunerative job in the industries or shops or farms or mines of the Nation;

The right to earn enough to provide adequate food and clothing and recreation;

The right of every farmer to raise and sell his products at a return which will give him and his family a decent living;

The right of every businessman, large and small, to trade in an atmosphere of freedom from unfair competition and domination by monopolies at home or abroad;

The right of every family to a decent home;

The right to adequate medical care and the opportunity to achieve and enjoy good health;

The right to adequate protection from the economic fears of old age, sickness, accident, and unemployment;

The right to a good education.

All of these rights spell security. And after this war is won we must be prepared to move forward, in the implementation of these rights, to new goals of human happiness and well-being.

The denial of human nature as the mooring for equal rights—no longer focusing on the fundamental things inherent in our humanity—changes the purpose of government. The inevitable result is that rights are asserted as claims for government benefits to which one is entitled in order to have economic security and independence. This leads to a redefinition of equality to be an *outcome*, to be achieved by government through various (and usually) unequal means.

This reinterpretation of equality and new sense of entitlement is the animating purpose of Lyndon B. Johnson's Great Society programs of the 1960s. With the creation of a large national bureaucracy and major new initiatives in housing, education, transportation, and urban renewal (most of which, like the "war on poverty," failed to achieve their goals) the Great Society was a vast expansion of the national government and its involvement in society building on the accomplishments of the New Deal. The Great Society took the argument one step further by asserting that the purpose of government is no longer "to secure these rights," as it says in the Declaration of Independence, but to "Fulfill These Rights." That was the title of President Johnson's 1965 commencement address at Howard University in which he laid out this shift from equality of opportunity to the government creation of the political and economic conditions that would guarantee an equality of outcome.* "It is not enough to open the gates of opportunity. All our citizens must have the ability to walk through those gates," Johnson proclaimed. "We seek not just freedom but opportunity. We seek not just legal equity but human ability, not just equality as a right and a theory but equality as a fact and equality as a result." The idea of an independent, self-governing citizenry pursuing equal opportunity has been replaced by individuals and groups who see the federal government as the guarantor of economic security and the primary provider of social services. Rather than basic or temporary programs, benefits come to be virtually permanent government aid to which one is entitled.

This inevitably leads to a shift from an emphasis on individual rights, inherent in the nature of each person, to a concept of rights based on the various material needs and practical demands of groups. We often speak nowadays of specific rights that are said to belong to categories of individuals defined by group characteristics. This is a misconception, to say the least. From the Founders' point of view, rights are inherently possessed by each and every individual and are turned into civil rights that apply equally to all persons through the constitutional process. There are no such things as "women's rights," or "black rights," or "gay rights," just as there are no "men's rights," "white rights," and "heterosexual rights." Associating the legitimacy of rights with interest groups and political advocacy, rather than recognizing its proper grounding in nature, not only gives rise to unlimited (and unbounded) rights claims and endless legal battles, but also leaves the core rights with which we are endowed to wither as mere values, subject to shifting political opinion and court majorities.†

---

* On the shift from equality of opportunity to outcomes, see Charles Murray's *Losing Ground: American Social Policy, 1950–1980* (1984), and on the failures of Great Society social policies, see Myron Magnet's *The Dream and the Nightmare: The Sixties' Legacy to the Underclass* (1993).

† On the modern rights revolution, see Mary Ann Glendon's *Rights Talk: The Impoverishment of Political Discourse* (1991).

A Great National Community

Under the Founders' constitution, government was limited in order to maintain and protect a wide realm of liberty. It established a framework for exercising rights and practicing the habits of self-government, protecting a thriving and decentralized system of states, local communities, and civil society wherein traditional institutions would help shape the lives and characters of free citizens. Under the protection of property rights and contracts, economic markets would flourish, creating opportunity and prosperity. Within a diverse and expansive civil society, countless private institutions—families, schools, churches, associations—would moderate the passions and dampen their influence, thereby encouraging deliberation and republican government. The purpose of government was to secure the pursuit of happiness—defending life, upholding the vast opportunities provided by liberty, and protecting the goods associated with happiness.

The modern theory of government based on evolving rights and an expanding state has vast implications for every aspect of American life. The objective of the new thinking, and a major cultural component of modern-day liberalism, is to transform America from a decentralized self-governing society based on a framework of limited government, free markets, and traditional cultural institutions into a great progressive society, built around a homogeneous national community focused on *national* ideals and the achievement of *social* justice. By this is meant not a just society but a society in which equal justice—understood especially to mean economic egalitarianism—is brought about in every aspect of society.

An important element of this argument is a new understanding of economics. The progressives maintained that the old system—based on private property and the inviolability of contract, free markets and the pursuit of economic opportunity—encouraged greed and selfishness, creating widespread inequalities and poverty that far outweighed any public benefit. They advocated a new system of reform economics that would curb the excesses of capitalism by focusing on changing sociological conditions through government regulation of the private economy and solving socioeconomic problems through the redistribution of goods and benefits within society.

The clearest formulation of this nationalizing and socializing aspect of progressive thought is found in an influential book by Herbert Croly called *The Promise of American Life* (1909). Croly, who later became the editor of the flagship progressive magazine, *The New Republic*, argued for a "subordination of the individual to the demand of a dominant and constructive national purpose." The essential instrument of this new national community would be an active, central national government which would regulate corporations and property for social purposes, be responsible for the distribution of wealth, and begin to alleviate economic inequalities through the progressive taxation of income and by expanding social-welfare programs—goals which were made possible by the development of the scientific management of government.

When it came to the political community's authority and control of the individual, the progressives did not see much difference between what they advocated and socialism. "In fundamental theory socialism and democracy are almost if not quite one and the same," wrote Woodrow Wilson. "They both rest at bottom upon the absolute right of the community to determine its own destiny and that of its members. Men as communities are supreme over men as individuals. Limits of wisdom and convenience to the public control there may be: limits of principle there are, upon strict analysis, none." While Croly was "not concerned with dodging the odium of the word," he preferred that his theory "be characterized not so much as socialistic, as unscrupulously and loyally nationalistic."

In order to achieve this purpose, reformers had to first overcome the moral authority of the old order. In his 1922 book *Principles of Sociology*, the progressive thinker Edward Ross complained that America was weighed down by "thousands of local groups sewed up in separatist dogmas and dead to most of the feelings which thrill the rest of society." The traditional institutions of civil society—especially faith-based groups, churches, and private associations—were a problem, from the progressive point of view, as they kept citizens focused on local communities rather than national ideals, and on "separatist dogmas" (read: moral convictions and absolute principles) rather than ideas of progress. The progressive solution to the "problem" of civil society was twofold. There was to be the "widest possible diffusion of secular knowledge" throughout society in order to check the influence of the moral and religious opinions propagated by these institutions. And there would be a general centralization of politics under the national government, as "removing control farther away from the ordinary citizen and taxpayer is tantamount to giving the intelligent, far-sighted and public spirited elements in society a longer lever to work with." In order to bring about social progress and reform, the influence of the institutions of civil society that emphasized moral character and religious conviction—indeed, the very idea of self-government—had to be weakened and overcome, replaced by government-created and government-directed national community.

In the old system, moral character was emphasized to temper the passions and dampen their influence on politics, thereby promoting self-government. But with administrative government, there is much less a concern with moral character: There is little reason to worry about emancipating the passions, because popular opinion will be guided by progressive political leaders and public policy will be administered by apolitical experts. The moral virtues—based on old distinctions between virtue and vice, right and wrong—no longer have public implications (recall the anti-foundation of relativism) but must be limited to the realm of private opinion and personal values. The political virtues (qualities such as self-control, restraint, circumspection, and political moderation) are replaced by a new virtue of faith—faith in government action, faith in bureaucratic experts, and faith in the inspired vision of progressive leaders.

Nationalized public education was to be the key vehicle for creating this new sense of community. John Dewey (recall his commitment to "historic relativity" and "experimentalism") was the chief architect of progressive education, and a leading advocate of what he called "collectivist liberalism." He argued that the whole American education system, historically focused on transmitting received knowledge and accumulated learning, must become the centralizing focus of progressive ideas and social change. In a 1937 essay on "Education and Social Change," Dewey wrote that schools should "take an active part in directing social change, and share in the construction of a new social order." Rather than upholding the ideas and traditions of the "old order," schools should foster change and reform and teach students to "take part in the great work of construction and organization that will have to be done" for the sake of social progress. New schools of education would be created to prepare teachers for their new task. This theory of progressive education, which became dominant in schools and the universities in the mid-twentieth century, revolutionized the American education system.*

This new kind of education would be liberating from past ideas and assumptions. The core assumptions of the Founders were dangerous illusions—remember, there are no fixed principles or moral standards—from which Americans need to be emancipated, and so education becomes a project not only of intellectual but also of moral liberation. Traditional subjects like literature, philosophy, the humanities, and history—in particular, American history and the ideas and institutions of the American Founders—had to be "deconstructed" to reveal and emphasize progressive theories of value relativism, historical consciousness, and social awareness.

While citizens used to be educated by a school system designed around concepts of core knowledge and learning, and by local community institutions that were foremost responsible for moral formation, under the new view, individuals were to be shaped by a system of progressive education and molded to serve the ends of social justice through individual participation in national endeavors and government programs. "Democracy must stand or fall on a platform of possible human perfectibility," Herbert Croly wrote. "If human nature cannot be improved by institutions, democracy is at best a more than usually safe form of political organization. . . . But if it is to work better as well as merely longer, it must have some leavening effect on human nature; and the sincere democrat is obliged to assume the power of the leaven." By liberating individuals from the narrow confines of traditional culture, the development of a new progressive democracy and a national community will lead to the transformation of human nature itself—"the development of a better quality of human nature," as Croly put it. Indeed, the goal was now understood as freedom *from* human nature.

Liberty is no longer the freedom of self-government in the context of constitutional order and the institutions of civil society, but becomes the autonomous pursuit of personal self-realization within the horizon of national social ideals.† Freedom now means liberation of the human will.

---

* On this, see *John Dewey and the Decline of American Education: How the Patron Saint of Schools Has Corrupted Teaching and Learning* (2006), by Henry Edmondson.

† A recent example of this thinking is Richard Rorty's *Achieving Our Country* (1998).

"At the heart of liberty," Associate Justice Anthony Kennedy wrote in the 1992 Supreme Court decision *Planned Parenthood v. Casey*, "is the right to define one's own concept of existence, of meaning, of the universe, and of the mystery of human life." If all values are relative, it is hard to define any moral limits or defend any moral restraints. Yet it is the job of the national government to assure more and more evolving rights, and provide more benefits and new entitlements to achieve that personal happiness.

A New "Living" Constitution

For much of American history, judges and courts—the officers of the law and institutions designed to uphold the rule of law—were the bulwark of legal stability and constitutional fidelity, keeping our politics moored to the Constitution and its system of separation of powers and limited government. The inevitable changes in society were to be reflected in politics through the mechanisms of constitutional government, which included a formal process for amending the Constitution by popular consent. This process of consensual change would temper popular impulses at the same time that it would encourage larger interests and views of the common good, as well as an adherence to fundamental political principles.

The progressives saw things very differently. The Constitution's focus on controlling and restricting government power and moderating democratic opinion was not only misguided but had become a serious barrier to the new activist government necessary for progressive reforms. The assault on the Constitution began in the academy, where scholars like James Allen Smtih, Charles Beard, and others argued that the document represented the triumph of moneyed elites protecting their economic interests in the face of a populist revolution.* Based on the same assumptions, progressive historians asserted that the democratic forces of the American Revolution, having produced an idealistic Declaration of Independence, were later defeated by reactionary forces that produced an antidemocratic constitution, an argument that is still widely maintained as the key dynamic of American political history.

---

* This economic interpretation of the Constitution was powerfully refuted in *Charles Beard and the Constitution* (1956) by Robert Brown, and *We The People: The Economic Origins of the Constitution* (1958) by Forrest McDonald.

But the aim of the new thinkers was not to get rid of the old constitution—that was neither desirable nor possible, given its elevated status and historic significance in American political life. Their aim was to transform the Constitution to be flexible and pliable, and thus capable of growth and adaptation in changing times. The original constitution was to be replaced by the idea of a "living" constitution that would update (and uproot) the old system of individual rights and limited government in favor of evolving rights and an activist (and unlimited) federal government.

While every aspect of government was to be shaped by this new approach, the judiciary was to play a central role in this process, as this transformation was to be achieved primarily through innovative and forward-looking interpretations of the Constitution. The easiest way to bring new lifeblood into the dead body of the law would be through the constant transfusion of changing meanings into the Constitution itself.

The doctrine of the living constitution is closely connected to the misguided notion, as Supreme Court justice Charles Evans Hughes once approvingly observed, that the Constitution is "what the judges say it is." This is the idea that the meaning of the Constitution is decided by courts alone, resulting in the widespread assumption—taught in most law schools and generally accepted in the legal profession—that the most recent decisions and opinions of the Supreme Court amount to being the Constitution at that point in time. This idea is inconsistent and incompatible with the Founders' concept of limited constitutional government.

The great progressive jurist Oliver Wendell Holmes (who served on the Supreme Court from 1902 to 1932) famously argued that the life of the law was nothing more than experience, and that the most crucial factor in the development (and interpretation) of the law was a consideration of "the felt needs of the time." In this view of outcome-oriented jurisprudence, sometimes called "legal realism," judging is not distinct from legislating, but merely a different form of it, filling in the gaps, so to speak, created by general laws. Judges determine not only what the Constitution says about certain questions but also, in effect, what policies will best harmonize the document's allegedly vague presumptions with the popular needs of the time.

This view came into maturity during the New Deal. At first, the Supreme Court struck down many of Roosevelt's programs—regulating agriculture, manufacturing, labor, transportation—as unconstitutional. But eventually—after President Roosevelt threatened to "pack" the Supreme Court with additional judges to get his way—a few judges began to embrace the New Deal initiatives by changing their interpretation of the Constitution to accommodate the previously unconstitutional laws. In particular, the court began to interpret expansive new authority in the Commerce Clause—making anything (even wheat grown by a farmer for his own consumption!) subject to federal regulation, whether it was manufactured for interstate commerce or not—and read the Tenth Amendment (and so the doctrine of federalism) to be nothing more than "a truism that all is retained which had not been surrendered." And so the Constitution was changed not by the democratic process of amendment but by the *interpretation* of a handful of appointed judges, amounting to what some have called a constitutional revolution.*

We can see this new jurisprudence expressed in the difference between the old and new views of judicial review. The Founders' view was that the Supreme Court in deciding particular cases would consider whether the laws in question were consistent with the text of the Constitution. The new view is that judges should decide according to whether the law comports with their own (not the Constitution's) standards of reasonableness and rationality, shaped by the spirit and course of developing court decisions and constitutional interpretation.

What is especially troubling is the extent to which the new jurisprudence, having removed the content of the Constitution, seeks to replace it with new substance. The modern Supreme Court seems less concerned with protecting old-fashioned constitutional rights than with advancing the cause of new, evolving rights. As a result, the theory of the living constitution has extended the actual Constitution to protect unspecified rights and liberties having to do with race, ethnic identification, and sexual orientation, often based on unwritten meanings found in the document. There is no direction or limit as to where this evolving sense of rights might take our politics in the future.†

---

* See *Progressivism and the New Science of Jurisprudence* (Heritage First Principles Essay #24) by Bradley C. S. Watson. A good overview of constitutional history, including the New Deal shift, is *The American Constitution: Its Origins and Development* (1991) edited by Alfred Kelly, Winfred Harbison, and Herman Belz.

† See *From Constitutional Interpretation to Judicial Activism: The Transformation of*

Perhaps the clearest example of this development is the right to privacy. In *Griswold v. Connecticut* (1965), the Supreme Court's majority argued that the "specific guarantees in the Bill of Rights have penumbras formed by emanations from those guarantees that give life and substance," and those penumbras formed by emanations—literally, partial shadows and emissions—"create zones of privacy." This right, created in *Griswold* and extended in cases like *Roe v. Wade* to include a right to abortion, turns out to be a general right to autonomy that can be applied to strike down virtually anything, as has been seen in various cases recently concerning the meaning and substance of marriage.

"The genius of the Constitution rests not in any static meaning it might have had in a world that is dead and gone," wrote Justice William Brennan in a 1986 law review article, "but in the adaptability of its great principles to cope with current problems and current needs." It is the particular responsibility of judges to provide that adaptation, he concluded, through "a personal confrontation with the wellsprings of our society."

If the Constitution is little more than majestic generalities waiting to be given purpose through the interpretive process itself, and it contains no fixed meanings, the judge's challenge is to identify and define the open-ended values that the Constitution seeks to fulfill—such as democracy, freedom, and equality—and then impose an outcome relevant to achieving that value at the current time.* But of course the times change and so do the values. That is why the new jurisprudence, as Justice Anthony Kennedy put it recently in *Roper v. Simmons* (2003), has "established the propriety and affirmed the necessity of referring to the evolving standards of decency that mark the progress of a maturing society." Constitutional meaning does not stem from the Constitution—in this thinking, interpretation seems to have no real association to the document at all—but develops from the judge's ever-changing views of evolving standards.

Rather than making sure the age adheres to the spirit and the letter of the Constitution, the new role of the judiciary is to adapt the law (and deconstruct the Constitution) to bring American society forward, accord-

---

Judicial Review in America (Heritage First Principles Essay #2) by Christopher Wolfe.
* A recent example of this argument can be found in Justice Stephen Breyer's *Active Liberty: Interpreting Our Democratic Constitution* (2005).

ing to judges' views of societal change. In this world, the Constitution is an empty vessel. It means whatever judges say it does, according to their personal speculations. Which is to say that it means anything—or nothing.

Is It Too Late?

The rise and dominance of progressive ideas among our political elite, in our colleges and universities, and in key parts of our popular culture has given us a very different understanding of ourselves and our nation.

Thinkers like Woodrow Wilson, Herbert Croly, and John Dewey argued that the forces of industrialism and urbanization had shattered America's traditional social order, and that the conditions of the modern world required a new activist government to better manage political life and human affairs. This new liberalism set out to transform the old constitutional structure of limited government into a "living" governmental system that is progressive, increasingly centralized, and focused on national social reform. The rise of the modern administrative state, the growth of government at every level, and the increased benefits the American people expect from government have changed the idea of self-government in America. The anti-foundational assumptions they established within that tradition can be seen playing out over the course of the twentieth and now twenty-first centuries, and have become widely accepted in our society.

These ideas have also changed how we look at the world. The progressives argued that the United States must be actively engaged in international affairs—not to defend itself, its national interests, or even the cause of liberty but to "make the world safe for democracy," as Woodrow Wilson said in his War Message to Congress in 1917. The progressive theory of government applied writ large in the world: A powerful sense of idealism and the suppression of national interests gave the United States a new moral imperative to use American influence and strength to bring progress—in terms of evolving human rights, altruistic diplomacy, international organization, and world community—to every corner of the globe.

Consistent with the view that trained bureaucrats were best suited to run government at home, the new thinkers maintained that America had an obligation to manage the affairs of less civilized peoples and the conditions of less developed nations. Senator Albert Beveridge, a prominent advocate of a progressive foreign policy, maintained that as "trustees of the world's progress, guardians of its righteous peace," it was the "divine mission of America" to be "the master organizers of the world [and] to overwhelm the forces of reaction throughout the earth." Although less confident in America's goodness and while using more sophisticated language—global justice, interdependence, social transformation, and the creed of multilateralism—many modern-day thinkers still pursue what has come to be called a Wilsonian approach to the world.

The result of all this is that America seems to be moving ever further away from its original principles and constitutional design. While progressive ideas have not completely won the day, and in many important ways those ideas have had to adapt to the realities still defined by the American political tradition, the dominance of these arguments—in our schools, in the public square, and in our politics—has significantly weakened the very foundations of American constitutionalism, making it all the more difficult not only to defend but more importantly to recover the ideas and institutions of America's Founders.

Is it still possible to revitalize our country's principles and to renew our liberty? To that challenge we now turn.

11

❧

American Renewal:
The Case for Reclaiming Our Future

"If destruction be our lot, we must ourselves be its author and finisher," Abraham Lincoln observed in 1838. "As a nation of freemen, we must live through all time, *or die by suicide.*"

By any measure, the United States of America is a great nation. Thirteen colonies are now fifty states covering a vast continent. The American economy accounts for almost a quarter of the world's annual gross domestic product. The strongest military force in the world allows the United States to extend its power anywhere on the globe. The American people remain one of the most hard-working, church-going, affluent, and generous in the world. Just as George Washington predicted, the United States is a sovereign nation "in command of its own fortunes."

And yet it seems we are on a course of self-destruction.

A national government once limited to certain core functions has an all but unquestioned dominance over virtually every area of American life, restricted only by expediency, political will, and (less and less) budget constraints.

Congress passes massive pieces of legislation with little serious deliberation and is increasingly an administrative body overseeing a vast array of bureaucratic policymakers and rule-making bodies. Although the Constitution vests legislative powers in Congress, the majority of "laws" are promulgated by administrative agencies in the guise of "regulations"—a form of rule by bureaucrats who are mostly unaccountable and invisible to the public.

Federal and state courts, meanwhile, don't adjudicate the law, as much as they rewrite it, and sometimes make it up, regularly usurping the power of the political branches in ways that expand government power and diminish the authority of popular consent. Many of the most important decisions in Americans' lives, and the final answers to virtually every major question of public policy in America today, are made by unelected judges. It is not too much to ask whether there is a single clause of the Constitution left that has not been traduced by judicial reinterpretation.

Beset by a Congress that is increasingly administrative and a Supreme Court that is more and more legislative, the modern president constantly campaigns for a mandate that is subject to the enormous powers wielded by the other branches. The bureaucracy is so overwhelming that it is unclear whether modern presidents actually can be held constitutionally responsible for "tak[ing] care that the laws be faithfully executed." Presidents now appoint numerous policy "czars"—megabureaucrats operating outside of the existing cabinet structure—to forward their objectives over the inertia of their own administrations.

America is covered by an intricate web of government policies and procedures. States, localities, and private institutions still exist, subsumed under national programs—states increasingly as administrators of policy emanating from Washington, supplicants seeking relief and assistance from the federal government. Growing streams of money flow from Washington to every state and locality, thousands of private and nonprofit organizations, and millions of individuals, who are in turn increasingly subject to federal rules and regulations.

A nation of citizens is becoming a society of consumers who pay more and more taxes to purchase more and more government-controlled programs and services. The United States is nearing the point that a majority of its citizens will have no federal income tax liability, yet the government continues to act without regard to the future, leaving the bill for future generations. If spending continues at the current rate, the United States will accumulate more debt in the next ten years than the combined debt built up over the course of all previous American history.

A New Form of Despotism?

As a people, we have fallen into the habit of expecting government to solve all problems, removing risk from our lives and providing for all our needs and wants. It is commonplace now for individuals to look to government to relieve their most ordinary concerns, support their basic endeavors, and make good on the simplest injuries anticipated in daily life. As more and more citizens look to government for benefits and services, they come to depend on them, and the government. Are Americans becoming the clients of government rather than its self-governing master?

Dependency encourages a politics in which government benefits and programs are treated as payoffs to existing or potential voter groups—a modern-day patronage approach to building political majorities. As benefits expand beyond primary needs to include middle-class entitlements, conflicts will arise between competing self-interests and a long-term, common interest that favors self-reliance, personal responsibility, and civic independence. Has dependence on government created a class of Americans who are "united and actuated by some common impulse of passion, or of interest, adverse to the rights of other citizens, or to the permanent and aggregate interests of the community"? This was James Madison's definition of a faction. And the Founders warned that majority faction was the chief threat to the very existence of free, republican government.

In *Democracy in America*, Alexis de Tocqueville warned of a tendency of democracies, bent on bringing about equal results in all cases, to succumb to a centralized and consolidated government that promises to master every social condition and outcome in pursuit of this elusive goal. The combination of egalitarianism and the regulatory power of centralized administrative government, Tocqueville feared, could lead to a new form of despotism that would destroy the human spirit. In this future, he foresaw "an innumerable crowd of like and equal men who revolve on themselves without repose, procuring the small and vulgar pleasures with which they fill their souls." Government would become the all-powerful instrument serving these insatiable appetites. Self-governing citizens would degrade themselves into passive subjects of an impersonal, bureaucratic nation-state.

Written almost 170 years ago, Tocqueville's analysis of a form of despotism that democratic peoples should most fear seems ever more prophetic with the passage of time:

> Above [the people] an immense tutelary power is elevated, which alone takes charge of assuring their enjoyments and watching over their fate. It is absolute, detailed, regular, far-seeing, and mild. It would resemble paternal power if, like that, it had for its object to prepare men for manhood; but on the contrary, it seeks only to keep them fixed irrevocably in childhood; it likes citizens to enjoy themselves provided that they think only of enjoying themselves. It willingly works for their happiness; but it wants to be the sole agent and sole arbiter of that; it provides for their security, foresees and secures their needs, facilitates their pleasures, conducts their principal affairs, directs their industry, regulates their estates, divides their inheritances: can it not take away from them entirely the trouble of thinking and the pain of living?

The problem is not that such a government is hard, or even harsh, but just the opposite. It promotes selfish, petty interests because it caters to them, and by doing so deforms the character of self-governing citizens, rendering "the employment of the free will less useful and more rare." It creates a therapeutic society under the authoritarian rule of bureaucrats and experts. Such a power, Tocqueville concluded, "does not destroy, it prevents things from being born; it does not tyrannize, it hinders, compromises, enervates, extinguishes, dazes, and finally reduces each nation to being nothing more than a herd of timid and industrious animals of which the government is the shepherd."*

Once its citizens have given up liberty for comfortable security and the responsibility of self-government for the ease of government-as-parent, democratic government can become a type of soft despotism—less coercive in its methods and more benign in its intentions but despotic nonetheless. And as Tocqueville surely knew, the shepherd cares for his defenseless sheep for the ultimate purpose of fleecing and consuming them.

* See "What Kind of Despotism Democratic Nations Have to Fear," in volume two of Alexis de Tocqueville's *Democracy in America* (1840). The best modern edition is the translation (with an introduction) by Harvey C. Mansfield and Delba Winthrop.

Is this to be the failed destiny of the greatest experiment in self-government mankind has ever attempted?

The Path of Decline

Our politics have always been debates about the meaning of America. From Abraham Lincoln's "new birth of freedom" to Franklin Delano Roosevelt's New Deal to Ronald Reagan's New Beginning, America's greatest debates have turned on how we understand ourselves, our principles, and our national purpose.

The view of America that dominates the academy, journalism, major foundations, and most segments of the American intellectual community—and as a result, major portions of America's political leadership in both parties—was marked out at the start of the last century by progressive thinkers when they launched their grand project to remake America. They repudiated the Founders' principles, holding that there are no self-evident truths—in the Declaration of Independence or elsewhere—but only *change* in the constant search for progress without final goals. There are no permanent rights with which man is endowed, but endlessly evolving rights that develop and grow (just as our old rights whither and shrink) based on new demands. Our fidelity must be to a "living" Constitution that adapts to fit the demands of the times. Progress requires a new form of government able to control social conditions and engineer a better society, assuring equal outcomes and redistributing wealth through a distant and patronizing welfare state that regulates more and more of America's economy, politics, and civil society.

As America's principles have been assaulted, undermined, and redefined in our culture, in our universities, and in our politics, we have taken significant steps down this path. The Progressive movement laid the intellectual groundwork, but the basic infrastructure of the modern welfare state was established under the New Deal and expanded in regulatory scope and social purpose under the Great Society and its progeny. We are in the beginning of a new and perhaps decisive move in this direction.

For a glimpse at the future of this America, look across the ocean. The grand nations of old Europe are stifled by regulated economies, nationalized industries, and socialized health care, ruled more by bureaucrats in

Brussels than by their own elected legislatures. With more allegiance to international organizations than their own nation-states, Europeans are disinclined to defend themselves in the world. Magnificent cathedrals are now empty testaments to their postmodern faith in secularism. The cultures of Europe are in steep decline; it is unclear whether they will ever be able to recover. In a matter of a generation or two, the Europe we have known for millennia as the home of Western civilization will exist only in museums and history books.

This is not progress, but the decline of a civilization. It is movement not forward but backwards, away from human equality, popular consent, the rule of law, and constitutional government and toward failed, undemocratic, and illiberal forms of statism. Denying the truth of America's principles for the sake of such "change" can make no claim to progress at all.

President Calvin Coolidge made this very point with unsurpassed clarity in a speech on the 150th anniversary of the Declaration of Independence in 1926, when the progressive attack on America's principles was still in its initial phase.

About the Declaration there is a finality that is exceedingly restful. It is often asserted that the world has made a great deal of progress since 1776, that we have had new thoughts and new experiences which have given us a great advance over the people of that day, and that we may therefore very well discard their conclusions for something more modern. But that reasoning can not be applied to this great charter. If all men are created equal, that is final. If they are endowed with inalienable rights, that is final. If governments derive their just powers from the consent of the governed, that is final. No advance, no progress can be made beyond these propositions. If anyone wishes to deny their truth or their soundness, the only direction in which he can proceed historically is not forward, but backward toward the time when there was no equality, no rights of the individual, no rule of the people. Those who wish to proceed in that direction can not lay claim to progress. They are reactionary. Their ideas are not more modern, but more ancient, than those of the Revolutionary fathers.

The Promise of American Renewal

There is another way forward. The slow Europeanization of America is not inevitable, and it's not too late. But it will take a monumental effort to get our country back on track.

The primary reason the United States has not gone the way of Europe—though there are clear parallels throughout our society—is that our country has long maintained a political culture grounded on America's moral and constitutional principles, which has kept it moored in the Western tradition of reason and faith, protected from the radicalization (and the emptiness) of modern thought that has devastated Europe. Indeed, the European-style arguments that American progressives imported in the last century have not fully succeeded here precisely because they are working *against* rather than *with* the deep currents of America's ideas and institutions.

We don't need to remake America, or discover new and untested principles. The change we need is not the rejection of America's principles but a great renewal of these permanent truths about man, politics, and liberty—the foundational principles and constitutional wisdom that are the true roots of our country's greatness.

We must look to the principles of the American Founding not as a matter of historical curiosity, but as a source of assurance and direction for our times. In a world of moral confusion, and of arbitrary and unlimited government, the American Founding is our best access to permanent truths and our best ground from which to launch a radical questioning of the whole foundation of the progressive project.

Renewing America's principles doesn't mean going back to the eighteenth century, or some other time for that matter. Think of principles as the unchanging standards that inform changing experiences. The question is not, "What Would the Founders Do?" but what will we do as we go forward toward an unknowable future with these fixed principles as our trustworthy guides. It is not about looking *back* to the past, but rather looking *down* at our roots in order to look *up* to our highest ideals.

Nor does it mean that today's problems are to be solved by formulaic appeals to our principles. It is the job of prudence, keenly aware of the necessities of particular circumstances and the realities of practical outcomes, to advance principles under prevailing conditions by relating particular actions to their ends. But the key to making prudential decisions, as well as distinguishing between reasonable compromise and self-defeating reforms, is a deep understanding of and commitment to core principles. It is just this sure commitment to principles that can transform prudence from mere timidity into bold and courageous action when the times call for it. And serious, thoughtful leaders cannot doubt that we are living in just such a time, calling for prudence at its very boldest.

It is not the affirmation of a peculiar set of antiquated claims that tie us to America as much as it is our common recognition of transcendent truths that bind us all together and across time to the patriots of 1776. Only with this sure foundation can we go forward as a nation, addressing the great policy questions before us and continuing to secure the blessings of liberty to ourselves and our posterity.

The challenge is to faithfully maintain, vindicate, and fulfill our principles in the face of constant, and thoughtless, demands for change.

Educating for Liberty

The Department of Education reports that more than half of high school seniors lack even a basic knowledge of American history. Many college students, another study finds, can't identify the Gettysburg Address and don't know that James Madison was the father of the Constitution.

Like the canary in the coal mine, this ignorance of facts and figures alerts us to the real problem. Modern education has shifted away from civics and social studies in elementary education. High schools largely ignore, minimize, or disparage the story of America's Founding in the classroom. Students can graduate from the top colleges and universities in America without taking a single course in U.S. history. Dominated by relativism and historicism, too many of our schools, colleges, and universities ignore the American Founding because it is considered outdated and too difficult to explain to modern students, or instead fixate on the flaws or errors of the American Founding in light of modern values. By doing so, they are subverting the principles of liberty and constitutional government.

We must reverse this course by making a commitment at every level of education to promote an awareness and appreciation of the true principles of the American Founding. The meaning and power of these ideas will be lost in the course of a lifetime if they are not taught to each generation of students. The public mission of our schools in the past was to transmit this knowledge to young Americans as the most important requisite for democracy. This must be the mission of our schools again.

Americans must be familiar with the history of the American Revolution, the ideas behind the Declaration of Independence, and the deliberations and debates surrounding the formation of the Constitution. They should be well-versed in the primary documents of the founding—not because they are historical relics, but because they have enduring meaning for public life today. A basic understanding of our history—with its many inspiring achievements and noble triumphs, as well as its imperfections, flaws, and failures—should be required knowledge for every citizen.

Civic education is not indoctrination; quite the opposite. The Founders themselves didn't agree in every respect, and neither do we. Taking their arguments seriously in the classroom, though, invites students to consider the most important questions, then and now, and prepares them for meaningful participation in our political system. The revival of traditional history and civics in K–12 schools and rigorous academic programs that improve history and civics instruction should be strongly encouraged, as should the many private organizations that are promoting and assisting in such educational work throughout the United States.

The key to improving instruction and student knowledge in this area is the teaching and training of teachers of American history, government, and constitutionalism. There are several excellent organizations that work with high school teachers and college professors, assisting them in developing a deeper understanding of the subject matter, better courses and curricula, and more appropriate and effective classroom materials. At the college and university level, a growing number of independent centers on campuses foster the teaching and serious study of American principles and history. All of these efforts ought to be supported and expanded.

Legal education is a particular problem, as it has relentlessly promoted the gradual deconstruction of the Constitution. For decades now, law schools have downplayed the written constitution, focusing on the history of recent judicial decisions and developing progressive legal doctrines rather than the meaning and history of the document itself. This has changed somewhat in recent years with a renewed interest in constitutional studies and the roots of constitutionalism in the foundational principles of liberty, the rule of law, and popular consent. But more needs to be done—on the part of students, faculty, and alumni, as well as independent scholars and outside organizations—to make sure that law schools seriously teach (and take seriously) the rule of law and constitutional government, and that the importance of original constitutional meaning extends beyond legal scholars to once again become the basic method for understanding the Constitution.*

An Expression of the American Mind

Education must not be confined to the classroom or end with the conclusion of the formal education process. The popularity of histories, biographies, and television miniseries about America's Founding is evidence of an abiding general interest in our national narrative, but it does not replace an understanding and appreciation for the purposes behind the personalities and events of that story. We must continue to teach the principles of liberty and the rights and responsibilities of self-government to all Americans, in order, as James Madison once put it, "to refine and enlarge the public views."

Participatory democracy requires popular deliberation. But our political discourse too often is stifled by the political correctness of self-appointed social critics on the one hand and the closed-minded ideology of single-issue advocates on the other. Neither makes a real attempt to persuade or listen. The debate among our political leaders is more narrowly partisan than it is broadly political, driven by immediate interests more than considerations of the common good. Rather than throwing up our hands and withdrawing from the public debate, though, we need to engage it in new ways by making a clear and forthright defense of core principles, applying them creatively to the questions of the day, supporting positions consistent with those principles, and generally reframing the national debate about the most serious issues before us.

---

* A brief list of such organizational resources can be found at the end of the bibliographic essay.

We need more popular scholarship and scholarly popular writing that is accessible and compelling to the general public, designed to shape the public mind and not just contribute to the dusty shelves of university libraries or the passing attention of the latest website. A scholarship of freedom would not only explain modern liberalism's sweeping rejection of America's principles and the Western tradition in which they are rooted; it would also intellectually defend those principles and that tradition and provide scholarly depth to the public debate about the meaning and purpose of American liberty.

This task requires correcting several misconceptions, two of which are particularly pernicious.

There is great confusion about the source and status of our rights. Under the progressive theory, rights emerge from a government that constantly creates and redefines those rights—ex nihilo by judicial decree, or de facto by Congress in the form of entitlements—to keep up with the times. We need to reestablish the proper understanding of rights in the American political tradition—the principle that each person equally possesses the unalienable rights with which he or she is endowed according to "the Laws of Nature and Nature's God." Political thought in the last half century has led to a serious reevaluation of the Founders' conception of natural rights and natural law, giving rise to an extensive scholarship which needs to become more broadly influential, legitimating and bolstering what most Americans believe to be the case.

There is also much confusion about the meaning and status of the Constitution. While not fully comprehended, the "living" Constitution concept is widely accepted. It is generally supposed that judges have the final say concerning every constitutional question, giving modern government wide latitude and significant cover for its unlimited activities. These arguments need to be challenged and overcome in the public view, both as a matter of historical accuracy and a necessary condition for reinvigorating limited government, constitutionalism, and the rule of law. By allowing the Constitution to be treated as a malleable document, we should not be surprised that the "living" Constitution has deadened the political mind of many Americans.

The Declaration of Independence, Jefferson later recorded, was "neither aiming at originality of principle or sentiment, nor yet copied from any particular and previous writing, it was intended to be an expression of the American mind." Our aim must be a clear expression and forthright defense of America's principles in the public square so that they become, once again, an expression of the American mind. Despite constant criticism and scorn by academic elites, political leaders, and the popular media, most Americans still believe in the uniqueness of this country and respect the noble ideas put forth by the American Founders. We must give voice to all those who have not given up on their country's experiment in self-government, have not concluded that the cause of liberty and limited constitutional government is lost, and have not accepted America's decline as inevitable.

The goal must be to restore the liberating principles of the American Founding—its philosophical grounding, its constitutional wisdom, and its limitless spirit of self-government and independence—as the defining public philosophy of our nation. As it has been for most of American history, so it can be again.

A New Era of Constitutional Responsibility

It is not sufficient that we recover America's principles in our classrooms, or even in the popular mind. If these principles have permanent significance, they must inform our politics and shape public policy. A commitment to enduring principles means that these principles are applicable to the past, as well as the present, and the future.

We need political leaders who understand and uphold America's principles. Public officials take a solemn oath to support the Constitution of the United States, which means they have a moral obligation to abide by the Constitution in carrying out their duties of office. For members of Congress, this means determining constitutional authority before passing legislation. For the executive, it means considering the constitutionality of legislation presented to them, and withholding approval of unconstitutional legislation, as well as executing the law in a constitutional manner. This admittedly is difficult in the current political environment; constant recurrence to constitutional authority by itself can be self-defeating. But this is no excuse for not prudently making constitutional arguments and taking constitutional actions that—in addition to being the right thing to do—will begin to change the environment in favor of limited government. One small step in this direction would be to require all legislation to contain an explanation of its constitutional authority, compelling at least a consideration of each proposal's constitutional legitimacy.

While judges are in a unique position to spell out the meaning and consequences of the Constitution, it is imperative to understand—and for them to recognize—that they are not above, outside, or immune to the constraints of that document. The Constitution limits judicial power just as it does for the executive and legislative branches, and all are bound by its strictures. Indeed, judges are more constrained in that they have a special obligation to impartially uphold the Constitution in cases before them, despite political pressures and changing times. This enables the lawmaking branches of government to address current challenges in the stable context of the constitutional rule of law. Though progressive jurists increasingly look to the laws of other nations, the Constitution—and the very nature of constitutional government based on the consent of the governed—also compels judges not to give foreign law any binding authority or persuasive consideration in the U.S. legal system.

We need learned judges who take the Constitution seriously and follow it faithfully. Anything less should disqualify a judicial nominee and raise a legitimate inquiry about a sitting judge. Insofar as these matters cannot be left to judges alone to define, judicial appointments and confirmations are important opportunities for presidents, nominees, and the Senate to advance, debate, and explain the proper role of judges and the legitimate parameters of constitutional interpretation.

Upholding the Constitution is a responsibility of all three branches of government. Government must be limited, but also energetic in fulfilling its legitimate, constitutional functions. Just as important, each branch of government must also be *responsible* (and held responsible) for its actions according to the structure and distribution of government authority set out in the Constitution. The Founders didn't rely on the enumeration of powers alone to limit government, and neither should we. The "auxiliary precautions" of the Constitution, in particular the checks and balances that place institutional interests in competition, need to be reinvigorated so that officers in separate branches of government will actively defend their own constitutional powers, and challenge the constitutional claims of the other branches.

Too much of government today occurs outside of the confines of the Constitution, in unaccountable administrative agencies. Not stemming from the consent of the governed, these agencies lack basic legitimacy in our constitutional system. The Constitution creates three branches of government, yet administrative agencies operate in practice as a headless fourth branch, beyond the control of the executive and limited largely by budgets they carefully negotiate with congressional committees and staff. Rather than spending its time micromanaging the bureaucracy and trying to influence the casework of various agencies, Congress should reassert its authority as the nation's legislature, avoid delegating its power to administrative agencies, and take responsibility for all the laws which govern us. At the same time, Congress should unambiguously place government administrators under the authority and direction of the president to assure that those laws are faithfully executed.

Too many programs, once started, are automatically reauthorized and become part of the permanent bureaucracy. A good way to correct this would be for Congress to periodically review and authorize anew every major program, creating an ongoing mechanism that would work against the steady, automatic expansion of government. Rather than assuming their permanence, Congress should subject government programs to regular reevaluation of their authority, purpose, and effectiveness.

One of the most important tasks of public officials is to articulate how the principles and limits of their constitutional responsibilities inform and guide their actions and the public-policy choices they make. This not only maintains popular support for principled policies but also instructs the public in ways that can effectively change political opinion over time. Congressmen should do this in committee deliberation and floor debates on proposed legislation, judges in their written opinions interpreting the real meaning of the Constitution in the cases before them, and presidents in executive orders, legislative signing statements, and especially in official addresses. Political leaders should speak more about the meaning of America's principles and institutions in speeches, statements, and official communications, making common-sense, principled arguments even when not making specific proposals, decisions, or policy pronouncements. Public statements should be an occasion for informing and educating American citizens about their obligations, as well as their natural and constitutional rights. The modern abandonment of this practice has much to do with the widespread cynicism and scorn in which our political leaders of both Left and Right are held today—an attitude which does not bode well for the future of democratic government.

Defending Free Markets and Fiscal Responsibility

In addition to being the primary engine of our economic growth and prosperity, the fundamental right to acquire, possess, and sell property is the very backbone of opportunity, a crucial measure of liberty, and the most practical of means for pursuing human happiness. It needs to be protected in principle and—along with the free-enterprise system that stems from it—as a basic element of American political culture.

When it comes to popular economic knowledge, our nation is running a deficit. Americans need to understand the essential workings of political economy—not the equations and statistics of the academic theorist but the basic human actions of common exchange, general budgeting, and everyday commerce. More and more, these are the key tools necessary to analyze the major issues of today's politics. Most important, simple economic knowledge is needed to appreciate the relationship among individuals, markets, and government, and to comprehend the striking difference between a free market system based on rewarding the dynamism of the human spirit and a centrally planned system that suppresses capitalism in order to redistribute wealth and limit individual opportunity.

Too much government regulation of our economic system subverts the very foundations of liberty. American commerce is increasingly stifled by burdensome taxes, extensive regulations, and other government-imposed requirements that suppress investment, discourage risk-taking, and increase the cost of starting or operating a business, thus weakening the American economy, impeding job creation, and undermining America's competitive position in the world. The United States government now owns significant portions of formerly private banks, controls a major insurance firm, has nationalized significant lenders of home loans, and has stock ownership in leading automobile companies. Many banks and corporations that have received significant bailout money from the federal government are finding it difficult to get out from under the debt and regulatory control that came with the loan. Economic recovery plans such as these threaten to leave government permanently larger, more intrusive, and even more costly for the American economy—and every American.

Annual federal spending has increased by 221 percent since 1970, nearly nine times faster than median household income. The annual federal government budget did not reach $1 trillion until 1988, but exceeded $2 trillion in 2002 and $3 trillion in 2009. Total government spending in the United States has reached 40 percent of the total national economy (gross domestic product). The expansion of federal government spending is mostly being driven by the growth of guaranteed entitlements, now more than half of all program spending, and expected to nearly double over the next decade. Without major reforms, entitlement spending will consume all federal tax revenues by 2052. In addition to fundamental entitlement reform, we need to seriously consider the institution of new legal and constitutional mechanisms to enforce fiscal discipline on the federal government, such as an overall spending limitation keyed to a percentage of the national economy, a supermajority vote requirement to raise taxes, and a requirement for a balanced federal budget.

All of this has come at a great cost. While Americans have been taken aback by massive government spending in recent years, consider that the unfunded obligations for social security and Medicare are *more than sixty-one times* the cost of the $700 billion Troubled Asset Relief Program (TARP) intended to purchase toxic assets and equity from financial institutions weakened by the recent economic downturn. As a result, the current national debt (about $68,000 per household) will double in five years and triple over the next ten years—this before the long-term costs of any new programs or entitlements (such as a health-care entitlement) are added to the ledger.* Is it morally responsible to place such unsustainable debts on our own children and grandchildren, who have not consented to such an overwhelming burden?

The better approach to economic issues, consistent with the ideas and principles of the American Founders, is to view government as the framework—through the constitutional rule of law, the protection of

---

* These numbers (and more analysis) are available in various papers by my colleagues at The Heritage Foundation.

property and contracts, and a limited regulatory structure—for promoting unlimited opportunity and widespread prosperity. The key is to increase incentives to produce by removing barriers to work and investment: decreasing tax rates, reducing government spending, and preventing the overregulation of private enterprise. Such an economic program would bring greater dignity, better options, and higher rewards to those who work and create wealth, which in turn stimulates the overall economy and brings more opportunity and prosperity for everyone. The best thing we can do for the less fortunate is to offer them a hand up through job growth and economic opportunity, rather than a handout through the perverse incentives of a welfare state that discourages self-reliance, family cohesiveness, and financial independence.

It must not be forgotten that the marketplace is an institution of civil society, and we need to defend it as such. Built on property ownership and the freedom to contract, the elements of economic opportunity—stable employment, better household income, job flexibility, upward mobility—are important aspects of American life. The fruits of hard work and entrepreneurship for the sake of improving the conditions of self and family, as well as the opportunities that have long been associated with the pursuit of the American dream, are moral goods and contribute to human happiness. All have the added virtue of harnessing enlightened self-interest to serve the common good and limited constitutional government. Now more than ever, we must connect the economic arguments for liberty and prosperity with the moral case for equal opportunity and free enterprise in order to make a full defense of the American system of democratic capitalism.

The Revival of Self-Government

America's principles define the very nature of our national identity, but that identity can be sustained only by citizens of firm convictions and sound character. From the beginning, America's creed and culture have developed together, nourishing each other for their common good. There is a critical connection between a thriving civil society and limited, constitutional government.

In assuming more and more tasks in more and more areas outside of its responsibilities, modern government has caused great damage to

American self-rule. By feeding the entitlement mentality and dependency rather than promoting self-reliance and independence, administrative government encourages a character incompatible with republicanism. The extended reach of the state—fueled by its imperative to impose moral neutrality on the public square—continues to push traditional social institutions in to the shadows of public life, undermining respect for institutions meant to strengthen the fabric of America's culture and civil society.

In order to stop the erosion of our social capital and restore a culture of *self*-governing citizens, we must challenge, engage, and reject the relativism and historicism that infect our culture and have caused such great turmoil in our politics. What does it say about our moral discernment when an endangered snail is protected more than a six-month-old child in his mother's womb, or when we are unable to agree whether defining marriage as a union between man and woman serves any rational purpose? In a world of moral confusion, we must restore the accepted understanding of a human nature limited by the unchanging ground of right and wrong. The Declaration of Independence asserts self-evident truths according to "the Laws of Nature and of Nature's God" that we too must honor: All persons are created equal and possess equal human dignity, regardless of race, color, sex, age, or religious creed. All are endowed with the same unalienable rights to life, liberty, and the pursuit of happiness. While we acknowledge man's weaknesses, we must also recognize his great capacity for virtue.

Deeply embedded in Western civilization and the worldview of America's Founders, the family, centered on marriage, must be defended and preserved as the core natural or prepolitical institution of free society. We must shore up all the institutions of civil society that are increasingly under progressive assault—families, churches, schools, and private associations—for their own sake, but also so that they can sustain and cultivate the virtues and character required for republican government. Government must recognize its paramount interest in upholding equality before the law; defending life, liberty, and property; and protecting religious liberty and the freedom of private association. It must also—primarily in state but if necessary in federal laws—preserve the integrity of marriage and the family. In the end, though, addressing the fundamental problems we face in our nation will require extensive work—

such as efforts to rebuild fatherhood in the inner cities, help mothers choose adoption rather than abortion, and expand charitable work and volunteerism to help the poor—well beyond the ability of government and properly in the domain of civil society itself.

There is a clear connection between America's growing social ills and the abandonment of traditional moral norms most Americans acquire through religion. Rebuilding a society of individual and political self-government requires a return of religious and faith-based institutions to a central place in our civic and public life. We have never been and should not try to become a nation defined by a particular or official religious denomination, but Americans are a religious people—the Supreme Court said in 1952 (and reiterated in 1963, and again in 1984), "We are a religious people whose institutions presuppose a Supreme Being." Because of our disavowal of sectarianism, the United States has not experienced the religious hatreds and conflicts that plagued much of the world for more than a thousand years, and continue with horror in many places today. America must return to a more reasonable and historically accurate understanding of religious liberty, like that of our Founders, which upholds religious and moral conscience as an invaluable support for both healthy republican government and human happiness.

True self-government cannot be revived without a decided reversal of administrative centralization in the United States. This requires that we seriously revisit the classic argument of federalism, but not by merely shifting bureaucratic authority to states that are themselves bureaucratic and increasingly dependent on the federal largess. What we need is a significant decentralization of power and of vast areas of policymaking from the federal government to states, local communities, neighborhoods, families, and individual citizens.* Public welfare, education, and health care—all issues that in recent decades have become federal government concerns but are better dealt with at the state and local levels of government (not to mention by families, community organizations, religious congregations, or private markets)—are ripe for this kind of reform. We cannot claim to govern ourselves if every question, problem, and aspect of our lives demands a new government program.

---

* On this, see *A Moral Case Against Big Government: How Government Shapes the Character, Vision, and Virtue of Citizens* (Heritage First Principles Essay #9) by Ryan Messmore.

One area where the government plays a legitimate and extensive role in civil society, not at the federal but at the state and local level, is education. For America's Founders, widespread public education was the key to equal opportunity, to individual improvement, and to the pursuit of human happiness. Today, widespread educational failure imposes unquantifiable costs on individual lives and communities, and weakens the foundations of self-government. For decades, built on the mistaken assumptions of progressive educational theory, modern education policy has increased government spending, bureaucracy, and federal control, but yielded little improvement in student performance and achievement, leaving countless millions to fall permanently into the ranks of the underclass. The decentralized approach, encouraging innovation and competition, restoring greater parental control over the education of their children, and making states take seriously their traditional responsibilities, is the most principled and effective way to improve American education.

Our experiment in self-government cannot survive if we become a nation of disconnected, autonomous individuals. The American system of decentralized governance, which allows political bodies closest to the people to decide a multitude of issues within their own purview, not only is an important feature of our constitutional structure but also plays a crucial role in civic formation. It is through our relationships with neighbors, friends, and fellow countrymen—in local communities, churches, schools, and private organizations, in workplaces and through economic exchange—that we acquire the habits, practices, and spirit of Americans, strengthening our virtues, work ethic, and mutual responsibilities. We need to reclaim the idea that self-governing citizens have a serious responsibility to defend the principles and practices of constitutional liberty. Too often we think of civil society as a collection of social units outside of or beyond "politics," but self-government compels knowledgeable citizens to assume their moral obligation to be involved in American public life, from the local school board up to the highest offices of the land.

Abraham Lincoln had a keen sense of his profound moral duty to serve his country. "As the patriots of seventy-six did to the support of the Declaration of Independence, so to the support of the Constitution and Laws, let every American pledge his life, his property, and his sacred honor," he once wrote. "Let every man remember that to violate the law, is to trample on the blood of his father, and to tear the character of his own, and his children's liberty." It was just such a man who took his obligation as a citizen seriously enough to save his country.

From an early age, we need to teach and habituate our children to practice the civic virtues that fit them to fully engage in participatory democracy. We must reflect these virtues in our own lives, and take more responsibility for shaping the course of this self-governing republic. An understanding of our deepest principles, as well as an appreciation of our history, tells us why this nation is a noble achievement, and worth defending. We must constantly rekindle an enlightened love of liberty, and of the country that is responsible for upholding the great principles of human civilization here and abroad. We need to take up the work of honoring liberty's patriots and making new ones.

Upholding Liberty in the World

A chief purpose and obligation of our constitutional order is to provide for the common defense. The fundamental freedom and rights of all are in danger when the nation is at risk. As a matter of principle, the United States must be able, willing, and prepared at all times to defend itself, its people, and its institutions from conventional and unconventional threats at home and from abroad. Americans have always been and remain a generous people, and will continue to be, but that does not conflict with the constitutional duty of the United States government to secure its international borders and preserve and protect its territorial integrity, to strengthen and preserve its constitutional government, and to promote the long-term prosperity and well-being of its people.

Without principled American leadership the world will become a more dangerous place—for Americans and for freedom. Transnational terrorism, rampant anti-Americanism, unaccountable international institutions, nuclear proliferation, and regional conflict all represent threats to our security, our liberties, and our prosperity. The ability of rogue nations and hostile nonstate actors to use weapons of mass destruction against the United States creates a new and compelling interest in America actively defending itself. The United States must have the will and the means to remain engaged in the world, not only to protect the nation and its citizens from freedom's adversaries, but also to defend its principles, policies, and vital interests wherever they are threatened. A complacent America, either at home or abroad, risks not only the peaceful and productive future of this country but also that of its friends and allies.

At the heart of our common defense is the need to defend at all cost the very ideas and beliefs that we hold in common, including the good character of our people and America's universal principles of human liberty. Our national allegiance stems not from deference to political leaders, ethnic categories, or an abstract state, but from a profound attachment to the country that protects and secures individual freedom, fundamental equal rights, and the constitutional rule of law. Because we hold that governments are instituted among men, deriving their just powers from the consent of the governed, a profound commitment to the concept of sovereignty must be at the center of our nation's policies toward other countries and the world. As opposed to the visionary argument of postnationalists that we are merely "citizens of the world," sovereignty imposes both principled obligations and limits on our actions. It demands that we defend our nation and advance its principles and interests, but also uphold and respect the rightful claim of other legitimate nations to sovereign status. At the same time, sovereignty requires, just as constitutional government necessitates, that we reject outright the claims of any international groups, organizations, or courts (as in the case of international criminal courts that assert jurisdiction over our legal system) that violate the Constitution of the United States.

As one nation among many that do not recognize or respect universal principles, let alone our interests, America must ensure a strong internal sense of our national identity and appropriately reflect this sense in our policies toward others. A profound example of this can be seen in our policies toward immigrants. Because of its founding principles, this country, with only a few exceptions, has always welcomed immigrants who come here honestly and legally, with their work ethic and appreciation of freedom, seeking the promise and opportunity American liberty generously offers. Yet by those same principles, we also insist that they embrace their adopted country, not by rejecting ethnic heritages and cultural identities but through a deliberate and self-confident policy of patriotic assimilation. We must maintain an effective naturalization process that ultimately forms immigrants into citizens who understand the principles and institutions of free government, speak a common language, reflect good character and civic virtue, and seek to earn a real stake in America's economic prosperity. It is the principles and institutions we hold in common that allow for the flourishing of our differences, prevent the American "melting pot" from becoming a cauldron of tribalism, and reflect a model of democratic governance to the world.

In the modern era, as in the past, it is crucial for the United States to prevail in the ideological challenges against us—from radical Islamic terrorism to resurgent transnational populism and other anti-American forces—and to spread and institutionalize economic and political freedom around the world. The way by which the United States teaches the rest of the world about America's ideas and political culture is through programs and activities in the international realm, called "public diplomacy." As we promote our national policies to other countries, it is important, especially when our way of life is challenged, to explain, defend, and promote America's unique concept of ordered liberty not only as good and just in and of itself but also as a signal to other nations about what we believe and will fight for. Public diplomacy must have real, substantive content, informed by our principles and shaped by our experience of constitutional government.* As we defend America's interests in the world, for instance, we must also stand up for religious liberty in the Middle East, democracy and the rule of law in Russia and the post-Communist world, national sovereignty in Europe, and government by popular consent everywhere.

By the very nature of the principles upon which it is established, the United States—more than any other nation in history—has a special responsibility to defend not only the cause of liberty but also its meaning at home and abroad. This is why the friends of freedom everywhere have always looked to this country and drawn great inspiration from its ideas, example, and actions. A confident understanding of America's principles, and a renewed sense of American independence and purpose, is a reaffirmation of what *we* hold to be self-evident. Anything less would be to deny our own birthright and undermine our moral standing in the world.

---

* See *Ideas Matter: Restoring the Content of Public Diplomacy* (Heritage Special Report #62) by Robert Reilly.

Our Noble Task

In the late spring of 1775, Boston was occupied by British troops, and its harbor commanded by British warships. Local militias from the neighboring towns and villages had harassed and chased the king's men all the way back to the city after the battles of Lexington and Concord, and were being replaced by fresh volunteer units, constituting the beginnings of a ragtag, ill-equipped rebel army. The Massachusetts Provincial Congress had relocated to safer quarters, but Joseph Warren, its new president and head of the public safety committee, remained in Boston to lead the American opposition.

A young medical doctor, Warren was the father of four small children, a widower engaged to remarry. He was the author of the Suffolk Resolves, the resolutions passed by the Continental Congress calling for wartime preparations, and it was he who sent Paul Revere and William Dawes on their famous rides to warn of an imminent British attack on Concord. His public life was dedicated to the patriot cause.

The Americans had moved their meager forces onto the Charlestown peninsula, constructing hasty breastworks on the heights of Breed's Hill, overlooking Boston from the north. Contemptuous of the "rabble in arms," the British planned a direct assault on their position. Although he had been elected a major general, Warren chose to fight as a volunteer private. He once said that he hoped to die knee-deep in the blood of his fellow countrymen.

Twice the British Regulars attacked, and twice the Americans, holding fire until the advancing regiments were in close range, decimated the British ranks and forced them to fall back. Short of powder and ammunition, and without reinforcements, the Americans were overwhelmed on the third assault, British soldiers swarming their redoubt, stabbing with their bayonets. Only later did they find Joseph Warren, in a trench, below the bodies of his fellow countrymen. He had gotten his wish.

Three months before his death, Warren spoke these powerful words, which speak to us today:

Our streets are filled with armed men; our harbor is crowded with ships of war; but these cannot intimidate us; our liberty must be preserved; it is far dearer than life.

No longer could we reflect, with generous pride, on the heroic actions of our American forefathers . . . if we, but for a moment, entertain the thought of giving up our liberty.

Our country is in danger, but not to be despaired of.

Our enemies are numerous and powerful; but we have many friends determining to be free, and heaven and earth will aid the resolution.

On you depend the fortunes of America.

You are to decide the important question on which rest the happiness and liberty of millions yet unborn.

Act worthy of yourselves.

If history taught the American Founders anything, it was that freedom was very difficult, and usually short-lived. They knew that the success of their own accomplishment could not be assured and that America's experiment would be constantly tested over the long course of human events.

We Americans have the immeasurable benefit, the providential gift, of having inherited a great country, built on the rock of human liberty, with a firm confidence that free men and women are capable of self-government.

All nations change over time. We have wandered far for many years. Yet our constitutional faith has not been erased from our consciousness. Nor has it been defeated in our politics. Our principles always await rediscovery, not because they are written on faded parchments in glass cases, but because the immutable truths of liberty are eternally etched on the human soul.

Do we still hold these truths?

In times of peace and war, prosperity and poverty, political consensus and social unrest, every generation of Americans is challenged to vindicate the sacred cause of liberty.

This is our noble task now. Let us act worthy.

Bibliographic Essay

The quotations used in this book (and other quotations from the Founders, their leading critics, and modern interpreters) can be found in a searchable database at WeStillHoldTheseTruths.org. A more extensive bibliography can be found there as well, along with documents, materials, and other resources on the American Founding. What follows is an annotated list of the books I often turn to and recommend for the general reader interested in becoming familiar with the principles, events, and figures of the American Founding.

The best place to begin is with the Founders' writings. To know the minds of the Founders is to read their own words. There are many good collections of the writings of individual Founders: The Library of America has several fine one-volume editions of the letters, public papers, and documents written by most of the main figures. Beyond these volumes I would recommend in particular *George Washington: A Collection* (Liberty Press, 1995), edited by William B. Allen, a well-chosen collection of Washington's correspondence and writings from early, middle, and later life that provides a clear perspective on Washington's statesmanship. A nice collection of Hamilton's most important letters, speeches, and essays from 1775 to 1803 is *Selected Writings and Speeches of Alexander Hamilton* (American Enterprise Institute, 1985), edited by Morton J. Frisch; an excellent overview of Hamilton's political thought is provided through introductions and commentary. Marvin Meyers's *The Mind of the Founder: Sources of the Political Thought of James Madison* (Brandeis University Press, 1981) is a good collection of Madison's essays, letters, and speeches between 1774 and 1836, with a great explanatory essay on Madison, section introductions, and a brief note with each entry.

Jack P. Greene's *Colonies to Nation, 1763–1789: A Documentary History of the American Revolution* (W. W. Norton, 1975) tells the story of the American Founding using documents ranging from government papers and popular pamphlets to diary accounts and personal letters. Each section has a full introduction and every entry is prefaced by an introductory note placing the documents in a coherent framework. *American Political Writing During the Founding Era* (Liberty Press, 1983), a two-volume work edited by Charles Hyneman and Donald Lutz, includes pamphlets, articles, sermons, and essays written by various political authors between 1762 and 1805. It is a gold mine of seventy-six less well-known but equally interesting popular writings; each entry is introduced by a brief note on the author. *Political Sermons of the American Founding Era, 1730–1805* (Liberty Fund, 1998) is a superb collection of fifty-five complete religious sermons, edited by Ellis Sandoz. The array of denominational and theological viewpoints displays the religious seriousness of the time, as well as the importance of the pulpit to the American Revolution.

To truly understand the period, and what was accomplished, it is essential to get to know the American Founders through biographies of their lives, watching them grapple with the challenges of their day and seeing their ideas in action. While there are many good biographies of the Founders, and more keep coming, I would recommend a few. James Thomas Flexner's *Washington: The Indispensable Man* (Little, Brown and Co., 1984) is still the best one-volume biography of Washington from his most accomplished biographer, who has also written a comprehensive four-volume biography for the more adventuresome reader. *Founding Father: Rediscovering George Washington* (Free Press, 1996), by Richard Brookhiser, is not a life history of Washington but an analysis of his career and character as soldier, founder, and statesman, presented in highly readable, thematic chapters. David McCullough's *1776* (Simon & Schuster, 2005) is truly monumental, telling the story of that fateful year, centering on General Washington and those around him. Esmond

Wright's *Franklin of Philadelphia* (Harvard University Press, 1986) is a solid, modern biography that is a bit more scholarly but nicely readable. David McCullough's sweeping *John Adams* (Simon & Schuster, 2001) covers all of Adams's life, with due prominence given his relationships with wife Abigail and fellow patriot Thomas Jefferson, making a strong case for Adams's importance. John Ferling's *John Adams: A Life* (Henry Holt and Co., 1996) is more academic and less easy reading, but a good substantive biography that draws upon large amounts of original texts. Merrill Peterson's *Thomas Jefferson and the New Nation: A Biography* (Oxford University Press, 1970) is the standard and most balanced one-volume Jefferson biography for the general reader, providing a basic narrative and highlighting three dominant themes of Jefferson's career: democracy and popular government, the new American nationality, and philosophical enlightenment. Forrest McDonald's *Alexander Hamilton: A Biography* (W. W. Norton, 1990) is an excellent political biography, focusing on and explaining Hamilton's greatest contributions in finance, economics, and law, making the case for the first secretary of the treasury's importance to the political economy of the early American republic. A more recent and complete biography is Ron Chernow's *Alexander Hamilton* (Penguin Press, 2004). The best comprehensive Madison biography, accessible to general readers and scholars alike, is Ralph Louis Ketcham's *James Madison: A Biography* (MacMillan, 1971), a very thorough historical narrative and distillation of both the ideas and the man, with a good emphasis on his role in the Continental Congress and at the Constitutional Convention. Jack Rakove's relatively short but solid biography *James Madison and the Creation of the American Republic* (Scott, Foresman, 1990) focuses on Madison's public life, looking at him as a political thinker and leader to emphasize how he successfully combined serious ideas and practical politics.

On the period of the American Revolution, one of the best single volume histories covering the period from 1763 to 1789 is John Alden's *A History of the American Revolution* (Alfred Knopf, 1969), covering the political, military, social, economic, and constitutional aspects of the period. The best short history of the era is Edmund Morgan's *The Birth of the Republic, 1763–89* (University of Chicago Press, 1956), which tells the story of the American Revolution in a concise, readable fashion. John C. Miller's *Origins of the American Revolution* (Little, Brown and

Company, 1943) is an older popular history of the events leading up to the American Revolution, chronicling the various British acts against the colonials beginning after the French and Indian War up to the Declaration of Independence. A wonderful work that brings the American Revolution to life through important vignettes along the way, from James Otis in 1761 to George Washington at Yorktown in 1783, is A. J. Langguth's *Patriots: The Men Who Started the American Revolution* (Simon & Schuster, 1988).

Clinton Rossiter examines the meeting that created the Constitution in *1787: The Grand Convention* (MacMillan Company, 1966), a solid, readable work focusing on the setting, men, events, and consequences of the federal convention through the early years of the new republic. Max Farrand wrote a succinct and charming book on the events surrounding the Constitutional Convention, *The Framing of the Constitution* (Yale University Press, 1913), that is still available and very readable. Catherine Drinker Bowen's *Miracle at Philadelphia: The Story of the Constitutional Convention, May to September 1787* (Little, Brown and Company, 1966) is a popular narrative of the Constitutional Convention that focuses more narrowly on the participants and the day-to-day convention debate in almost novel-like form. A more recent work is David Stewart's *The Summer of 1787* (Simon & Schuster, 2007), which gives a lively account of the conflicts and negotiating that created the Constitution.

The Records of the Federal Convention of 1787 (Yale University Press, 1986), edited by Max Farrand, gathers into three volumes all the records written by participants of the Constitutional Convention of 1787, including the extensive official notes taken throughout by James Madison. Philip B. Kurland and Ralph Lerner edited *The Founders' Constitution* (Liberty Fund, 2000), an extensive work consisting of extracts from the leading works of political theory, history, law, and constitutional argument on which the Framers and their contemporaries drew, and which they themselves produced. Originally published by the University of Chicago Press to commemorate the bicentennial of the Constitution, Liberty Fund has prepared a paperback edition of the entire work in five volumes, which is also available online at http://press-pubs.uchicago.edu/founders. Don E. Fehrenbacher's *The Slaveholding Republic: An Account of the United States Government's Relations to Slavery* (Oxford University Press, 2001) is a detailed study, stretching from the First Continental Congress to the Civil War, which argues persuasively that early trends in the colonies were against slavery and that the U.S. Constitution was not a proslavery document, despite later policies that supported the institution.

The greatest commentary on the Constitution, and probably the greatest work of American political thought, are the essays written by James Madison, Alexander Hamilton, and John Jay under the title *The Federalist*, originally published as a series of pro-Constitution newspaper articles intended to sway New Yorkers in the debate over ratification. The classic edition, edited by the late Clinton Rossiter, has now been published by Signet Classics with a fine introduction and notes by Charles Kesler, as well as a historical glossary and other supplementary materials. Kesler has also edited a very approachable collection of essays, *Saving the Revolution: The Federalist Papers and the American Founding* (Free Press, 1987), explaining and interpreting this key Federalist writing on topics such as republicanism, federalism, foreign policy, the separation of powers, executive power, and the original purposes of the Constitution.

To understand the debate over the Constitution, and the full extent of early American political thought, one must also know something about the Anti-Federalists, those who opposed the ratification of the Constitution and wanted a small republic, more federalism, and a bill of rights, among other things. The classic introduction is Herbert J. Storing's brief *What the Anti-Federalists Were For: The Political Thought of the Opponents of the Constitution* (University of Chicago Press, 1981), which also considers their effect on enduring themes of American political life such as a concern about big government and the infringement of personal liberty. An accessible selection of leading Anti-Federalist writings is *The Essential Antifederalist* (University Press of America, 1985), edited by William B. Allen and Gordon Lloyd. After a nice interpretative essay by the editors, the selections are grouped to focus on the origins of Anti-Federalist thought and then Anti-Federalist views on federalism, republicanism, capitalism, and democracy. A good two-volume collection of Federalist and Anti-Federalist speeches, articles, and letters during the struggle over ratification of the Constitution is *Debates on the Constitution* (Library of America, 1993), edited by Bernard Bailyn. It focuses on debates in the press and correspondence between September

1787 and August 1788, and the debates in the state-ratifying conventions of Pennsylvania, Connecticut, Massachusetts, South Carolina, Virginia, New York, and North Carolina.

A classic and substantive work on the meaning of the U.S. Constitution by one of its early scholars and one of the greatest justices of the Supreme Court is Joseph Story's *Commentaries on the Constitution* (Carolina Academic Press, 1987), originally published in 1833. It includes histories of various colonies and of the Revolutionary and the Confederation periods, and straightforward commentaries on the clauses of the Constitution. A more recent work in the Story tradition is *The Heritage Guide to the Constitution* (Regnery, 2005), edited by David Forte and Matthew Spalding. It brings together more than one hundred scholars to create a line-by-line examination of every clause of the Constitution, explaining their original meaning as well as their contemporary understanding.

The Framing and Ratification of the Constitution (MacMillan, 1987) is a nice collection of twenty-one essays edited by Leonard Levy and Dennis Mahoney on the framing and ratification of the Constitution, addressing various topics ranging from our colonial background and the events leading up to the Constitutional Convention to questions of original intent and organization of the new government. Robert Goldwin's *From Parchment to Power: How James Madison Used the Bill of Rights to Save the Constitution* (American Enterprise Institute, 1997) is a clear and convincing historical study of the constitutional issues surrounding the creation of the Bill of Rights, looking at the philosophical arguments behind these guarantees, and how Madison crafted the first ten amendments and shepherded them through the First Congress. Stanley Elkins and Eric McKitrick's *The Age of Federalism: The Early American Republic, 1788–1800* (Oxford University Press, 1993) traces the development of the new nation from the time after the Constitutional Convention through its first three presidents. It is a comprehensive analysis of the early national period, including all the achievements and fights of the chief figures.

One can get a good taste of the interpretive debate over the founding from Alan Gibson's *Interpreting the Founding: Guide to the Enduring Debates over the Origins and Foundations of the American Republic* (University Press of Kansas, 2006), which discusses six approaches that have dominated the study of the American Founding: the progressive, Lockean-liberal, republican, and Scottish enlightenment interpretations, as well as the multiple traditions approach and the modern social history view. *Essays on the Making of the Constitution* (Oxford University Press, 1987) is a collection edited by Leonard Levy bringing together differing viewpoints of the roles and motivations of the framers of the Constitution. It includes a selection from Charles Beard's historic *An Economic Interpretation of the Constitution* and essays attacking and defending Beard's thesis. Thomas West's *Vindicating the Founders: Race, Sex, Class, and Justice in the Origins of America* (Rowman and Littlefield, 1997) debunks widely held politically correct opinions about the Founders by addressing their views on the controversial issues of slavery, property rights, women, the family, welfare, and immigration.

As this book includes a chapter on the progressives' assault on America's principles, a few book recommendations are in order. Once again, the best place to start is their own writings. Ronald Pestritto and William J. Atto's *American Progressivism: A Reader* (Lexington Books, 2008) is a good collection that runs the gamut of progressive thought, from political principles to Social Gospel writings to foreign policy speeches. It also includes a fine introductory essay explaining the basic views of the progressives. An honest and comprehensive overview from a historian sympathetic to the reform efforts of the period is Eric Goldman's *Rendezvous with Destiny: A History of Modern American Reform* (Alfred Knopf, 1952). Several recent works have delved more deeply into the progressive rejection of the American Founding. A good introduction to this scholarship is *The Progressive Revolution in Politics and Political Science: Transforming the American Regime*, edited by John Marini and Ken Masugi (Rowman and Littlefield, 2005), with essays on the progressive critique of American constitutionalism, as well as on progressive ideas in theory and practice. An important volume that treats Woodrow Wilson as a political thinker as well as a politician, Ronald Pestritto's *Woodrow Wilson and the Roots of Modern Liberalism* (Rowman and Littlefield, 2005) reveals Wilson's progressive philosophy, derived from nineteenth-century German thought, and its profound and continuing influence on progressive liberalism in America. Bradley C. S. Watson's *Living Constitution, Dying Faith: Progressivism and the New Science of Jurisprudence* (ISI Books, 2009) explains how modern legal thinking began with the progressive rejection of America's principles and its creation of a new theory of the "living" Constitution. A heavily researched and deliberately provocative book, Jonah Goldberg's *Liberal Fascism: The Secret History of the American Left, from Mussolini to the Politics of Change* (Doubleday, 2008) chronicles many of the excesses of the progressive movement, and explains how those excesses were connected to some of the basic principles implicit in progressive philosophy.

~

Organizational Resources

There are many good groups and organizations working to strengthen and advance America's constitutional principles in our schools, on college campuses and in the public square, but here are a few I would especially recommend.

The Lehrman American Studies Center (lehrman.isi.org), sponsored by the Intercollegiate Studies Institute, provides excellent teacher resources in the field of American Studies (including syllabus materials and classroom modules) and partners annually with the James Madison Program at Princeton University for a summer seminar for advanced graduate students and junior faculty. The Intercollegiate Studies Institute (isi.org) is itself a great resource for college students and faculty, sponsoring conferences and fellowships for college and graduate students, maintaining a network of campus groups and college newspapers, and supporting an active publishing house. It also is home of the American Civic Literacy Program, designed to study and strengthen the teaching of America's history and institutions at the college level.

The James Madison Program in American Ideals and Institutions at Princeton University (web.princeton.edu/sites/jmadison) is a leading example of an independent academic center on a college campus that is advancing America's first principles. It awards visiting fellowships and postdoctoral appointments each year to support scholars conducting research in constitutional law and political thought, promotes civic education through lectures, seminars, and conferences, and supports an Undergraduate Fellows Forum for Princeton students.

The Jack Miller Center for Teaching America's Founding Principles and History (jackmillercenter.org) supports academic centers on college campuses dedicated to teaching America's founding principles and history, and sponsors graduate student and postdoctoral fellowships. In addition, the Miller Center sponsors summer seminars on American history and workshops to assist graduate students and young professors.

Hillsdale College in Michigan (hillsdale.edu) is one of the few colleges in the United States that requires a course on the American Constitution as part of its core curriculum. The Hoogland Center for Teacher Excellence at Hillsdale sponsors seminars across the nation to educate high-school teachers in the liberal arts tradition, including the classics of American political thought. The Kirby Center for Constitutional Studies and Citizenship is an extension of the college in Washington, D.C., that sponsors educational activities for Hillsdale students as well as political leaders and their staff, and the general public.

The Federalist Society for Law and Public Policy Studies (fed-soc. org) is dedicated to advancing constitutional principles throughout the legal community. A national membership organization of law students, law school faculty, and lawyers, it has established chapters at every one of America's accredited law schools, and lawyers chapters may be found in many cities across the United States. It sponsors campus lectures, debates (many of which are posted on its website), conferences, and legal practice groups, and is a good educational source for anyone in the legal profession or interested in the rule of law.

The Bill of Rights Institute (billofrightsinstitute.org) is a great resource for high-school teachers interested in educating their students in the history and principles of the American Founding. It provides curriculum materials (essays, interactive activities, assessments, etc.) and promotes teacher education through year-round constitutional seminars as well as summer programs facilitated by academic experts and master teachers. The Bill of Rights Institute also sponsors a weeklong Constitutional Academy in Washington, D.C., for high-school juniors and seniors, as well as an essay contest for students in grades 9–12 who are attending public, private, religious, or charter schools, or being home-schooled.

TeachingAmericanHistory.org is an affiliate project of the Ashbrook Center for Public Affairs (ashbrook.org) at Ashland University in Ohio. The website is an excellent resource of primary and secondary documents in American history and on the Constitutional Convention and the ratification period. The Ashbrook Center provides educational programs for high-school history and government teachers and under-graduate and high-school students, as well as public events for citizens interested in America's principles and history. Teachers interested in pursuing a Masters of American History and Government should con-sider Ashland's summer degree program of intensive one-week seminars focused on the substance of history and government.

In addition to the online resources already mentioned, the Gilder Lehrman Institute of American History (gilderlehrman.org) supports several academic fellowships and awards three national book prizes. It also offers various resources and interactive website features for students and teachers. The Constitutional Sources Project (consource.com) is an online archive of important documents, texts, and writings on the Constitution and the founding which is authoritative (documents are uploaded alongside their originals from the Library of Congress), quite extensive, and very user-friendly (allowing users to build their own doc-ument libraries).

The Claremont Institute for the Study of Statesmanship and Politi-cal Philosophy (claremont.org) publishes the *Claremont Review of Books*, sponsors programs for college students and young up-and-coming con-servative leaders (the Publius Fellows Program and the Lincoln Fellows Program), holds panels for scholars at the annual American Political Science Association, and houses a variety of public policy programs, including a Center for Constitutional Jurisprudence and the Salvatori Center for the American Constitution. It supports several educational websites: founding.com (resources on the Declaration of Independence and the Constitution), foundingfather.com (dedicated to the statesman-ship of George Washington), and vindicatingthefounders.org (support-ing Thomas West's book by the same title).

Among its many activities and programs, The Heritage Foundation (heritage.org) has launched a nationwide effort to reclaim America's constitutional principles in our political and public life called the First Principles Initiative. It also houses the B. Kenneth Simon Center for American Studies, which sponsors lectures, seminars, and conferences, and produces numerous publications with the objective of teaching up-and-coming and current leaders, as well as reminding American citizens, about the foundations of liberty. The various papers, monographs, and books that are the substance of the First Principles Initiative are available at heritage.org, as are many of the studies and analyses—on economic policy, family and social policy, and defense and international policy—that inform the last chapter of this book. Additional resources, educational tools, and products on the themes of the book can be found at WeStillHoldTheseTruths.org.

Acknowledgments

The chapters of this book grew out of the lectures and seminars I have given over the years to hundreds of college students participating in the Heritage Internship Program and to congressional staff enrolled in the Heritage Congressional Fellows Program. Several senior congressional staff in our James Madison Fellows Program also commented on aspects of the manuscript. I thank them for their comments, questions, and critiques, all of which made the book better.

My work, along with the many educational programs Heritage conducts, is possible because of the half a million supporters of The Heritage Foundation. In particular, I am grateful to Jack Miller and Doris and Richard Pistole for supporting this book project, as well as the Lynde and Harry Bradley Foundation, the Herrick Foundation, the Albert and Ethel Herzstein Charitable Foundation, and the Philip M. McKenna Foundation for supporting the First Principles Initiative of The Heritage Foundation. Henry Salvatori and Ken Simon, two great patriots and successful entrepreneurs, made my work at Heritage possible in the first place.

All of my colleagues at Heritage have encouraged this project, and I have benefited immensely from their extensive research and generous assistance. Ed Meese has given me guidance and support throughout my work. In addition to my current and former staff at the B. Kenneth

Simon Center for American Studies—my assistant director, Joseph Postell, along with Julia Shaw, Spencer Anderson, and Carolyn Raney—I must thank a series of research interns for their work: Laura Arnold (University of Texas at Arlington), Kevin Brooks (University of Notre Dame), Caitlin Carroll (Berry College), Benjamin Cole (Baylor University), Lianne Cottrell (Villanova University), Sandra Czelusniak (Cornell University), Suzanne Fagan (University of Dallas), Shauneen Garrahan (Amherst College), Ruth Bailey Grandy (Hillsdale College), Jonathan Green (Northwestern University), Kathleen Hunker (Hofstra University), Jaron Janson (Utah State University), Nathan Jerauld (Hillsdale College), Nicola Karras (Yale University), Kevin Kearns (Ashland University), Verlan Lewis (Brigham Young University), Caitlin Poling (Ashland University), Charles Quigg (Amherst College), Elizabeth Thatcher (Hillsdale College), and Jonathan Walker (Hillsdale College).

Several individuals remain central to my thinking about American political thought and statesmanship, and I am deeply grateful to them, especially Harry V. Jaffa and Charles Kesler of Claremont McKenna College, and Thomas G. West of the University of Dallas. My friend and colleague Dennis Teti carefully read the entire manuscript and provided many insights and much counsel throughout. As this book is intended for a wide readership, I also want to thank three outside readers for their perspectives: Stacy Moses, who teaches U.S. history at Sandia Preparatory School in Albuquerque, New Mexico; Catherine O'Connor, a homeschooling parent and co-op instructor in Spotsylvania, Virginia; and Ron Weisbrod, who teaches American history and AP European history at St. Xavier High School in Cincinnati, Ohio.

Jed Donahue and his staff at ISI Books, and Genevieve Wood and Keesha Bullock at The Heritage Foundation, made this book project a reality. Those in my own "seminary of the republic"—my wife, Elizabeth, and Joseph and Catherine—were as patient with my work as they were endlessly supportive.

Index

About the Author

❧

Matthew Spalding is director of the B. Kenneth Simon Center for American Studies at The Heritage Foundation, where he also is the project leader of the First Principles Initiative. He has taught at George Mason University, the Catholic University of America, Claremont McKenna College, and Hillsdale College, and is the author or editor of several books, including *A Sacred Union of Citizens: Washington's Farewell Address and the American Character*, *Patriot Sage: George Washington and the American Political Tradition* (available from ISI Books), and *The Founders' Almanac: A Practical Guide to the Notable Events, Greatest Leaders, and Most Eloquent Words of the American Founding*. He is executive editor of *The Heritage Guide to the Constitution*, a clause-by-clause analysis of the United States Constitution. A fellow of the Claremont Institute for the Study of Statesmanship and Political Philosophy, and an adjunct fellow of the Kirby Center for Constitutional Studies and Citizenship at Hillsdale College, Spalding lives with his family in northern Virginia.

About The Heritage Foundation

The future of liberty depends on reclaiming America's first principles.

Founded in 1973, The Heritage Foundation is a research and educational institution—a think tank—whose mission is to formulate and promote conservative public policies based on the principles of free enterprise, limited government, individual freedom, traditional American values, and a strong national defense.

We believe the principles and ideas of the American founding are worth conserving and renewing. As policy entrepreneurs, we believe the most effective solutions are consistent with those ideas and principles. Our vision is to build an America where freedom, opportunity, prosperity, and civil society flourish.

Heritage's staff pursues this mission by performing timely, accurate research on key policy issues and effectively marketing these findings to our primary audiences: members of Congress, key congressional staff members, policymakers in the executive branch, the nation's news media, and the academic and policy communities.

Governed by an independent Board of Trustees, The Heritage Foundation is an independent, tax-exempt institution. Heritage relies on the private financial support of the general public—individuals, foundations, and corporations—for its income, and accepts no government funds and performs no contract work. Heritage is one of the nation's largest public policy research organizations. Nearly half a million individual members make it the most broadly supported think tank in America.

The First Principles Initiative is one of ten Transformational Initiatives making up The Heritage Foundation's Leadership for America campaign. The publications and programs of this Initiative seek to provide a much-needed education for students, policymakers, and citizens about the ideas of liberty and constitutional self-government, with the objective of reorienting our politics and public policy to the principles of the American founding.

For additional information, or to support our work, please contact The Heritage Foundation at (800) 546-2843 or visit heritage.org.

For *We Still Hold These Truths* video, curriculum, and interactive resources, visit WeStillHoldTheseTruths.org.